Federal Paper Board at Seventy-five

Federal Paper Board at Seventy-five

The Intimate History of an American Enterprise

By Richard Blodgett

GREENWICH PUBLISHING GROUP, Inc.
Essex, Connecticut

*T*his book celebrates
the seventy-fifth anniversary of
Federal Paper Board Company, Inc.,
on March 3, 1991.

Library of Congress Catalog Card Number: 91-71374
ISBN: 0-944641-01-6

Published and produced by Greenwich Publishing Group, Inc.
Essex, Connecticut

First printing: May 1991

Contents

The Cast of Characters

WILLIAM G. SHORTESS   Large, outgoing and energetic, Shortess was a born salesman who loved to acquire paperboard mills – whether he could afford them or not. He worked day and night managing mills for others before striking out on his own to found Federal Paper Board Company in 1916. He survived a series of financial crises to control 5 percent of the U.S. paperboard market and gain recognition as one of the industry's important pioneers.

JOANNA D. SHORTESS   When her husband Will died in 1942, Joanna wanted to take charge as Federal's new president. The fact that she was 74 years old and had no previous business experience didn't seem to faze this deeply religious, soft-spoken — and tenacious — woman in the least. Wiser heads prevailed, and she agreed to sell the company. She remained an active member of Federal's board until her death at age 86.

JOHN R. KENNEDY, SR.   He led a group of three Federal employees who acquired the company from the Shortess estate in 1943 in a completely leveraged transaction, without a penny down. Witty, tough and aggressive, he built Federal from a marginally profitable, $7-million-a-year enterprise into a $200 million corporation listed on the New York Stock Exchange.

JOHN R. KENNEDY, JR.   He succeeded his father as Federal's chief executive in the early 1970s. A visionary leader with a penchant for large, calculated risks, he has spearheaded a massive investment program to make Federal a leading forest products company and the world's number one producer of bleached paperboard.

PLUS THOUSANDS OF OTHERS who have contributed importantly to Federal's success. . . engineers, paper testers, mill foremen, accountants, machine tenders, graphic designers, lumber graders, secretaries, salespeople, attorneys and many more.

The Plot

It's 1916, and 44-year-old Will Shortess quits his job following a bitter dispute with his boss. With a $50,000 investment, he purchases a paperboard mill — just across the tracks from his boss's mill in Bogota, New Jersey — and launches Federal Paper Board Company.

Today, Federal markets its products worldwide and has operating facilities across the United States and in the United Kingdom. Shortess's tiny company has grown into a major corporation employing nearly 8,000 people. It has annual sales in excess of $1.3 billion and a market value of $1.2 billion. It's a story of American enterprise at its best, filled with unexpected twists and turns along the way.

Our story begins in the present. . .

CHAPTER 1

Federal Today: 'A Method to Our Madness'

Among the most memorable, and frightening, events in the life of Jack Kennedy was the time he survived a plane crash. The date was August 6, 1986, and the affable chief executive of Federal Paper Board Company had driven his wife and teenage daughter to Vermont to look at colleges. Kennedy had arranged to return to New York in a chartered Lear jet for a dinner that evening, while his wife and daughter stayed behind. However, on taking off from the Rutland, Vermont, airport, the pilot mistakenly chose the shorter runway instead of the longer one required for the plane.

"I realized we were in trouble when the pilot slammed on the brakes," Kennedy relates. "We went right off the end of the runway, across two stone walls, across a road. Fortunately, we didn't hit any trees. There was a clearing after the second wall. The wheels came off and the plane was skidding through this field on its belly, on fire.

"It happened so quickly," he continues, "you don't have an opportunity to think about anything except getting out of there. That business about your whole life going before you — I was trying to get the door open!"

Miraculously, the copilot suffered only a black eye, and Kennedy and the pilot walked away unscratched. Kennedy lost his jacket and briefcase in the fire.

Jumbo rolls of paperboard coming off the No. 3 machine at Federal's Augusta mill. Paperboard is the heavy paper used to manufacture printed folding cartons, paper cups, posters and dozens of other products.

"Skidding Jet Burns At Airport," was the headline of the Rutland Herald *on August 7, 1986. All that was left of the Lear 55 was the nose and the tail; the rest of the plane was a pile of blackened, twisted metal.*

Federal is unusual among public companies in having had only three chief executives in its 75-year history. Federal's founder, William G. Shortess, headed the company from 1916 until his death in 1942.

After such an accident, many people would head for the nearest bar. But Kennedy had other thoughts: he wanted to get back to work the next morning. So he phoned his wife at a nearby college and asked her to pick him up at the airport. Kennedy and his wife then drove straight home to Connecticut, a five-hour trip, arriving at close to midnight. He was at his desk the next morning.

This incident illustrates three points about Jack Kennedy. First, business has a very high priority in his life. Second, he is cool under pressure. And third, he is sometimes blessed with extraordinary luck.

THREE CHIEF EXECUTIVES IN 75 YEARS

For as long as most people can remember, a Kennedy has been associated with Federal. Based in Montvale, New Jersey, Federal is a leading manufacturer of paperboard — the heavy paper used to make packaging, brochure covers, baseball cards, paper cups and numerous other products.

Jack's father, John R. "J. R." Kennedy, Sr., joined the company in 1935 as assistant to the president and became its president in 1942. He served as chief executive until the 1970s, when he was succeeded by Jack. Jack is today the president and chief executive officer, and his brother, Quentin, is the executive vice president.

The history of Federal can be divided into three periods of approximately equal length, each coinciding with the stewardship of one of its three chief executives. In the first, from 1916 to 1942, founder William G. Shortess saw opportunity in the newly emerging paperboard business. He took many risks and had narrow escapes from financial disaster. After 26 years of struggle, he left something worthwhile on which others could build.

Then came the maturing era, from 1942 into the early 1970s, when J. R. Kennedy and his two partners, Howard Brown and Guy Freas, expanded the company through acquisitions. In the 1960s, J. R. Kennedy took a big chance by building a large new paperboard mill in Sprague, Connecticut. This facility helped revitalize Federal at a time when its business was sagging.

But it is in the third period, from the early 1970s to the present, that Federal's most dramatic growth and change have occurred. In fact, Federal has been on an almost nonstop growth streak for the past 20 years. According to an August 1990 study by *Financial World* magazine, Federal was the eighth-fastest-growing "big" company (sales over $1 billion) in the United States for the period 1985-90.

Jack Kennedy has fueled this growth by investing large sums to modernize and expand Federal's paperboard operations and move into new businesses.

Shortess was succeeded by J.R. Kennedy, an employee who had joined Federal in the mid-1930s to help straighten out its tangled financial affairs.

J.R. Kennedy was succeeded in the 1970s by his son, Jack Kennedy.

STRATEGIES FOR GROWTH

In the United Kingdom, Kennedy sees a unique opportunity to grow by capturing market share from Scandinavian paper companies. Two years ago, Federal bought Thomas Tait & Sons Ltd., which operates a mill in the Scottish town of Inverurie. Tait manufactures "uncoated freesheet," primarily white paper for copy machines and laser printers. With Tait under its wing, Federal is taking dead aim at the Scandinavians, who control 43 percent of the uncoated freesheet market in the U.K. Kennedy figures Tait has a cost advantage over the Scandinavian producers. He intends to capitalize on that advantage by nearly doubling the capacity of the Tait mill over the next three years. Projected capital cost: $140 million.

In 1989, Federal entered the paper cup business through acquisition. One year later, it bought a second cup manufacturer. Combined cost of the two acquisitions was $250 million. Federal now holds 14 percent of the paper cup market in the U.S. and sees a big opportunity if it plays its cards right. Kennedy notes that the cup market is moving away from styrofoam, back to paper, for environmental reasons. In addition, Fort Howard Corporation, which was the largest paper cup manufacturer in the U.S., went private in a leveraged buyout in 1988 and one year later sold its cup operations to a newly organized company, Sweetheart Holdings Inc. "That's created a vacuum in the industry which we think we can fill if we hurry up," Kennedy observes. He hopes to expand Federal's cup business by a hefty 18 percent a year.

Meanwhile, Federal recently completed a major expansion of its Sprague, Connecticut, mill. This mill stands at the center of one of the important trends of our time: recycling. Each day, the mill takes in more than one million pounds of wastepaper — corrugated cartons, newspapers, envelope clippings, data punch cards, cancelled government checks, etc. — and turns it into high-quality recycled paperboard. Demand for its product has never been greater.

Federal also manufactures "folding cartons" — the ubiquitous paperboard boxes in which hundreds of different products, such as crackers, macaroni and perfume bottles, are sold to consumers. (They're called folding cartons because they can fold at the creases and are shipped flat from the carton manufacturer to the consumer products company. A breakfast-cereal box is an example.) Federal was once one of the leading U.S. manufacturers of folding cartons, but recently trimmed sail and sold most of its plants. "Folding cartons are no longer a growth industry," Kennedy explains. "In addition, we were generalists making commodity-type cartons and the rates of return in that part of the business are inadequate. If we were to reenter folding cartons, it would be in specialty niches." Federal's one remaining carton plant — in Durham, North Carolina — makes 1 billion cartons a year for the cigarette industry.

Then there's the giant Riegelwood, North Carolina, paperboard mill. Acquired by Federal in 1972, it got the company started on its growth spurt. This facility not only produces lighter grades of paperboard, primarily for brochure covers, posters and other printing applications; it also makes "market pulp" — sheets of processed wood fiber shipped in 560-pound bales to paper companies around the world. The foreign-produced paper you buy may actually contain fiber from the vast timberlands of North Carolina.

But Federal's most ambitious expansion program of all is at its huge paperboard mill in Augusta, Georgia. This mill makes heavier grades of paperboard, primarily for the packaging industry, and also supplies stock to Federal's newly acquired paper cup plants. The Augusta mill highlights Kennedy's willingness to accept short-term sacrifice for long-term gain. Seven years ago, when Federal announced plans to acquire the facility, the price of Federal stock plunged 26 percent! Many investors unloaded the stock, fearing Federal was biting off more than it could chew. But Kennedy went ahead with the acquisition and Augusta has been an enormous success. Today, Federal is completing Phase II of a $1.1 billion, three-stage expansion that will raise the mill's capacity to 2,500 tons of paperboard a day by the mid-1990s. The facility will then be the largest paperboard mill in the world. Phase III was supposed to be the end. However, Kennedy is never one to stop thinking about growth. Jaws dropped in surprise at a recent meeting of investment analysts when he let out the word, rather offhandedly, that Phase III might be followed by a Phase IV that would lift the Augusta mill's capacity to 3,000 tons.

"One of the things we've been preaching is there's a method to our madness," the 60-year-old executive asserts. That method is a network of interrelated operations. "We go from the tree to the sawmill to the pulp mill to the pulp dryer to the paperboard machine... and then to folding cartons, paper cups and copy paper. So all the businesses we're in are interconnected. Our future is to add on to those branches."

The Federal of today reflects a dramatic change in a company that, during its first 55 years, concentrated solely on the manufacture of recycled paperboard from wastepaper and the manufacture of folding cartons. Among the dozens of recycled paperboard companies that existed as recently as the 1950s, Federal is one of the few that still exists and has successfully transformed itself into a diversified forest products enterprise.

How did Federal get to be the company it is today? How did it adapt to change? And what does its story tell us about risk, opportunity and entrepreneurship in America? Let's find out.

Chapter 2

Where There's a Will, There's a Way

THE JOKE about Will Shortess was that he couldn't drive by a paperboard mill without buying it. Shortess was a large, gregarious man who founded Federal Paper Board Company in 1916 and served as its president and owner until his death in 1942.

Between 1916 and 1941, he acquired nearly a dozen paperboard mills throughout the Northeast, many at sheriff's auctions and bankruptcy sales. However, success did not come to him quickly or easily. Like so many pioneering American industrialists, he was highly individualistic and a born risk-taker. While some of his risks paid off, others did not. Moreover, he treated money as if it was not something to worry about; he constantly borrowed more than he could handle and, on at least one occasion, drove his company to the very brink of bankruptcy.

Yet, Shortess managed to succeed in time through sheer doggedness. By the early 1940s, he controlled nearly 5 percent of the paperboard market in the Northeast, and his customers included Nabisco, Lever Brothers, H. J. Heinz and other well-known consumer products companies. In a 1941 article, the *New York Times* recognized him as one of the paperboard industry's pioneers and important leaders.

"We Didn't Really Think of Him as Old"

Who was William Shortess, and what were his contributions to Federal and the paperboard industry?

Born in Pennsylvania in 1871, he was the youngest of six children — four girls and two boys. He grew up at a time when the paperboard industry was in its infancy. As a young man, sensing the opportunities that lay ahead, he was drawn to the business like a bear to honey. Thereafter, paperboard became his consuming passion. He loved the business and worked at it ten to twelve hours or more a day, including Saturdays and Sundays — a habit he maintained over the course of a half-century career in the industry.

His energy and stamina were legendary, so that when he passed away at age 71, no one could quite believe he was gone. "It was a shock to us all when he died," says Pauline Conrad, who joined Federal in 1926 as a 19-year-old bookkeeper and stayed with the company 45 years before retiring. "I don't ever remember thinking of him as on in years. He was always active and around, and we didn't really think of him as old."

Shortess was a specialist in the operations and sales aspects of the paperboard business. His major contributions were to assemble the largest group of affiliated mills in the eastern United States and to develop new customers and markets for the mills' output.

Prior to striking out on his own, Shortess had a long association with W. J. "Old Man" Alford, owner of the Continental Paper Company and one of the paperboard industry's colorful early figures. Alford had initially earned his money by purchasing worn-out railway wheels and recycling the metal to make shovels. Early in this century, he began reinvesting his profits in the newly emerging paperboard business.

The first mill that Shortess managed for Alford was the Haverhill Box Board Company operation north of Boston. Then in 1912, when Alford purchased the Bogota (rhymes with pagoda), New Jersey, mill of the defunct Traders Board Company, Shortess was assigned to manage that operation as well. Two years later, Alford purchased the Thames River Specialties Company mill in eastern Connecticut, and Shortess was once again enlisted to take charge. Shortess traveled from facility to facility by train, frequently spending three or four nights a week on sleeping cars.

Although Shortess was the corporate secretary of Continental and one of three members of its board of directors, he was a salaried employee rather than a partner. This bothered him. He pressed Alford for a 10 percent stake in the Bogota operation and believed he had won a pledge that he would receive it. Alford apparently saw matters differently. "I spoke to Mr. Alford several times regarding the stock promised me," Shortess later wrote, "but each time was put off."

Frustrated and angry, Shortess quit his job in March 1916 and started his own company, purchasing a mill just across the

Federal Paper Board's original facility was a small mill in Bogota, New Jersey, acquired for $125,000. It was located across the tracks from a mill owned by Shortess's former employer, W.J. "Old Man" Alford.

tracks from Alford's Bogota operation. Shortess called his new corporation Federal Paper Board Company, Inc. Sales that first year were $460,000, and Federal earned a respectable $40,000 profit. Shortess was 45 years old when he founded Federal.

EARLIER ACQUISITION OF THE VAN REED MILL

Actually, the Bogota mill was not the first he acquired. Seven years earlier in 1909, while working for Alford, Shortess had purchased a mill in Reading, Pennsylvania, at a sheriff's auction for the astonishingly low sum of $7,500. This facility, located in the heart of Pennsylvania Dutch country, is known as the Van Reed mill. Shortess ran the facility as a sideline business while in Alford's employ — as if he didn't already have enough work to keep himself busy.

The story of the Van Reed mill is interesting in its own right, and provides a firsthand look at the early history of papermaking in the United States.

John Van Reed was a prosperous farmer and miller who, in 1820, converted one of his grist mills to the production of paper. He was 73 at the time. There wasn't anything fancy about the way paper was made at this original Van Reed facility. Straw or rags were chopped into fine pieces and mixed with water and chemicals to produce a pulp that looked like cottage cheese. The pulp was then spread across a screen; excess water was squeezed out; and when completely dry, the result was a rough-hewn but serviceable sheet of writing paper. All the work was done by hand.

John Van Reed died within weeks of entering the paper business. His son, also named John, then took over the operation. The younger John died three years later, whereupon his brother, Henry, took charge — though he too passed away three years after that. The next Van Reed, Henry's son Charles, managed the mill for more than a decade and then leased it to his son Henry Z. Van Reed, a sagacious businessman who secured a contract to supply paper to the State of Pennsylvania for the printing of official documents. Henry Z. Van Reed operated the business for nearly 30 years.

In 1853, as demand for paper continued to grow, Henry opened Mill Number Two (on the site of the mill that Shortess would later purchase), this time converting a sawmill to paper production. Papermaking technology was advancing rapidly, and in 1879 Henry and his sons purchased their first papermaking machine. As the business prospered, the Van Reeds became one of the wealthiest and most influential families in the county.

Then the bad times arrived. In 1888, a fire broke out at Mill Number Two. The Neversink Fire Company was summoned by phone. But the firehouse was more than five miles from the mill, and the horses pulling the engine soon gave out. By the time a team of mules could be dispatched to haul the engine the rest of the way, the mill was a total loss. Borrowing $32,000, Charles L. Van Reed (who had inherited the business from his father, Henry Z. Van Reed, in 1879) rebuilt on the same site; this new mill was the facility Shortess would later acquire.

The next blow came two years later, when a flood destroyed the dam that supplied power to the mill. Rallying again, Charles borrowed $28,000 and constructed a new dam. In the early 1890s, he began to build a railway from the mill to the main line some 20 miles away at Pottsville. But the train was wishful thinking; it never arrived. Although Charles Van Reed completed the roadbed, he was out of business before he could lay the track.

The fatal blow was struck by the Panic of 1893, which ushered in a nationwide economic depression. Financially overextended, Charles closed the business, and the buildings and equipment were sold at sheriff's auction. He scraped together his remaining resources to open a paper warehouse in Reading, which he operated until his death in 1924.

Legend has it that Henry Z. Van Reed paid $5 and a quart of whiskey for this 1872 painting of his paper mill and farm. He liked it so much he commissioned the artist to paint four more — one for each of his children.

The mill building on the stream, towards the left of the picture, burned to the ground in 1888 and was replaced by the mill in the photograph on the opposite page.

At the sheriff's auction, Mill Number Two passed into the hands of Francis P. O'Reilly, who ran it for nearly 15 years until he too was forced out of business by the Panic of 1907. Shortess acquired the mill in 1909. Perhaps one measure of Shortess's determination and staying power as an entrepreneur was his ability to survive the greatest panic of all, the Depression of the 1930s, and keep the Van Reed mill going for 33 years until his death in 1942. The mill was subsequently merged into Federal, which operated the facility until 1980 and then sold it.

The Reading, Pennsylvania, mill was acquired by Shortess in 1909 and still operates commercially today — a rare antique in an age of giant manufacturing facilities.

Today, a visitor to the Van Reed mill is surprised to find it still operating in much the same manner and with essentially the same machinery as it did a century ago. The mill is located in a lovely wooded area on the outskirts of Reading, near a neighborhood of stately eighteenth-century homes. It is operated around the clock, seven days a week, to meet demand. "All we do is run the machinery and patch it up," says Dick Wieder, the mill's office manager. "Very little capital is put into it." Phil Klahold, the plant superintendent, says that getting spare parts is the biggest challenge. Sometimes, parts take up to 20 weeks to obtain because they have to be custom-made. The facility is owned by Reading Paper Board Company and is the oldest paperboard mill in operation in the United States.

The Van Reed facility is a quaint, improbable antique in an industry dominated by large manufacturing complexes. Its annual production of 13,000 tons of paperboard is equivalent to less than 2 percent of the annual output of, say, the Federal mill at Augusta, Georgia. Robert McCabe, a former Federal employee who is Reading Paper Board's president, says the Reading mill survives and earns a steady profit by filling specialty orders for regional customers — orders too small for the big mills to bother with. "In the early days, little mills like Reading built Federal and were cash cows," he states. "Strangely enough, the Reading mill is doing equally well today."

The Bogota mill is shown in 1953 with Interstate 80 under construction in the background. It was closed in 1960, no longer able to compete with more modern, efficient facilities.

MEMORIES OF THE EARLY YEARS AT BOGOTA

The Bogota, New Jersey, mill — which launched Federal — was a mid-sized facility, with a production capacity about three times as great as that of Reading. Bogota is a small residential/industrial community about ten miles west of New York City. Driving by today on Interstate 80, one can still see the original Federal smokestack — with the company's name running down the side — just north of the highway near exit 67.

Federal closed the mill in 1960 (the building was recently being used by another company as a factory to make blue jeans), and moved its headquarters to Montvale, New Jersey, in 1968. Yet, memories of the Bogota corporate headquarters and mill are still dear to the hearts of many Federal retirees and long-time employees.

Miss Conrad, the bookkeeper who knew Shortess for many years, was born and raised in Bogota. She had never heard of Federal until a friend suggested she apply there for a job. She joined the company in 1926 at a starting salary of $100 a month — "which was actually considered good money for that time," she reports.

Miss Conrad looks back fondly to the close-knit family atmosphere of the company in those early days. Shortess was a fatherly boss who knew all his employees and watched out for their interests. His door was always open to discuss their concerns and personal problems. Until the Depression, he gave each of his employees a cake or a tin of cookies at Christmas and Easter.

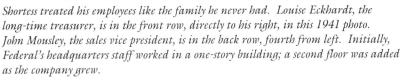

Shortess treated his employees like the family he never had. Louise Eckhardt, the long-time treasurer, is in the front row, directly to his right, in this 1941 photo. John Mousley, the sales vice president, is in the back row, fourth from left. Initially, Federal's headquarters staff worked in a one-story building; a second floor was added as the company grew.

Jeanne Derato, who joined Federal in 1927 as a secretary, still has one of these treasured tins — given to her by Shortess more than 60 years ago — and uses it to this day as a cookie box.

Federal's administrative and financial offices were located in a small one-story building. Later, a second story was added, and subsequently the building was expanded again. Federal's headquarters staff in the early years totaled about 20.

The company's treasurer was Louise Eckhardt, who had joined Federal at its founding and was second in authority to Shortess. She was outspoken and opinionated and would complain vehemently to Shortess whenever he was considering the purchase of a mill she felt he couldn't afford. He would invariably ignore her and buy it anyway.

Miss Eckhardt was responsible for the hiring of administrative and financial personnel, and she believed in employing single women. Married women were, in her view, not reliable because they might have babies. As a result, all female employees used their maiden names, whether single or not. One time, an employee who was secretly married became pregnant. To everyone's surprise, Miss Eckhardt accepted the news graciously and immediately started fussing over the mother-to-be to make sure she ate a proper diet.

Most employees, particularly the women, addressed each other by their last names — Miss Williamson, Miss Conrad, Miss Davies, Miss Bentley, Miss Lamartin and so on. Despite this formality, the women became good friends and often got together outside the office for dinner or tea. When the Depression struck, five of them had to be let go. Shortess and Miss Eckhardt apologized personally to each of them.

The sales staff was headed by a charming gentleman named John Mousley, who stayed with Federal more than 40 years before retiring in 1961. The real chief salesman, however, was Shortess himself. His ability to find new customers and win orders helped keep Federal afloat through many difficult times.

Situated between the office and the mill was a pond. It was surrounded by weeping willows and was a favorite spot for employees to gather for lunch. Employees brought their own food. An elderly timekeeper sold fruit to those who wanted it. Later, Federal opened a cafeteria and began serving hot meals.

The mill superintendent was Jack Reynolds. He ran a tight ship and was well respected by his men. The Bogota mill was not the largest Shortess ever owned; production capacity at his biggest mills was nearly twice that of Bogota. Nonetheless, the Bogota facility was one of his best, turning out a quality product and operating consistently in the black.

Given the fact that Shortess was not a rich man, it's interesting to speculate how he was able to buy the Bogota plant and establish Federal. Records from the period seem to indicate that Federal paid about $125,000 for the mill, putting up $50,000 in cash and borrowing the rest. They also show that Shortess had a silent partner named Stephen B. Fleming.

Fleming was a native of Indiana who served 16 years in that state's legislature before moving to New York in 1900 to pursue a career in investments and business. When Federal was organized, Fleming owned slightly more than half its common stock, Shortess owned slightly less than half. How Shortess met Fleming, and what role the latter played in organizing and financing the company, are matters unknown. By 1918, however, Shortess owned all of Federal's stock, and Fleming was suddenly out of the picture. Perhaps Fleming was a friend and financial backer who agreed to help Shortess get started, or perhaps there was some kind of dispute and Shortess bought him out. In any event, Fleming went on to a long and distinguished business career, eventually retiring as president of a bakery in Indiana at age 92.

EXPANDING TO VERSAILLES

Less than six months after acquiring the Bogota facility, Federal purchased a second mill — this one in Versailles (pronounced Ver-sáils), Connecticut. With an annual capacity of 60,000 tons of paperboard, the Versailles plant was the largest facility owned by Federal during Shortess's lifetime.

Shortess had, by now, established a pattern he would follow for the next 25 years: buy old mills, modernize their equipment

In 1916, the same year he founded Federal, Shortess acquired a mill in Versailles, Connecticut. The Versailles plant was the largest ever owned by Shortess.

The Steubenville, Ohio, mill was acquired by Shortess in 1927. It was so old it had a dirt floor.

Howard Brown, top, joined Federal in 1916 as manager of Versailles. He eventually became chairman of the board. Guy Freas, bottom, came to Federal in 1928 to manage Steubenville and later became executive vice president.

and improve their operations. At the time of Federal's founding, the banks of America's streams and rivers were lined with hundreds of paper and paperboard mills, mostly owned by local entrepreneurs. These facilities were sometimes traded back and forth among a succession of owners like chips in a poker game. Shortess became a leading player. By the late 1920s he had acquired eight mills, and by 1941 he owned nearly a dozen. Throughout his career, he sold only one mill — a small operation in Virginia's Shenandoah Valley.

All of his mills made "recycled" paperboard — board produced from wastepaper. Many were run-down and desperately in need of modernization when he bought them. The Versailles mill had been built in the mid-nineteenth century and was originally designed to make paper from straw. The Steubenville, Ohio, mill had a dirt floor when Shortess acquired the facility in 1928. He later installed a concrete floor.

Shortess visited his mills frequently to see how operations were going. Actual day-to-day operations, however, were left to each mill manager. Versailles was managed by Howard Brown, who joined Federal in its first year. Brown would later purchase a one-third interest in Federal and become chairman of the board.

Brown had worked previously with Shortess at Haverhill and was just 24 years old when he took charge of the Versailles facility. Gardner Macintosh, who was related to Brown by marriage, says

Shortess didn't blatantly hire Brown away from Haverhill Box
Board Co. — that wasn't Shortess's style. "He just said, 'Howard,
I'm leaving Haverhill and going into business on my own. I will
be there if some day you become interested.' I guess Howard
took the hint and went to work for him."

Paperboard was a growth industry, but the volatile nature of
the market made it difficult to earn consistent profits. Furthermore, during the Depression many mills could drum up only
enough business to operate two or three days a week, so that
competition became cutthroat and prices plummeted. The largest
customer of Versailles during the 1930s was Worcester Paper Box
Company, which was secretly owned by Shortess (we'll come back
to that in the next chapter). Worcester purchased paperboard
from Versailles and converted it to folding cartons for Lever
Brothers and other consumer product companies. "Howard
would have to wait until Worcester had an order from Lever to be
able to buy coal to start up the boilers and open the floodgates
and activate the mill and fulfill that order," says Macintosh, who
was a salesman at Versailles. "That's how tough it was."

The Steubenville, Ohio, mill — Shortess's second largest
after Versailles — was managed by Guy Freas, who joined Federal
in 1928 when he was 31 years of age. Freas would later purchase
a one-third interest in the company and become executive vice
president.

*Employees in Bogota posed
for this photo in 1941, when
Federal reached its 25th
anniversary. Jack Reynolds,
the mill superintendent, is
in the front row, far left.
Adele Lamartin, the
accounting supervisor to
whom Shortess's widow would
later turn for advice, is in
the front row, far right.
Third from right in the
front row is Jeanne Derato,
the secretary who joined the
company in 1927. Pauline
Conrad is standing directly
behind Shortess.*

*Federal's administrative
and financial group was
staffed by bright young
women who were hand-
picked by Miss Eckhardt; she
is standing next to Shortess,
to the left of the bannister.*

Arthur Freas, Guy's son, says, "When my father was in Steubenville and they had no orders, he'd go into Pittsburgh and hustle up some business and come back. He'd call in the crew and get the plant running. Sometimes he'd have to go down to the express office and plead with them to give him supplies that had been sent COD. He didn't have the money to pay for the darn stuff, and he'd convince them if he didn't get the supplies he couldn't make the paper to pay the COD bill."

One of Steubenville's customers in Pittsburgh was Grant Paper Box Company, owned by Walter Grant. Grant Paper Box made folding cartons for bakeries, toy companies and other customers. "During the Depression, not only was Walter Grant struggling to keep the business alive but his customers were doing the same," says Ray Hall, who joined Grant Paper Box in 1931 as

One of a series of trade advertisements from the 1960s extolling the benefits of paperboard packaging. The products of various customers were featured next to Federal's logo.

REVOLUTION IN PACKAGING

The far-reaching role of paperboard in your life may surprise you. Per-capita consumption of this heavy paper has increased more than 15-fold since the turn of the century, and Americans today consume an average of well over 350 pounds of paperboard per person per year — more than their consumption of newsprint, writing paper and printing paper combined!

Paperboard is used to make many different products, from paper cups to paperback book covers. One of the markets served by Federal in the 1980s was clue cards for the Trivial Pursuit board game. But most importantly, growth in demand for paperboard has been driven by a revolution in packaging.

Back in the "good old days," our grandparents or great-grandparents took a little wooden box to the store to buy eggs and a small can to buy milk. They scooped sugar from a barrel at the grocer's. And when they got sick, they bought a medicine formulated by a local pharmacist.

However, as Americans moved from farms to cities and living standards improved, they began to seek greater shopping convenience, increased product choice and higher standards of product integrity, including protection against damage, spoilage and contamination.

The paperboard packaging industry was born in response to these needs. Its roots date back to a mistake by a printer in 1879 — 37 years prior to Federal's founding by William Shortess. The printer was running an order of heavy-duty paper bags for a seed company and failed to notice that the printing plates were cutting the paper. Although the bags were ruined, the mistake sparked the a salesman. "As a result, they would fall behind in paying for cartons. Walter Grant had an old overcoat, with frayed sleeves and a tattered lining. He would get a list of customers who were past due, and he would put on his old overcoat and go plead poverty. In the majority of cases, it worked. They felt so sorry for him they would pay." Grant Paper Box was acquired by Federal in 1954. Hall joined Federal at that time and retired 14 years later as senior vice president in charge of Federal's folding carton division.

One time, the Steubenville mill fell behind on its taxes, and the tax collector came for a visit. Freas simply put a gun on his desk (whether it was actually loaded is unknown), and the tax man got up and left. The taxes were paid later when there was sufficient cash.

interest of the plant's owner, Robert Gair. He added special dies to his printing plates — some with sharp edges to cut paperboard into the proper shape, others with dull, rounded edges to make crease lines for folding the shape into a box. The result: the first "folding carton." Even today, folding cartons are the main type of box in which we buy facial tissue, crackers, cosmetics, breakfast cereal and hundreds of other products. They are called folding cartons because they fold at the creases and can be shipped flat from the carton plant. Prior "set-up" boxes were rigidly fixed at the creases and were shipped fully assembled from the manufacturer to the company ordering the boxes — an inconvenient and expensive arrangement.

With the invention of the folding carton, individual packaging became economically viable for the first time, permitting the mass distribution of consumer goods and allowing food products to be kept fresh on grocers' shelves for extended periods. In 1896, National Biscuit Company introduced Uneeda biscuits in a folding carton with a waxed paper liner — the first national brand packaged in that manner. It was an immediate hit with consumers, and other companies began to embrace the new marketing concept. In the 1930s, demand for paperboard packaging was further spurred by the opening of the first supermarkets, their shelves lined with packaged products.

Today, paperboard continues to be one of the most widely used packaging materials. It is versatile and affordable. Its smooth surface accommodates quality printing. And it is biodegradable and recyclable — important considerations as Americans become more concerned about protecting the environment.

A sampling of the many printed folding cartons Federal produced for leading manufacturers.

"THE OLD GENTLEMAN TYPE"

Somehow, Shortess was able to rise above the rough-and-tumble nature of the business. He had a unique personality that seemed to fit his role as a successful business executive. Tall, heavy-set and bald, he was a distinguished-looking gentleman who was known to all his employees as Mr. Shortess.

In 1941, when Shortess acquired the Packerack mill near Reading, Pennsylvania, he hired Frederick Hesser to restart it. Now retired in Florida, Hesser remembers Shortess as "the old gentleman type, always gracious and courteous... a wonderful man to work for." Hesser adds, "He said to me, 'Look, it's a hell of a thing getting one of these mills started. But as long as you're willing to do it, I'll stand by you.' And he called every night. Of course, that meant I had to stay down at the mill waiting for his calls. Nevertheless, when I got the mill running, he said, 'This is as good as Bogota now.' So he was happy."

Shortess could be uncommonly generous to employees in need. When Howard Brown's daughter, Eleanor, graduated from high school in 1935, she wanted to go to college, but her father couldn't afford the cost. "Daddy told Mr. Shortess," Eleanor recalls, "and Mr. Shortess said, 'Don't you worry. Just go ahead and send her.'" Eleanor got her college education. She never learned the details, but believes that Shortess either gave her father a raise or paid part of her college expenses out of his own pocket.

But there was another side to Shortess's personality — a tendency to overpromise if that was what it took to keep an employee happy. Perhaps this tendency was common among early industrialists struggling to make ends meet. Certainly, Shortess claimed that Alford, his former boss, had failed to deliver on a promise to him, and it's easy to understand how a business owner might promise too much when the very survival of his company is at stake. Some employees viewed this aspect of Shortess's personality with bemusement, a "there he goes again" attitude. Others, however — including Miss Eckhardt, the treasurer — found it extremely exasperating. Miss Eckhardt's disputes with Shortess came to a head in 1940, when she asserted that he had fallen behind on her salary despite repeated promises to catch up. Under threat of legal action, Shortess agreed to settle for $100,000. Although Miss Eckhardt stayed with the company, Shortess never did pay a penny of the agreed-on amount — and when he died in 1942, the new owners were left to make good on his pledge. Several other employees accepted low salaries in the belief they would inherit a piece of the company when Shortess died. To their shock and dismay, he left the entire business to his wife, Joanna. He did, however, leave small cash bequests to a number of long-time employees.

There was still another side to Shortess: the flamboyant promoter. One of his trademarks was the patriotic "1776" telephone number. During the 1920s, phone numbers were mostly four or five digits in length, and through sheer persistence he was able to obtain 1776 as the local number for nearly every one of his facilities. To this day, the phone number of Federal's headquarters in Montvale ends with the digits 1776.

Although Shortess was married, his marriage was not the focus of his life. He lived mainly at the exclusive New York Athletic Club in Manhattan, while Joanna stayed at their large, well-maintained home in Ridgewood, New Jersey. They did not have any children. It would be inaccurate, however, to suggest their relationship was hostile. They apparently got along even though they didn't see much of each other. Joanna was a deeply religious woman, active in the Baptist Church and known almost universally as "Mother" Shortess. Will gave her moral support by sending donations to her favorite religious causes, and he sometimes spent weekends with her at their home. When he died, he left her his business and a $300,000 trust fund.

ONE STEP AHEAD OF HIS CREDITORS

Although Shortess was a notable pioneer of the paperboard industry, he had one glaring weakness — he was inept when it came to managing his company's finances. This weakness dogged him throughout his career. Virtually from the founding of Federal in 1916 to his death in 1942, he was running one step ahead of his creditors.

An official of Gottesman & Company, a New York City pulp dealer that was one of Federal's major suppliers, described Shortess as an optimist who constantly expanded his business on the basis of anticipated earnings. This approach enabled Federal to grow faster than many of its competitors. On the other hand, it left little room for error in the event of an earnings downturn.

Federal's finances reached rock bottom in early 1929. Shortess owned his mills through a series of interlocking companies — Federal Paper Board Company, Inland Paper Board Company, Acme Paper Board Company, Liberty Paper Board Company, Midvale Paper Board Company and others. Some of these companies were profitable, others were not. Furthermore, they had borrowed from one another and guaranteed one another's debts. Shortess himself had pledged his Federal stock to the Trust Company of New Jersey as security for a loan.

As Shortess purchased more mills during the 1920s, and as his companies added more debt to finance these purchases, Federal and its affiliates fell behind on interest payments. On January 30, 1929, creditors stepped in and took control. They allowed

Shortess to continue to manage the business, but forced him to submit a letter of resignation to be exercised at their pleasure. When the stock market crashed just nine months later, his position might have seemed hopeless to some — but not to Shortess. Optimistic and energetic as ever, he struggled back and managed to repay his creditors in full, including interest — pulling off this feat during the worst years of the Great Depression! Under the watchful eyes of creditors, he had cut costs, stopped buying mills for a period of five years and focused on the basics of operating the ones he had. With the very survival of his business at stake, he had managed to generate enough cash to make good on his obligations (except perhaps to Miss Eckhardt and other hopefuls). In less dire circumstances, however, it was the thrill of the chase — acquiring more mills, finding new customers, being a successful and respected businessman — that seemed to interest him more than increasing profits or worrying about debt.

His resignation was never exercised, and the creditors' committee was disbanded in 1933. But that was merely the most dramatic in an ongoing series of financial crises.

To be sure, Shortess never came close to a soup kitchen. He had expensive tastes and always found ways to indulge them. Even in the most difficult times, he kept his chauffeured limousine and nicely tailored clothes. He so outspent his income that he personally owed $600,000 to his various companies, including Federal, by the early 1930s. He repaid at five cents on the dollar — and then had Federal pay him a $56,000 cash dividend!

In 1935, at the suggestion of creditors, he hired J.R. Kennedy as Federal's first professionally trained financial executive. Kennedy succeeded Shortess as president of Federal on the latter's death.

The financial woes of the company eased after Kennedy was brought on board. However, Shortess continued to treat his personal finances as if he didn't have a care in the world about money. In 1941, the year before his death, he paid more than $7,000 of interest on past-due income taxes — equivalent, after inflation, to more than $50,000 today.

CHAPTER 3

Opportunity Knocks — Not Once, But Twice

DESPITE his lack of aptitude for finance, William Shortess was in many ways a genius. Part of that genius was his ability to recognize opportunity and seize upon it. He was always ready to take a gamble if he thought it would help his business. Two examples occurred in 1928, when he acquired Worcester Paper Box Company, and 1935, when he purchased S-C-S Folding Box Company — both at fire-sale prices.

Worcester and S-C-S made folding cartons, and Shortess saw the benefits of entering that business. At a time when many other paperboard operators were content to manufacture paperboard and nothing else, Shortess realized he could lock up a guaranteed market for some of his paperboard if he owned factories that converted board to cartons. His idea proved farsighted; during the Depression, as numerous other paperboard companies were forced out of business because of a paucity of orders, Federal managed to survive — due in part to the business it obtained through Worcester and S-C-S.

These acquisitions foreshadowed Federal's decision, in the late 1940s and 1950s, to diversify downstream into folding cartons as a way to sell more paperboard and get closer to the ultimate consumers of its product.

THE ACQUISITION OF WORCESTER

The 1928 secret purchase of Worcester Paper Box Company, located in Medford, Massachusetts, just outside Boston, was one of the most interesting deals of Shortess's career. The acquisition was kept secret not because there was anything improper about it. The problem was that Harry Posner, Worcester's popular and charismatic owner, didn't want it known that his company had gotten into financial trouble and needed to be bailed out. Even today, some of Posner's friends and associates express surprise that Worcester was owned for nearly 15 years by Shortess.

Posner was one of the most beguiling characters in Federal's history. Barely five feet tall, he was a Russian Jew who sprinkled his conversation with amusing anecdotes and parables. It is sometimes said that Posner managed to succeed in business without ever having learned to read or write. However, the belief that he was illiterate, like so much of the lore of Harry Posner, is subject to interpretation. Posner was such a grand raconteur (and the details of his stories having perhaps been embellished over the years in the retelling) that it is often difficult to be sure where fact ends and fiction begins. The truth about Posner's "illiteracy," according to William Guiney (who was hired by Worcester in 1946 and became its general manager in the 1960s), was that Posner damaged his eyes as a young man and, consequently, required the services of an assistant to read to him and write for him. Even assuming that to be correct, his accomplishment in building a successful business, despite virtual blindness, was extraordinary in its own right.

Posner seemed to have a sixth sense that helped compensate for his poor eyesight. When bidding on a carton order, for instance, he was often able to figure out the proper price even before an estimator went through the formal process of determining the thickness and quality of the paperboard, analyzing all the costs and calculating a bid. "He could feel the size of a folding carton, the caliper of the board and such, and while the estimator was preparing the bid, he had already figured out the price in his head," says Guiney. "In fact, he would sometimes tell the estimator, 'I think you're wrong. Do it again.'"

HOW HARRY POSNER GOT INTO THE CARTON BUSINESS

Posner's life story reads like a melodramatic novel. He was born in Russia in 1881 and came to the United States at the turn of the century with barely a penny in his pocket. Although his father was a brewmaster, and the family lived comfortably, young Harry was a maverick who longed to leave home and get out from under the control of his parents. Another version has it that he fled Russia to avoid being drafted into the tsar's army, which thousands of immigrants did.

In any event, on arriving in New York he got a job helping to erect fire escapes on tenement buildings. (It was on this job, according to Guiney, that Posner's eyesight was damaged by sparks from a welding torch.) Thrown out of work by a strike, Posner moved briefly to Connecticut and then to Worcester, Massachusetts. In Worcester, he worked as a tailor, hustling vaudeville acts backstage to mend their costumes, and opened a clothes-cleaning business.

Then came the turning point in his life. "As my uncle told the story, there was another tenant in his building who made set-up boxes," says Robert Gold, Posner's nephew. "The tenant came to my uncle and wanted some money to expand his business, so my uncle lent him $2,500." In 1914, the box maker went broke and handed over his company to Posner in payment of the loan. "Harry said, 'Vat's the box business?' — he enjoyed telling the story many times," says Guiney, doing his best to imitate Posner's thick Russian accent. It so happened that one of Posner's customers was a successful Irish immigrant who owned a motorcycle company and was prominent in the city of Worcester. "He came into the store and found my uncle distraught because he had lost all his money in the ill-fated loan to the box company," says Gold. "This man talked my uncle into taking over the box business and running it." The motorcycle manufacturer enlisted two of his Irish colleagues to join him as financial backers, and the three — through their contacts with businesses in the Worcester area — were quickly able to secure customers for the carton plant.

"The real big event happened around 1916," says Gold. "This is the story I've been told. My uncle had a contract to purchase boxboard from National Folding Box [a New Haven, Connecticut, company later acquired by Federal] at a fixed price. The war in Europe literally doubled the price of boxboard in this country. He was afraid National would try to break his contract, so — this is the story he told me — he wrote to National and said, 'I have three partners and they don't believe you'll honor this contract.' And National wrote back and said it would provide all the boxboard he wanted at the contract price."

But National did try to void the contract, according to Gold, by shipping carload after carload of boxboard to Posner on the assumption he wouldn't be able to pay. However, Posner was up to the challenge. "My uncle told me he had boxboard stored in every barn and warehouse in Worcester, and he was selling it as fast as he could move it out," says Gold. "In 1916, he made a profit of over $300,000, which for a small business was an enormous amount of money."

The good times kept rolling when Posner secured a contract to supply folding cartons to Lever Brothers. Guiney, whose father was in charge of purchasing at Lever Brothers, says Lever started buying cartons from Posner to break up a cartel of other carton producers who were fixing prices. Gold says the version he heard was that some members of the Irish community in New England were organizing a boycott of Lever, an English-owned company. According to Gold, Posner went to Lever and said his Irish partners could get the boycott called off. They did just that, and Lever rewarded Posner by giving him a large order for cartons.

Whatever the case, Lever Brothers soon became Posner's major client and remained so for decades. The strength of their relationship was so enduring that years later in 1967, even after Posner had passed away, Lever put up nearly $2 million to help defend Federal against an attempt by an unfriendly investor to acquire a 43 percent interest in Federal. This unusual event is discussed in Chapter Nine.

THE NEAR-DEMISE OF WORCESTER PAPER BOX

Prospering under the guidance of Posner, Worcester Paper Box moved to a large new plant in Medford, Massachusetts, in 1926. Then in 1928, the motorcycle manufacturer's company foundered. The result was like the toppling of dominoes. The manufacturer withdrew his investment from Worcester Paper Box. With its capital suddenly diminished, Worcester was unable to pay its debts, and Posner was forced to scramble for cash. He turned to Shortess.

Shortess and Posner had first met in 1927, when they were brought together at a New York hotel by a paper salesman named Jesse E. Perry. Shortess and Posner were both successful, self-made businessmen, and Perry recognized that each had something to offer the other: Shortess was always eager to acquire another paperboard mill, so why not a folding carton plant? Posner might, in turn, agree to purchase paperboard from Federal. Perry spent so much time cultivating the development of a business relationship between the two that he ended up being fired from his job as a salesman.

In 1928 — just months before Federal itself ran into financial trouble and came under the control of a creditors' committee — Posner and Shortess met again, this time striking a bargain. Shortess acquired Worcester for $67,000, giving Posner the cash he needed. Hannah Posner, Harry's wife, received an option to buy back 50 percent of the company. And Harry remained the company's chief executive, with the understanding he would buy paperboard from Federal's Versailles mill.

Those facts are clear. What happened next is not. Once the deal was struck, Perry insisted he had been promised a finder's fee in the form of a 10 percent equity interest in Worcester, and also a 2 $\frac{1}{2}$ percent commission on all the paperboard that Federal sold to Worcester. Shortess apparently ignored Perry's entreaties for payment, and nothing more happened until 1943, one year after Shortess's death. Perry then threatened to sue Federal for $360,000. J. R. Kennedy, Federal's new president, found it "rather strange that Perry should wait some 14 or 15 years before making his claim." Posner, on the other hand, thought there might be some merit in Perry's assertions and urged Kennedy to settle, afraid that court hearings might "bring to light unpleasant skeletons of years ago." Those skeletons were, presumably, Worcester's financial troubles in 1928. With Posner mediating, Federal settled for $25,000.

As if that wasn't enough, there was the question of who really owned Worcester. Shortess had invested in Worcester personally, rather than through Federal, and after he died the executor of his estate assumed Shortess still owned Worcester lock, stock and barrel. Hannah Posner, on the other hand, said she had exercised her option during the 1930s and reacquired a 50 percent interest in the company. At first, neither side could prove its position to the other's satisfaction, but Hannah eventually received her 50 percent (the details of how this settlement was reached are today unknown), and the estate then sold the remaining 50 percent to the Posners for $162,500.

Remarkably, through all this disagreement and turmoil, Harry Posner remained on the friendliest of terms with J. R. Kennedy, and Worcester Paper Box continued to purchase its paperboard from Federal. Helping to cement the relationship, Posner's niece, Anne, served for many years as Kennedy's secretary.

DAILY STROLLS THROUGH THE FACTORY

One reason for Harry Posner's success was his keen sense of human nature. He arrived at work each morning shortly after seven o'clock and always entered the building at the back end, walking the length of the factory floor to get to his office. Gold tells about joining the company in 1950 and being warned by his uncle never to accompany him on these morning strolls. "He said people in the factory might be reluctant to approach him and talk about their problems if he wasn't walking alone," Gold recalls.

Worcester Paper Box had more than 400 employees. Posner took a personal interest in their lives, helping finance their homes and their children's educations and encouraging them to support philanthropic causes. Beginning in the early 1930s, he matched all their gifts to charitable organizations, a practice he continued for three decades until he sold the company.

He himself had a lifelong interest in medical research and education and became an important contributor to Tufts University in Medford. In 1948, he established the Daniel E. Ziskin Memorial Research Laboratory at the Tufts School of Dental Medicine in memory of Hannah's brother, a pioneer in oral

While some said that Harry Posner, second from right, could barely read or write, his success as a business owner was so great that he was awarded an honorary doctorate from Tufts University in 1952.

pathology at Columbia University. In 1953, the Posners gave $1,086,000 to Tufts "as part payment of the debt we owe this land of freedom and opportunity." The donation, at the time the second largest ever made by an individual or individuals to Tufts, was earmarked for medical education. It enabled construction of Posner Hall, a dormitory for medical and dental students.

In 1952, Tufts awarded Posner the honorary degree of Doctor of Commercial Science in recognition of his business achievements and philanthropic endeavors.

FINAL SALE

Federal acquired Worcester for good in 1961, paying $3 million in common stock and notes. To welcome Posner and his people into the Federal fold, Kennedy held a small dinner party — and Posner, now 80 years old, proved once again that he had a story for every occasion. John P. Murphy, who was a member of Federal's management committee at the time, reports that J. R. Kennedy stood up at one point during the evening and commented that Federal had made a favorable deal in acquiring Worcester. "Then Posner got up and said in his Russian accent, 'Jack, I want to tell a story.' And J.R. said, 'Sure Harry, go ahead.'" Posner told about a traveling salesman who lost a costly hat while visiting a customer. The salesman put the hat on his expense account for reimbursement, but his boss disallowed it. Week after week the salesman kept seeking reimbursement without success, until his boss finally warned he would be fired on the spot if the hat showed up one more time. Thereafter the hat didn't appear again, and after a few weeks the boss congratulated the salesman on his good sense. Murphy continues: "And the salesman said, 'Well boss, that hat is on my expense account, but you find it.' Then Harry turned to J.R. and said with great humor, 'On this deal you think is so good, Harry is coming out very well — but you find it!' And J.R. roared with laughter."

Posner died in August 1962, one year after selling his company to Federal. He and Hannah had no children. He left the bulk of his estate to Hannah and Tufts.

THE ACQUISITION OF S-C-S BOX

In 1935, Shortess made another deal to lock in a captive customer for the Versailles mill: he acquired an 80 percent interest in S-C-S Box Company of Palmer, Massachusetts. Like Worcester, S-C-S was a financially distressed company that was a natural outlet for paperboard produced at Versailles.

The S-C-S Box Company plant in Palmer, Massachusetts, produced jigsaw puzzles when there weren't enough carton orders to keep its employees busy.

S-C-S had been founded in Willimantic, Connecticut, by three men named Sherman, Colgan and Scoucher (hence, the initials in the company name). "Sherman was the designer of the molded egg carton, Colgan had the money and Scoucher did the selling," says William Coulter, who retired from Federal in 1986.

S-C-S moved to Palmer, in central Massachusetts, in 1934 or 1935 to obtain more manufacturing space for egg cartons. However, technical problems in producing the cartons drove the company deeply into debt, and when it was unable to pay some $100,000 to Federal for board purchased from the Versailles mill, Shortess accepted an 80 percent equity interest as payment.

Although S-C-S specialized primarily in the manufacture of egg cartons, clothing boxes and bakery boxes, when business got slow it produced jigsaw puzzles to generate cash. These were sold through local five-and-ten-cent stores at a retail price of ten cents each. Subsequently, S-C-S became one of the leading producers of tomato boxes for A & P and other supermarket chains. These colorful little paperboard containers, holding three or four tomatoes covered with cellophane, were popular throughout the '40s and '50s.

Even though the S-C-S plant in Palmer was one of Shortess's smaller facilities, it held a unique distinction for many years — it was the last Shortess-owned facility still operated by Federal. By the late 1970s, every other plant and mill owned by Shortess had been sold or closed. Only Palmer — generating annual revenues of some $8 million (about one-half of one percent of Federal's total annual sales) — survived as a part of the company.

But even the Palmer carton plant saw its day in the sun eventually come to an end. In December 1990, Federal announced that it would sell seven of its folding carton plants, including Palmer. With that sale, Federal will no longer operate any of the mills or plants owned by Shortess.

THE END OF THE SHORTESS ERA

Will Shortess died in New York on February 4, 1942, following a brief illness. Looking back today, we can see the first third of Federal's 75-year history as the Shortess era — a time of risk-taking, growth, consolidation and narrow escapes from financial disaster.

Like so many early industrialists, Shortess was a highly individualistic, self-made man of incredible initiative and determination. He had the courage and skill to start a business and make it grow. Through years of struggle, he left something worthwhile on which others could build.

Will Shortess did everything with style. The ornate floral piece on his desk, in the shape of papermaking machine, celebrated Federal's 25th anniversary in 1941.

The plaques on the table show the growth in Federal's production from 34 tons of paperboard a day in 1916 to 230 in 1941.

TWENTY-FIFTH ANNIVERSARY

OF THE

FOUNDING

OF

FEDERAL PAPER BOARD COMPANY, Inc.

BOGOTA, N. J.

TESTIMONIAL DINNER TO
WILLIAM G. SHORTESS
COMMEMORATING TWENTY-FIFTH ANNIVERSARY
OF THE FOUNDING OF
FEDERAL PAPER BOARD COMPANY, INC.
HOTEL COMMODORE   APRIL 19, 1941

Federal held a grand banquet at New York's Commodore Hotel to celebrate its 25th anniversary. The New York Times *reported the event, describing Shortess as one of the paperboard industry's pioneers and important leaders. He is seated at the head of the table, with Howard Brown seated to his left. J.R. Kennedy is standing, second from left.*

The program for the anniversary dinner contained a quotation from Sophocles: "Success, remember, is the reward of toil."

CHAPTER 4

'Mother' Shortess Takes Charge

ANYONE who has been involved in the sale of a family business knows how complex and emotionally charged such a transaction can be. The sellers may have second thoughts about giving up control of an enterprise that has been in the family for years. They may want assurances that the business will continue to be managed in a way that reflects the ideals of the founder, or that valued employees will be treated fairly by the new owners. Or they may simply feel at loose ends, wondering what they will do to keep busy after the company has been sold.

All these elements — and more — came into play during the 1943 sale of Federal Paper Board Company.

Within weeks of Will Shortess's death in February 1942, two contradictory viewpoints emerged:

Joanna Shortess, who had inherited the business from her husband, wanted to become active in its management and assume its presidency. The fact that she was 74 years old and had no previous business experience didn't seem to faze this deeply religious, soft-spoken — and tenacious — woman in the least. "Mother" Shortess, as she was called, framed the issue in highly subjective terms: she loved her husband, his business was his pride and joy, she had a strong desire to manage it — and that was that. Still grieving over the loss of Will, she was looking for something positive to hold onto in her life, and "to talk business," she explained to a friend, "peps me right up." Since she was now Federal's sole owner, who was to tell her she couldn't be its president?

Wishing you a Merry
Christmas & Happy New Year
from Florida

Mother Shortess.

Mother Shortess was an avid letter writer and always sent cards at Christmas and Easter.

On the other hand, three of William Shortess's chief lieutenants — J. R. Kennedy, the 42-year-old assistant to the president, who had brought financial stability to the various companies owned by Shortess; Guy Freas, 45, manager of the Steubenville, Ohio, mill; and Howard Brown, 49, manager of the Versailles, Connecticut, mill — wanted to buy the company and operate it themselves. Together with Archibald Maxwell, a vice president of Guaranty Trust Company who was executor of the Shortess estate, they assumed day-to-day management responsibility while the estate was being settled. Shortess had indicated a number of times that he planned to leave an equity interest in Federal to each of his three valued associates when he died. Now that Shortess was gone, and the business had in fact been left entirely to Joanna, the three executives joined forces in seeking to purchase Federal and its affiliated companies. Though not close friends, they realized that Mother Shortess would never sell to one of their number and risk offending the other two. Thus, they were brought together by the practicality of common interest. They referred to themselves as "the syndicate."

A REMARKABLE PROPOSAL, A REMARKABLE RESPONSE

To be fair to Mother Shortess, she knew very well that she didn't have the knowledge or training to manage Federal by herself. So she proposed an astonishing deal: She had no children; the people at Federal were her "family." Consequently, she would give each of the three men a 10 percent ownership interest as "an outright gift and without strings." Such a gift, she noted, would have a value of approximately $450,000, or $150,000 per man, and "would be payment for their brains in running the business." She herself would retain a 70 percent interest and become active in the company's affairs as a full partner. When she died, the three men would inherit her 70 percent interest in equal shares.

It was an extraordinary offer, a once-in-a-lifetime opportunity for Kennedy, Freas and Brown to acquire a $7-million-a-year corporation at absolutely no cost — the only condition being that Mother Shortess would become Federal's new president and retain a 70 percent ownership interest for the rest of her life. Their response was equally remarkable: they politely turned her down and continued to negotiate to purchase the company. To appreciate their decision, one must first understand Joanna Shortess's personality and interests.

A small, energetic woman of strong opinions, she was a devout Baptist who lived by the teachings of the Bible in everything she did. For the previous 15 years, she had journeyed each winter to South Carolina to study at the Columbia Bible College, generally staying three or four months before returning home.

A prolific letter writer, she once estimated that she had written over 60 of them to friends during one four-week period. Moreover, her letters weren't just little notes. They were long, emotional missives filled with Biblical quotations. Mother Shortess sometimes complained that friends didn't write her as often as she wrote them, but who could possibly keep up?

She could be gracious and charitable — quick to help out a friend in need, for instance, or chip in money for a favorite cause. Following a brief hospitalization in 1946, she spontaneously donated $1,200 to the hospital library in gratitude for the care she had received.

On the other hand, she could come across as formidable and overwhelming. Mother Shortess lived with her maid Agnes in a

Whether she has wintering at Columbia Bible College in South Carolina or travelling in Europe, Mother Shortess deluged her friends with letters. The quotation on the stationery reads: "Thanks be to God, which giveth us the victory through our Lord Jesus Christ. 1 Cor. 15:57."

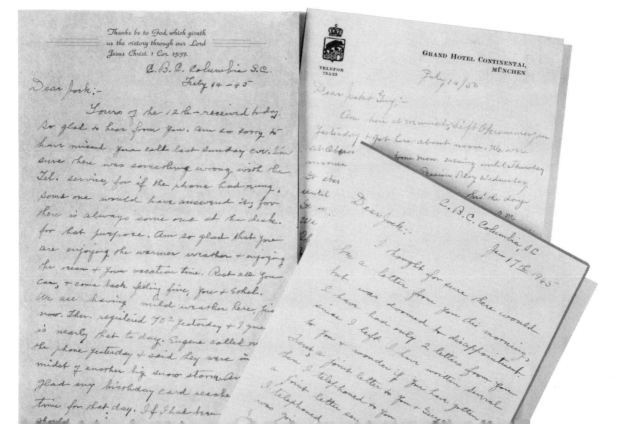

*J.R. Kennedy, his wife Ethel,
and two sons visit with Mother
Shortess at her home in
Ridgewood, New Jersey, in the
early 1940s.*

large, Tudor-style home in Ridgewood, New Jersey — a lovely, wooded suburban community some 15 miles northwest of New York City. She invited Guy Freas and his family for dinner one evening. Looking back, this is how Guy's daughter, Leanne Freas Trout, remembers the occasion:

"I was eight or nine at the time and had never met Mother Shortess before. As I recall, she was quite short, and she was very conservative in the way she dressed. What I remember most, though, was how long it took before dinner was served. The food was on the table, but first she said a lengthy grace. Then she passed around a little box shaped like a loaf of bread. Inside were 'bread slices' — cards with Biblical verses on them. Each person had to pick a card and read the verse out loud. And then she gave a little sermonette on each verse after it had been read. I couldn't wait to eat!"

Mother Shortess was adamantly opposed to tobacco and alcohol, and this too could lead to awkward moments. She had traveled to Norwich, Connecticut, to visit Howard Brown and his wife (teetotalers themselves, though not so outspoken in their views). As it happened, the Browns' daughter, Eleanor, was visiting from Arizona with her newborn baby. "My doctor had recommended that I drink beer to help the flow of milk," Eleanor recalls. "My folks wanted me to follow the doctor's orders, but they didn't want Mrs. Shortess to be unhappy." So Eleanor slipped down to the basement to sip her brew while Mother Shortess, unaware, remained engaged in conversation upstairs. Staying in Mother Shortess's good graces was especially sensitive at that time because Brown, Freas and Kennedy were in the midst of their attempt to buy Federal.

Why did they turn down Mother Shortess's offer to give them the company free? The hitch, of course, was her desire to play an active role in management — an idea they viewed as unworkable, given her strong-willed personality and total lack of business experience.

A Bid to Acquire the Company Without a Penny Down

In truth, Kennedy, Brown and Freas were in a tight spot. The problem was this: They were all family men who had worked many years for modest wages and had very little money. Consequently, having said no to an outright gift of the company, their only hope was to convince Mother Shortess to sell it to them on credit — without so much as a penny down. That, in itself, was ironic, since each of the three was, by nature, staunchly conservative when it came to matters of finance. However, they had no other choice: going deeply into debt was the only way they could afford to buy Federal.

To complicate matters further, Mother Shortess was under great pressure from some of her Baptist friends not to trust the three would-be acquirers. Shortly after Will's death, she briefly considered — and rejected — the idea of donating the company to the church. Even with that decision behind her, she continued to be admonished by friends not to sell to the three-member syndicate. In a long, rambling letter, one minister warned: "Please do not think I am questioning the integrity of these men. I believe they are wonderful men to run the business. I also believe that they are entirely honest. But you must remember two things. One is that men will naturally act for their own advantage. An honest man will do that when it can be done honestly. The other thing to remember is that these men, even those who are Christians, are not spiritual men and do not look at things the way you do. They certainly would have no understanding of our conception of the work of the Lord."

The minister reminded her that she had agreed to fund a missionary program — and if she sold the company, he said, she might not have the financial resources to do so. He also warned that the three men, once they had acquired the business, might pry into Mrs. Shortess's personal affairs and seek to prevent her from making any further donations to religious causes. He said that Joanna needed a "trusted banker" or other adviser. Still further, he asked to see a copy of her will and warned that she shouldn't sign anything without first giving him a chance to review it.

But Mother Shortess, iron-willed as ever, rejected the minister's advice. Scribbling comments throughout the margins of his letter, she told herself that she knew instinctively she could trust the three men. Moreover, she wrote, she didn't need an outside adviser to protect her: "I think I already have a helper in Miss Lamartin. Will trusted her and I can too."

Dear, devoted Miss Lamartin. An accounting supervisor who had worked at Federal for many years, she was both meticulous and loyal. She had often handled personal financial matters, such as tax returns and insurance problems, for the Shortesses, and Joanna knew her well and trusted her absolutely. It is highly unlikely, however, that Mother Shortess actually consulted Adele Lamartin on the disposition of Federal. And in any case, Miss Lamartin would almost certainly have shrunk from the idea of giving advice on a decision as momentous as whether to sell the company.

The episode indicates, nonetheless, just how desperate Mother Shortess had become. Consider her quandary: Her husband had never told her anything about the business, nor had he left any instructions regarding its future once he was gone. Now forced to decide on her own, she was under conflicting pressures and didn't really know where to turn for advice.

Colonel Joseph M. Hartfield, right, senior partner of White & Case, helped convince Mother Shortess to sell Federal to the three-man syndicate. He is pictured with Paul Pennoyner, the firm's managing partner.

COLONEL HARTFIELD TO THE RESCUE

The delicate task of convincing Joanna that the only realistic course was to sell the business fell to the colorful Joseph M. Hartfield, senior partner in the Wall Street law firm of White & Case, and to Archibald Maxwell, executor of the estate. Both men had been advisers to Will Shortess, and both ended up playing critical roles in Federal's history over a period of years.

Hartfield was born in Kentucky and was a devoted partisan of the state. Early in his life, a Kentucky governor had bestowed on him the honorary title of colonel. From that day forward, he bore it in public print, in the courts and in all the circles in which he moved.

Dapper and bald — and barely five feet tall — the Colonel had a unique and dynamic personality. Once, chairing a meeting of lawyers in a corporate board room, he simply took off his shoes, climbed onto the board of directors' table and conducted the meeting while seated cross-legged on it — a practical, if inelegant, solution that enabled everyone in the room to see him.

Not only was he a leading New York trial attorney, he also enjoyed the good life and was prominent in cultural affairs. One newspaper account described him as a lifelong bachelor who was sometimes seen traveling about town with a beautiful woman on each arm. He served for a number of years as chairman of the executive committee of the Metropolitan Opera and was long-time counsel for the American Red Cross. He was also a Chevalier of the Legion d'Honneur of France.

It is hard to imagine an odder pair than the worldly Colonel Hartfield and the pious Mother Shortess. However, Joanna respected men of accomplishment in business, and she placed great stock in Hartfield's advice. When the diminutive Colonel was enlisted to help negotiate the sale of Federal, he was 62 years old and at the height of his career.

Though his credentials were less dazzling, Archie Maxwell was a man of considerable experience and competence in his own right. He had founded a bank in 1926 and had later joined the Guaranty Trust Company of New York (now Morgan Guaranty Trust Company) as a vice president. Maxwell was 61 years old at the time of the negotiations, and although he would retire from the Guaranty Trust Company four years later, he remained a member of Federal's board of directors for a decade after that.

"I KNOW YOU WILL STAND BY ME"

Clearly, the negotiations to give up control of Federal were very stressful to Joanna Shortess. By January 1943, eleven months after Will's death, negotiations had reached the critical point and were being conducted by telegram, letter and telephone back and forth between Mother Shortess at the Columbia Bible College in South Carolina, Maxwell and Hartfield in New York, Kennedy in New Jersey, Brown in Connecticut and Freas in Ohio. In a lengthy and emotional letter dated January 23, 1943, Mother Shortess made a final plea to Kennedy: "I only want to say this to you, and I've written to Howard [Brown] and told him that all I want is a partnership in Will's business with you three men. While I live let me have what I feel Will would want me to have.... Jack, there never was a widow left so absolutely alone as I. There isn't a soul I can turn to but you three men, and I trust you all perfectly. I know you will stand by me."

Finally, one of Colonel Hartfield's associates traveled by train to South Carolina, meeting with Mrs. Shortess at the Columbia Bible College on February 2, 1943. He gently broke the news that, while Colonel Hartfield proposed that she retain a seat on Federal's board of directors after the sale, her active involvement in the day-to-day management of the business would be out of the question. Perhaps worn down by the lengthy negotiations, she gave in and agreed to sell the business. The papers were signed that very afternoon, just two days short of the first anniversary of her husband's death. As we shall soon discover, it turned out to be a decision she would never regret — a decision that not only brought her financial security and peace of mind, but also a new spirit of independence and adventuresomeness that saw her, among other things, off in the Middle East riding a camel in her eighties. The sale became a turning point in this memorable lady's life.

SELLING FEDERAL TO "MY BOYS"

It was also a turning point in the lives of Brown, Kennedy and Freas. In agreeing to the sale, Mother Shortess had bestowed upon them her customary generosity. She sold the business to "my boys," as she now began to call them, for a $1.5 million, non-interest-bearing, 90-day promissory note secured by the common stock of the companies — without a penny down, just as they had hoped. (Obtaining immediate cash from the sale had never been a priority for Joanna. In addition to bequeathing her his business, Will had left a $300,000 trust fund on which she lived comfortably.)

Included in the sale were four companies:

Federal Paper Board Company, with five paperboard mills in New Jersey, Connecticut and New York;

Acme Paper Board Company, with four mills in Pennsylvania and Maryland;

Liberty Paper Board Company, with one mill in Ohio; and

S-C-S Box Company, which manufactured folding cartons at its plant in Massachusetts.

The estate had already sold Shortess's interest in Worcester Paper Box Company to the Posners, so that Worcester was not included in the sale to Kennedy, Brown and Freas.

The three partners quickly merged all paperboard operations into Federal, which became their flagship corporation.

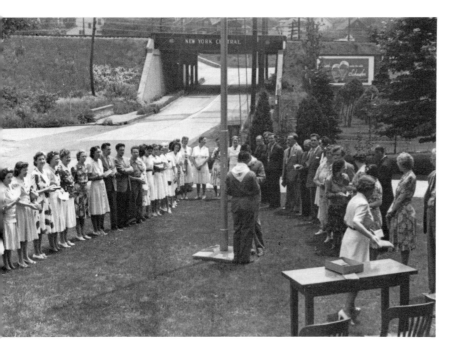

A flagpole in front of Federal's Bogota headquarters was dedicated to the memory of William Shortess one year after his death. Mother Shortess attended the ceremony and later told J.R. Kennedy she had been deeply moved.

SEVEN TIMES EARNINGS

Was $1.5 million a fair price? To find out, let's look at Federal's sales and earnings results over a six-year period — from 1942, the year before the acquisition, through the five years after:

FEDERAL PAPER BOARD COMPANY AND AFFILIATES

	Sales	Net Income
1942	$ 7,000,000	$ 415,000
1943	8,400,000	225,000
1944	9,900,000	206,000
1945	10,300,000	159,000
1946	12,500,000	1,168,000
1947	18,600,000	2,921,000

Based on 1942 financial results, the price was less than four times earnings, suggesting that the buyers got a very good deal. However, the U.S. economy was on a wartime footing, and Federal's profits were coming under severe pressure as a result of raw materials shortages and excess profits tax. The price reflected the reality that earnings would remain depressed so long as the war continued.

Financial results for 1943 (the sale was completed in February of that year) provide a more realistic yardstick. On that basis, the price was approximately seven times earnings, fairly typical of market values for small industrial companies at the time. Although Federal's records are not entirely clear on this point, the price was apparently established by Maxwell in his role as executor of the Shortess estate and accepted by all parties without question.

"IT SEEMED LIKE ALL THE MONEY IN THE WORLD"

As we shall see in the next chapter, the new owners worked hard to increase sales, streamline operations and reduce costs, and these efforts — together with a booming postwar economy — led to stunningly higher profits beginning in 1946. Federal was on its way to dramatic growth, and there could no longer be any doubt that they had made a wise decision in buying the company.

Yet, no one could possibly have foreseen this success in 1943. The world was then engulfed in war. Federal's cash flow was poor. Its facilities were old and in need of modernization. Furthermore, in acquiring the company entirely on credit, the buyers were taking an enormous personal financial risk.

Today, the three partners are gone. But in talking with their children, themselves now in their fifties and sixties, one hears many vivid memories of this exciting, and traumatic, period in their families' lives — memories of their fathers coming home and declaring that Mother Shortess had finally agreed to sell, and nervous talk about being more than $1 million in debt. "My mother told me that Daddy had just borrowed a million dollars. It seemed like all the money in the world," says Leanne Freas Trout.

A DESIRE TO BE MORE THAN A LENDER

The $1.5 million, non-interest-bearing note that the buyers gave Mother Shortess was not intended as permanent financing. It was an interim step, providing time for the new owners to secure long-term capital from other sources. They did just that three months later, in May 1943, borrowing $1,050,000 from the Metropolitan Life Insurance Company. Using that money, they repaid the note by giving Mother Shortess $1,050,000 in cash and a five-year, $450,000 note bearing 5 percent interest. Later, she exchanged the $450,000 note for 5 percent preferred stock, reflecting her desire to be more than just a lender to Federal. She held onto the preferred for the rest of her life.

These events could well have marked the end of Mother Shortess's role in the history of Federal Paper Board Company. Having acquired Federal, the three partners might just as easily have gone about their business without further concern for her interests and needs. However, they felt a moral responsibility to an unspoken side of the bargain — an aspect that involved more than money.

It had been clear from the beginning that Mother Shortess, in selling Federal, was seeking friendship and a "family" as much as cash. Recognizing this, the three men stuck by her and became surrogate sons. They wrote her often. They talked with her by phone. They invited her to their homes. They found doctors and nurses when she needed special care. They visited her when she was ill. They assisted her in making travel arrangements. They recommended professionals to manage her finances. They sent her flowers.

J.R. Kennedy became like a son to Mother Shortess after the death of her husband and visited her often. He was a dignified-looking man and a dapper dresser.

Kennedy, Brown and Freas borrowed $1,050,000 from Metropolitan Life Insurance Company to help finance the acquisition of Federal. The money was deposited in Federal's account at Guaranty Trust Company and, with this check, was paid to the Shortess estate. The check is endorsed on the back by four of Federal's five directors: Kennedy, Brown, Freas, and Archibald Maxwell, executor of the estate.

Mother Shortess, in turn, remained on Federal's board of directors until her death in 1954, opening each board meeting with a prayer. In addition, with her new-found freedom and wealth, she emerged as a different woman. While religion continued to be the focal point of her life, she seemed to be more relaxed and adventuresome, journeying twice to Europe in her eighties on grand tours. On one of these trips, J. R. Kennedy, a devout Catholic, arranged for Mother Shortess, a died-in-the-wool Baptist, to have an audience with the pope. Following the audience, she wrote Kennedy to express her thanks and delight.

"THE UNCERTAINTY OF LIFE"

Born in 1868, just three years after the end of the Civil War, Joanna Shortess had witnessed in her lifetime the rise of America's industrial might, inventions such as the airplane, automobile, wireless and television, the Great Depression, two world wars, the dawn of the nuclear age and much more.

Irrespective of the confusing and sometimes shattering change that had occurred in the world around her, she remained unshaken in her faith. Once, on hearing of the death of a friend, she had written: "It only reminds us of the uncertainty of life, and the necessity for preparing for the change which must come to us all. It is a blessed thing to know that The Blood of Jesus Christ, shed on the cross for all sinners, cleanses us from all sin; and by faith in Him we have eternal life; and so, when the time comes to go, we need not fear."

Mother Shortess was 86 years old when she died on September 27, 1954, following a four-month battle with colon cancer. Fittingly, her "boys" arranged her funeral and Federal paid for it, later being reimbursed by her estate.

She left bequests of $175,000 to the Columbia Bible College to build a chapel in memory of her husband, $192,000 to other religious institutions, and varying amounts to nieces and nephews, as well as small bequests to a number of long-time Federal employees, including Miss Lamartin, the accounting supervisor. Neither did she forget Archibald Maxwell, the banker, nor her three "boys." Now successful and well-to-do themselves, the four men were hardly in need of money. She nevertheless continued to shower them with generosity even after she was gone, leaving each an amount in excess of $100,000. They had, after all, become her "family."

Chapter 5

Rule of Three

Despite their eagerness to acquire Federal and its affiliates, the three buyers understood from the beginning that it would be difficult to make their investment pay off.

In 1943, Federal was still a relatively small company with 700 employees. Its sales were spread among a dozen mills, some of which were making money while others were losing it about as fast as it could be made. On top of that, having borrowed to finance the purchase, the new owners faced the need to meet heavy debt service requirements at a time of reduced paperboard demand and higher raw material costs due to the wartime economy.

While Federal was marginally profitable following the acquisition, cash flow was negative. "There was no money available for experimenting, there was no money available for mistakes," J. R. Kennedy would later say. "We had to be right and we had to work fast." The new owners immediately adopted an austerity program, similar to the measures taken four decades later by managements of many companies acquired through leveraged buyouts in the 1980s.

They suspended dividend payments on the common stock and reduced capital expenditures to conserve cash.

They slashed costs, including their own salaries. They drew $15,000 each in their first year of ownership, compared with the nearly $65,000 annually that Shortess had collected prior to his death.

They reviewed the company's operations for opportunities to prune and consolidate. Four mills — the Tulpehocken and Packerack facilities in Pennsylvania and the Windsor and Midvale plants in New York — were sold or closed.

They entered negotiations with suppliers for extended payment terms. Federal made its paperboard primarily from wastepaper, combined with wood pulp in some instances. "We first arranged for a meeting with our wastepaper suppliers through the National Association of Waste Material Dealers," Kennedy later recalled. "Without the cooperation of these suppliers, given so willingly, we would not have been able to continue."

However, paying for raw materials was one thing. As World War II continued and raw materials came into increasingly short supply, finding them became the single biggest challenge faced by Federal and other paperboard manufacturers. Fred Hesser, then working at the Steubenville, Ohio, mill, recalls scouring the nation to locate wastepaper. "I got it from people I knew in the business, all the way from Chicago to Philadelphia," he says. "Steubenville did well during the war. Oh my God, we ran seven days a week. Everybody else in the industry ran four or five. Nobody else could get enough wastepaper, but we did."

As for wood pulp, in May 1944 Kennedy reported to the board of directors, "The supply situation in pulp has progressed to the critical point. There are no definite signs of substantial relief before cessation of hostilities. It is, however, possible that the situation may be relieved by importation from Russia or Scandinavian countries after the latter's release from German domination." Somehow, Federal managed to get the pulp it needed.

In retrospect, the war years were a period of consolidation and survival for Federal. Earnings declined from $415,000 in 1942 to $159,000 in 1945, even as sales rose from $7 million to $10.3 million. The three men were happy just to keep the company afloat.

To be sure, Federal had the support of an unusual array of blue-chip advisers. Kennedy and his associates — and Shortess before them — knew how to pick the best. Federal's lead bank was Guaranty Trust Company, later merged with J. P. Morgan to form Morgan Guaranty Trust Company. Its major lender was Metropolitan Life. Its law firm was White & Case. Its public accountant was Haskins & Sells. And later, when it went public in 1953, its investment banker was Goldman Sachs. This was a powerhouse group for a company of any size, and it helped give Federal credibility with customers, suppliers and lenders. Morgan Guaranty, White & Case and Haskins & Sells (now called Deloitte & Touche) are still affiliated with the company today, each having been continuously associated with Federal for half a century or more. Federal's largest lender today is Prudential Insurance Company of America, a heavyweight in its own right.

Moreover, the new owners took important steps to improve Federal's management practices and bring it into the modern age. Among other actions, they strengthened the company's financial controls, added group life and hospitalization insurance for salaried employees in 1943 and introduced the company's first pension plan in 1944.

MESSRS. KENNEDY, BROWN AND FREAS

Who were these three men, and what role did each play within the company?

In theory, they were equals. Each owned one-third of Federal and each drew exactly the same salary. Their salaries were raised in tandem to $25,000 in late 1943, and this policy of equal pay for equal partners was continued into the early '50s.

In practice, however, their roles and authority were quite different.

John R. Kennedy, Sr., was the hard-driving, demanding boss. He maintained offices in Bogota, New Jersey, and New York City and served as Federal's president, treasurer and de facto chief executive. Forty-two years old at the time of the acquisition, he was the youngest of the three and the dominant personality.

Howard T. Brown, 49, was a mill manager par excellence. He continued to manage the Versailles, Connecticut, facility, consistently Federal's biggest moneymaker. Quiet and unassuming, he was chairman of Federal's board of directors but, in fact, took little interest in overall corporate management.

A. Guy Freas, 45, was executive vice president. Following the acquisition, he moved from Steubenville to corporate headquarters in Bogota, assuming companywide responsibility for manufacturing.

The dynamics of the partnership were interesting. The three men were all in the same boat, dependent on the financial success of Federal, but didn't always get along. Kennedy and Brown, in particular, had strikingly different personalities and were not friends. To avoid problems, they stayed out of each other's way. Kennedy seldom went to Versailles, and Brown seldom attended board meetings in New York or New Jersey, generally sending a written proxy. Freas, who remained on good terms with both, sometimes acted as a go-between.

All three were extremely hard workers and were highly individualistic, self-made men. But the similarities ended there.

J. R. KENNEDY — "THE BOSS"

J. R. Kennedy, who headed Federal for more than a quarter of a century, has been described as the single most important person in its 75-year history. During his stewardship, sales went from $7 million in 1942 to nearly $250 million annually in the early 1970s, as he transformed Federal from a ragtag group of recycled paperboard mills into a more broadly based forest products company.

Kennedy was born in Brooklyn in 1900, the youngest of four children. His parents were Irish immigrants who met in the United States. J. R. grew up in Greenpoint, a working-class neighborhood in Brooklyn. Even as a youth, he had a work ethic and mental toughness that set him apart from many other boys in the neighborhood. He took his first job at age 12 as a part-time butcher's assistant. At age 16 — in the same year Shortess was founding Federal Paper Board Company — Kennedy left high school to work as a flagpole deliverer. In that job, he later recalled in his usual wry manner, he exercised "considerable thrift" by lugging 16-foot poles to customers on foot instead of paying a nickel to ride the trolley or subway.

Kennedy had quit school because of financial need. While working full time, he took special courses at night and received a high school equivalency diploma. He then enrolled in night classes at New York University while working days in various clerical, bookkeeping and administrative jobs. During this period he met his future wife, Ethel Rose Leavy — like himself, from an Irish immigrant family. Kennedy graduated from NYU in 1924 with a degree in business and accounting, and he and Ethel were married four years later.

In the early 1930s, J.R. Kennedy worked as the number two man in a trade association and met many of the leading industrialists of the time.

57

RULE OF THREE

Kennedy graduated in 1914 from St. Cecilia's grade school in Brooklyn. He's in the second row from the back, third from the left, in the group of boys in front of the school door.

When he graduated, he was already employed as the number two man in a trade group, the Copper Import Export Association, where he met the Guggenheims and other leading industrialists of the day. In 1933, a banker friend introduced him to Shortess, who was looking for an accountant to help straighten out Federal's tangled financial affairs. The two hit it off immediately, and Kennedy began working part time for Shortess as a consultant. In 1935, at age 35, Kennedy joined Federal full time as assistant to the president, becoming in effect the company's number two executive and chief financial officer. Under the tutelage of Shortess, his elder by 29 years, Kennedy learned the paperboard business.

The two worked closely together and often took lengthy train trips to visit mills and customers. These trips were invariably exhausting. "Shortess would talk about his companies' problems late into the night," explains Jack Kennedy, J. R.'s son. "Then he would go to bed and fall right asleep, while my father would lie awake worrying about the problems. My father couldn't figure out how Shortess managed to get a good night's sleep. Then he realized that Shortess worked at such a breakneck pace all day that he was exhausted and fell asleep for that reason."

Even though the hours were long and the pay mediocre, Kennedy stayed with Federal because he held Shortess in high regard and saw an opportunity to succeed him one day as the company's owner and president.

Kennedy possessed a unique and forceful personality. A little over six feet tall, distinguished-looking and always impeccably dressed, he was known around the office as "Mr. Kennedy" or "the Boss." He was a true American original.

J.R. and his sweetheart, Ethel Leavy, visit St. Patrick's Cathedral in New York. They were married in 1928.

J.R. smoked a pipe as a young man and in later years became partial to cigars.

On succeeding Shortess, he established a new direction for the company, stressing conservative financial practices and systematic expansion. He had a strategic vision of what the company could become and spearheaded three key developments to increase Federal's sales and improve its competitiveness: diversification into the folding carton business after World War II, growth through acquisition in the 1950s and the building of a large new mill at Sprague, Connecticut, in the 1960s.

Kennedy had an agile, probing mind and knew every detail of the company's operations. Nothing escaped him. When visiting a facility, he would grill employees about their jobs. If he wanted to talk with a sales clerk or accountant at corporate headquarters, he would call that person directly without regard for the corporate chain of command.

He was extremely loyal to valued employees, often going to great lengths to help in times of need — such as assisting with emergency medical bills. He also understood how to motivate people with little personal touches. Clark Fisher, who was a young salesman at the National Folding Box subsidiary in the 1950s, generally saw Kennedy once a year at National's annual customer party. "He always remembered who I was and took the time to spend a few minutes with me," according to Fisher. "And he would go out of his way to congratulate me on a new customer or something of that nature. In that respect he was very gracious and an outstanding leader."

At the same time, he could also be extremely demanding. "I would characterize him invariably as a very warm guy, a great guy, a true gentleman," says Francis X. O'Connor, who retired as a vice president of Federal in 1984. "But he could be merciless with people who didn't perform or made statements unsupported by fact. For example, somebody would say at a meeting, 'Potential tonnage from this customer is fantastic.' And he would turn on that guy and say, 'What do you mean fantastic?' He would rip him to shreds. He didn't want unsupported opinions. He wanted facts."

One of his pet peeves was employees who didn't answer their phones as quickly as he would like. If he dialed an executive down the hall and the phone went unanswered for two or three rings, he was likely to hang up and head to the executive's office to find out why. "I was the sales manager in the paperboard division, and he called one time from outside the office and the phone rang, I guess, six times," O'Connor says. "It was about 12:45 p.m. This poor, unwitting operator came back on the line and said, 'I'm sorry, Mr. Kennedy, the board division is out to lunch.' Well, you probably could see the fire in his ears. When he got back to Bogota, he told me in no uncertain terms that I'd better set up a schedule so that somebody was always there. Then he went on in his humorous way and kept saying, 'The board division is out to lunch!' He thought that was a riot."

A devout Roman Catholic, he was a stickler about ethical conduct and maintaining certain proprieties. Although he enjoyed a drink or two at a party, he did not tolerate drunkenness. His strongest swear words were "hell" and "damn."

It was his policy that everything at Federal be done first class. When the company reached its 50th anniversary in 1966, he arranged a gala dinner complete with musical revue at the renowned Plaza Hotel in New York. All the company's executives and customers were invited, and a replica 1916 automobile (the year of Federal's founding) was given away as a door prize. That was the Kennedy style.

He had a wonderful Irish wit — at times impish, at times self-deprecating, at times searing. On one occasion, he hired double-talk artist Al Kelly to speak at a meeting for security analysts. Kelly was not yet well known, and Kennedy introduced him with great flourish as an eminent economist. As Kelly began to deliver his "speech," the audience strained to figure out what in the world the fellow was saying. Slowly but surely the prank became apparent, and the analysts had a grand time listening to Kelly's garbled patter.

With his outgoing personality and reputation for integrity, Kennedy was Federal's best salesman. He was always prepared to visit a customer or prospect, large or small, at the sales department's request. As Federal grew, he bought a limousine and hired a uniformed chauffeur. He and the company's sales representatives would head off in grand style for their client visits. Few other chief executives in the paperboard industry became so directly involved with customers, and doing so helped Federal land and retain a number of major accounts.

Although Kennedy worked hard and expected others to do the same, he also liked to have a good time. He loved to dance and always enjoyed the company of his many friends. Peggy Chamberlain, whose husband, Baxter, was a Federal executive from 1965 to 1980, remembers him as a charming, gregarious gentleman. "It was always a pleasure to talk with him or sit next to him at a dinner party," she says. "He was so alive and full of energy. He enjoyed life to the fullest."

He also enjoyed playing golf, even though he was terrible at it. John H. Millikin, now retired as a senior vice president of Bankers Trust Company and a member of Federal's board of directors, held an annual golf tournament for clients and business associates. Almost invariably, Kennedy would finish last. "At dinner, we'd make our awards and Jack would always get up automatically — he'd make quite a point of it — and accept the booby prize," Millikin says. "One year, someone played even worse than he did. Jack had quite a good time insisting the prize was rightfully his and expressing mock indignation that he had somehow lost. He was absolutely a delightful man."

The invitation for Federal Paper Board's 50th anniversary celebration promised "a very special grand prize!" It turned out to be a replica 1916 automobile, won by a customer from Connecticut.

J.R. was a devoted and loving father. He is pictured here in the 1930s with Ethel, his baby daughter, and Jack.

Another leisure-time activity was pleasure boating. Kennedy bought his first boat in 1946, but seldom left the dock. His skills as a yachtsman, it was said, matched his talents as a golfer. Later he bought a 51-foot cabin cruiser and hired a captain to sail it for him — prompting Glover Johnson, a member of Federal's board of directors, to say tongue in cheek, "He has a captain to handle his boat to the end that his friends and guests relax in full confidence of a pleasant trip and a safe return to shore."

J.R. bought his first boat in 1946 and christened it the Ken-Quin *for five members in the Kennedy family. This was followed by the* Ken-Quin II *and, ultimately, a 51-foot cabin cruiser, the* Ken-Quin III.

Kennedy gained a certain amount of prominence in sports circles when he bought an interest in Yankee Stadium in 1955. He sold this investment after only a few years. The *New York Times* reported, "Mr. Kennedy found his share of ownership was financially pleasant but rather hard socially, particularly around World Series time when tickets were in short supply. A steadily mounting number of telephone calls as October approached was one factor in his decision to sell."

Together with work and family, his other great passion was religion. "As he got older he became very active in the church," says his son, Jack. "He was a Knight of Malta and a Knight of St. Gregory, and he was very generous to the Catholic Dioceses of New York and New Jersey."

Irish priests throughout the New York area knew John R. Kennedy as a friend. "Many of the local parish priests led lonely lives, and they tended to attach themselves to certain families," Jack Kennedy says. "They would sometimes drop by at the wrong time. My father was tolerant of this. My mother was less tolerant."

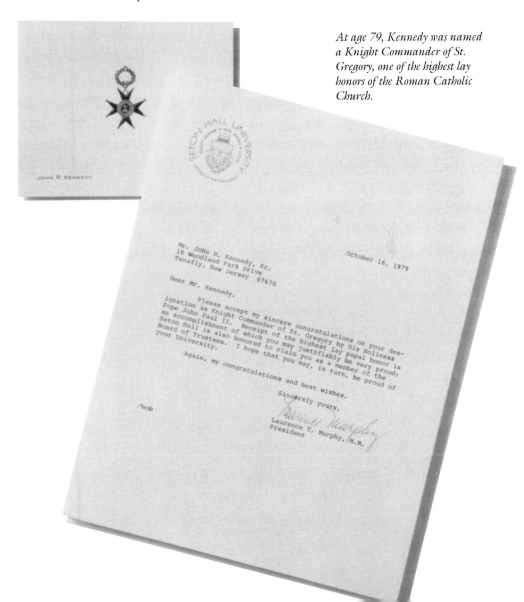

At age 79, Kennedy was named a Knight Commander of St. Gregory, one of the highest lay honors of the Roman Catholic Church.

J. R. and his wife were devoted to each other. She was a warm, gracious lady who was his close confidant, and he would often discuss business problems with her in the evening. When she died in 1974, he was devastated and never again seemed the same.

They had three children — Jack, Quentin and a daughter, Ethel. He was a loving father, but also a strict disciplinarian. As Federal prospered and he became personally wealthy, he was adamant that his children learn the value of work. John P. "Jack" Murphy, who joined Federal's folding carton division in 1948, recalls the time when Quentin took a summer job with the company while attending Georgetown University. "I called the old man and asked him what he wanted Quentin to do," Murphy says. "He answered, 'I don't care. Just give him the toughest job you have so he'll be tired at the end of the day.'"

J.R. and Jack, Quentin and young Ethel visit Hyannis, Massachusetts, in 1936.

The Kennedys' vacation home near Palm Beach, purchased in 1955, became a favorite retreat for Ethel and J.R.

Ethel and J.R. always enjoyed a good party. Here, they attend a 1969 reception at the Everglades Club in Florida. Guy Freas is in the background.

Kennedy was a hands-off manager. Even as he grilled employees for information, he would not tell them how to do their jobs. He gave his executives a great deal of leeway. When an executive failed to perform up to standards, though, the end came quickly. All of a sudden the executive would no longer be invited to important meetings, and shortly thereafter he would be gone from the company. But even in giving someone a pink slip, Kennedy attempted to be fair. "If you had to leave Federal, the best way was to get fired, because he was extremely generous," says one retired executive. "He was famous for that. You'd never get fired from Federal and have a complaint about the financial settlement. I knew guys who left and he agreed to pay them for six months. And after six months if they still didn't have a job, he would continue to pay them until they did."

Many employees were prepared to go to the end of the world for the Boss. Others found him intimidating. What he possessed in full measure was the intelligence, toughness and dynamic personality to succeed in a rough-and-tumble business. With someone less dominant at the helm, Federal would almost certainly have foundered, as happened to many other paperboard companies during the '40s and '50s. He was widely respected within the industry as one of its leaders. He served an unprecedented three terms as president of the National Paperboard Association from 1957 to 1960 and was the driving force in the creation of the American Paper Institute (API), now the forest product industry's preeminent trade group. He served as API chairman from 1970 to 1971.

J.R.'s desk contained shelves displaying many of the products made by Federal. He personally knew many of the company's customers and often went on sales visits.

*Ethel and J.R. had an audience
with Pope Paul VI in 1971.
J.R. was a devout Catholic who
became very active in the church
in his later years.*

*This photograph of J.R. Kennedy
is one of the favorites of his sons,
Jack and Quentin. It was taken
in 1971 when J.R. was 71 years
old and still the dominant figure
in Federal's management.*

He was also known for his charitable contributions. As his net worth grew in the 1950s, he established a private foundation even though his lawyers advised against doing so. "He went to White & Case and talked to them about having this foundation, but they told him, 'That's for the rich people like the Rockefellers,'" according to his son Quentin. "His reponse was, 'What's the difference, I have a little bit.' So that's how it got established." The foundation was funded principally with Federal Paper Board stock. Over time, he kept putting more stock into it. On his death, the foundation was divided into three separate foundations, each headed by one of his children. Today, those three foundations have combined assets of $6 million — all from the growth of the assets donated by J. R. Kennedy. These foundations support a variety of charitable and educational causes, including many of the organizations with which Kennedy was actively involved.

He served for many years as a trustee of the Holy Name Hospital in Teaneck, New Jersey, and was an important financial contributor. The Breslin-Kennedy wing at the hospital is named in honor of Kennedy and another long-time trustee, John Breslin, a New Jersey attorney. He served also as a trustee of Seton Hall University in South Orange, New Jersey.

J. R. Kennedy suffered the first in a series of strokes in 1972 and thereafter became less active in Federal's day-to-day operations. He retired as chairman of the board and a director in 1980 at age 80. He died in 1984.

He prided himself not only on his cribbage skills, but also on his abilities in high school as an offensive and defensive guard on the football team. Weighing barely 150 pounds at that time, "he was very fast and was able to get into the other team's backfield by either eluding or ducking underneath the opposing players," according to his daughter. "He was a letterman all four years and was really very proud of that fact."

On the other hand, he was reluctant to discuss his success in business. "You would never know he was one of the wealthiest men in Norwich," says Diogenes P. John, his accountant and tax adviser. "Everybody who met him really loved that man. A perfect gentleman, a rarity actually. He didn't brag about his accomplishments. He liked to say he was in the right place at the right time. I remember when he met my son, who was 13 or 14 years old at the time. I introduced them and they chatted for a while. After Mr. Brown left, my son asked, 'Who was that?' I said, 'That was Howard Brown.' My son said, 'The millionaire?' I said, 'Yes.' And my son said, 'You wouldn't think so. He's a regular guy.'

"The local Rotary Club sponsors a man of the year award," John adds, "and several years ago I was going to submit his name as a candidate. He was very upset with me. He didn't like notoriety."

One of Brown's pleasures was to dine out with his family. In later years, he would often take his wife to dinner and have her bring along her widowed friends. While dining out, he would sometimes strike up a conversation with the waitress or another diner, discovering in the process that this total stranger had a financial problem. Like the character in the old TV series "The Millionaire," he would direct Diogenes John to send some money discreetly.

He was charitable in other ways as well. He was a trustee of the Norwich Free Academy, a local school, and one of its important contributors. The local hospital and YMCA were among the other beneficiaries of his largess. He and another businessman bought a piece of land in nearby North Stonington and gave it to the YMCA to establish a summer camp. Later, with profits from the sale of Federal stock, he created the $500,000 Elsie A. Brown Fund, which today continues to give college scholarships to needy students from the Norwich area. He was an active member of the Congregational Church.

Macintosh describes Brown as a contented man who was happy with his accomplishments in life. "He said to me once, 'You know, Gardner, if you work for a firm you're never going to make any money. You've got to be in business for yourself.' He also said these words: 'I would rather be a big fish in a small pond than a little fish in a big pond.' In other words, he wanted to be a prominent person in a small community and be benevolent."

Brown died in 1979 at age 86.

Guy Freas is shown in 1948 at his country home in Pennsylvania. He was the shyest and most unassuming of the three partners.

GUY FREAS — A HANDS-ON MANUFACTURING EXPERT

Guy Freas, the third member of the triumvirate, was a still different personality. "Of the three men, I'd say Daddy was probably the shyest and most unassuming," according to his daughter, Leanne Freas Trout. "But he was a very smart businessman and was determined to be successful."

Freas was born in 1897 in the little community of Rohrsburg, Pennsylvania, where his father was a farmer. There were eight children in the Freas family and, in common with Kennedy and Brown, Guy was a youngest child. Like many a farm boy, he was a tireless worker and mechanically inclined. He also developed a lifelong passion for hunting and, in addition, became an avid reader.

Freas visits with the first of his five granddaughters in 1952. His children and grandchildren were very important to him, and he sometimes agonized that his work kept him away from home for long periods of time.

When Freas graduated from high school, first in his class, he was desperately needed as a teacher in the nearby town of North Berwick. At the school superintendent's request, he obtained a teaching certificate from the county and taught one year. He then took a job with the American Car and Foundry Company in Berwick, Pennsylvania, and after three years at ACF became a salesman for a small Pennsylvania papermaking company owned by his brother-in-law. He was hired by Shortess nine years later in 1928 to manage the Steubenville, Ohio, facility. Unlike Brown, Freas was actively involved in the day-to-day operations of his mill.

In Steubenville, Freas lived in a hotel and left his wife and two young children behind in Pennsylvania. Steubenville was a wide-open city at the time, rife with gambling and prostitution, and he didn't think it was a proper place to raise a family. He traveled home every second or third weekend. When home, he would sometimes pack the family in the car and drive around the Pennsylvania countryside visiting relatives who lived on farms.

"When we were young, we lived in Williamsport and Dad was working in Steubenville, and we didn't see a lot of him," his son, Arthur, recalls. "That's the way it was when we were growing up, and it lasted a heck of a long time. It may sound kind of strange to say, but his family was very important to him."

After having spent more than 15 years at Steubenville, Freas moved to corporate headquarters in Bogota following the 1943 acquisition of Federal by the three partners. He and his wife bought a home in Tenafly, New Jersey, and he finally had a family life. As executive vice president of Federal, he had primary responsibility for manufacturing and also took an interest in labor relations. He traveled frequently, visiting Federal's facilities to review their operations and evaluating mills the company was considering for acquisition.

Freas was down to earth and friendly. "He was the kind of person whose whole attention was focused on you when he was talking with you," Arthur's wife, Margery, says. "So you felt you were important to him when he talked. And what a remarkable salesman he was."

Although raised a Methodist, he was not religious. "He was spiritual rather than religious," according to Margery Freas. "He relied on his inner powers. If he faced a severe problem and couldn't make a decision, he'd go back to his room and sleep on it. He would wake up in the middle of the night and have an answer, and it would always be the right answer. He was very much aware of the power of the subconscious. Once in a while he would try another approach and it wouldn't work."

Freas was a trustee of Bucknell University in Lewisburg, Pennsylvania, for 25 years, from 1949 to 1974. On retiring from Federal in 1954 at age 57, he threw himself into his work as chairman of the university's buildings and grounds committee on virtually a full-time basis. Dennis O'Brien, who was Bucknell's president, said Freas was the type of person who would see a need and try to fill it. The university's athletic facilities were inadequate, so Freas and another long-time trustee, Robert Rooke, donated money to build the Freas-Rooke Swimming Pool and jointly made a challenge gift to start a campaign for a new field house. Later, the two men financed the building of the Freas-Rooke Computer Center. In the 1960s, Freas gave Bucknell a

In 1965, Freas laid the corner-stone for Bucknell's admissions office, Elisabeth Koons Freas Hall, dedicated to the memory of his first wife.

major contribution to build its admissions office, Elisabeth Koons Freas Hall, in memory of his first wife. Freas was awarded an honorary doctor of law degree by Bucknell in 1957. Both his children graduated from the university.

Freas remained on Federal's board of directors until 1978, retiring at age 81. He died four years later.

BRINGING THEIR INDIVIDUAL SKILLS TO THE PARTNERSHIP

Kennedy, Brown and Freas took over Federal at a time of world-wide conflagration and economic distress. Strong individuals were required to ride out the storm and make the company a success.

Each of the three brought something special to the partnership. Freas referred to Kennedy as "the man in the homburg," meaning J. R. was the financial expert and company leader. Freas knew the manufacturing end of the business. And Brown continued to do what he had done for more than 20 years in his own quiet way — manage the Versailles mill, generating a steady profit.

Freas, left, was a long-time trustee of Bucknell University and in 1975 received the Taylor Medal, that institution's highest honor. Also honored was Robert Rooke, a friend and fellow trustee.

CHAPTER 6

Postwar Boom

IN 1943, when Kennedy, Brown and Freas acquired Federal, one of their advisers estimated that the $1.5 million acquisition would pay for itself in ten years if the company earned an after-tax profit of $2 per ton on its paperboard. During World War II, as earnings sank to rock-bottom levels, that forecast must have seemed optimistic indeed.

But with the end of the war and a booming consumer economy, the payoff came suddenly and dramatically. As demand for folding cartons and paperboard surged, Federal's paperboard production — which had been essentially flat during the first half of the decade — jumped 20 percent in 1946 to 171,000 tons and rose another 5 percent in 1947 to 180,000 tons.

Reflecting higher board prices as well as increased demand, earnings zoomed to a level that would have seemed inconceivable when the three men bought the company in 1943. From $159,000 in 1945, net income soared to $1,168,000 in 1946 and then to an unprecedented $2,921,000 in 1947. Federal's profit in 1947 came to more than $15 per ton of board!

As might be expected in a cyclical industry, the paperboard market cooled in 1948 when the economy slowed. Federal's earnings receded from their 1947 peak, and the company's owners were left wondering what the future held. Business executives generally were in a quandary; some companies were expanding, while others were pulling back for fear that the postwar economic miracle might not last. Many executives were still haunted by the Great Depression. Standard & Poor's Corporation warned, in a 1948 forecast, that paper industry results would always be volatile and subject to "cut-throat" competition in a "serious recession." J. R. Kennedy and his partners retained an industrial engineering firm to assess Federal's prospects; the firm concluded that Federal's 1947 earnings were a fluke and that future profits might range between $750,000 and $1,000,000 annually. The engineering firm added ominously, "It should be appreciated, however, that this estimate must be qualified by any adverse effect which acute depression might create on the Company's volume, its net sales price realization and the adjustment of its costs of production to such unfavorable circumstances."

Ignoring these cautions and adopting an optimistic view, Federal's owners embarked on a major capital spending program to modernize facilities and acquire new plants. In the late 1940s, the company devoted an average of well over $1 million annually to capital expenditures — an aggressive program for a company of Federal's still-modest size. The average was upped to more than $2 million a year in the early '50s and was further increased to approximately $3 million annually in the second half of that decade.

The decision to invest proved right. The postwar boom continued, and Federal headed into the first of three great growth spurts in its history, the others occurring in 1972-78 and from 1985 to the present.

During this initial burst of growth, from 1945 to 1960, sales doubled every five years, shareholders' equity increased 15-fold and earnings rose 25-fold, as Federal raced forward at a breakneck pace with barely time to catch its breath:

FEDERAL PAPER BOARD COMPANY

	Sales	Net Income	Shareholders' Equity	Number of Employees
1945	$ 10,300,000	$ 159,000	$ 3,400,000	800
1950	19,100,000	1,734,000	10,600,000	1,100
1955	37,300,000	2,504,000	17,900,000	2,500
1960	83,100,000	4,000,000	51,300,000	5,600

Over the 15 years, Federal evolved from private to public ownership and began to come of age as an important American corporation. In a 1959 profile, the *New York Times* called J. R. Kennedy a "personality with few peers in paperboard" and recognized Federal as a leader in the growing field of paperboard and folding cartons.

The Bogota mill and office, located on the Hackensack River in northern New Jersey, were flooded in a 1949 torrential rainstorm.

It is interesting to review the sweep of change that occurred during this pivotal 15-year period. Major developments include:

1946 - Federal obtains a $900,000 loan from Guaranty Trust to finance capital investments.

1948 - Dividend payments are resumed on the common stock.

1952 - Preparatory to "going public," the three partners sell a 5.4 percent equity interest in Federal to 45 key employees — the first ownership outside the Kennedy, Brown and Freas families.

1953 - Federal completes a $3.4 million initial public offering of stock; the pricing of the issue establishes an $11.9 million market value for the company.

Federal begins to expand in earnest through acquisition, initially with the purchase of National Folding Box Company of New Haven, Connecticut.

At year end, Federal has 1,800 shareholders.

1954 - Acquisition of Grant Paper Box Company of Pittsburgh.

Mother Shortess dies.

Guy Freas retires as executive vice president, continues as a director.

Federal completes a second offering of stock, raising public ownership to nearly 50 percent of the company.

The company has 3,900 shareholders.

1955 - Federal's common stock is listed on the New York
Stock Exchange.

Archie Maxwell retires from the board.

1956 - Acquisition of Morris Paper Mills of Morris, Illinois.

1957 - Howard Brown retires as chairman, continues as a director.

1958 - Diversification into glassware through the acquisition of
Federal Glass Company of Columbus, Ohio.

1960 - Acquisition of Manchester Board and Paper Company of
Richmond, Virginia.

Federal's market value approaches $50 million.

The company has 4,600 shareholders.

DIVERSIFICATION INTO FOLDING CARTONS

Federal's growth during this critical 15-year period was driven,
more than any other factor, by the company's expansion into the
folding carton business. This expansion stands today as one of the
great successes in the history of the company.

Shortess had, of course, recognized the benefits of securing a
ready market for his mills' paperboard output by investing in
folding carton plants. By the late 1930s, he owned a 50 percent
interest in Worcester Paper Box Company and an 80 percent
interest in S-C-S Folding Box Company. On his death, the
interest in Worcester was sold back to the Posners and S-C-S was
merged into Federal.

When Kennedy and his associates acquired Federal, they
weren't quite sure what to do with S-C-S. At first, they retained it
as part of Federal, then in 1945 transferred it to a holding company with the intention of managing their paperboard and folding
carton interests separately. However, further consideration of this
policy brought its quick reversal, and in 1946 the partners merged
S-C-S back into Federal and decided to enter the folding carton
business in a serious way.

There were good reasons for this decision. Clearly, the
emerging trend within the paperboard industry was toward
downstream integration. Traditionally, the folding carton business had been dominated by small, independent factories. "After
World War II and in the early '50s, there was a move by board
mills to acquire some of these plants and assure a market for their
board," says David Trout, Guy Freas's son-in-law. Trout joined
Federal in 1951 and retired in 1986 as senior vice president in
charge of the packaging and printing division. In 1946, one of
Federal's major competitors, Continental Paper Company, had

*Paperboard is trimmed to
customer specifications, circa
1951. Federal was still a small,
privately owned company at the
time, but was about to enter a
period of dramatic growth
through acquisition.*

just built a carton plant and several others were planning to buy or build carton facilities. To maintain a market for its board, Federal had to do the same.

"We are the largest independent producer of folding board and, as such, cannot afford to remain as producers of board only," Kennedy remarked at a directors meeting in the fall of 1946. "The acquisition of properties for the manufacture of cartons is of primary importance to the future of our Company."

Federal bought its first carton plants in 1946 and expanded without letup for the next decade and a half. In 1947, folding cartons accounted for 16 percent of the company's dollar sales to customers. By 1952, the figure was up to 31 percent. And by 1957, carton sales reached a peak of 72 percent of the corporate total. (Those figures are, however, a bit misleading. Federal was still producing as much paperboard as ever. It was just bringing it to market differently — increasingly through its own folding carton plants, and less and less by selling board to others to make into folding cartons.) Folding cartons were also a very profitable business in the 1950s — another reason Federal wanted to expand into this industry.

In light of the company's changing direction, Federal's board of directors considered renaming the company Federal Packaging Corporation, but rejected the idea after much debate.

Federal's initial moves into the folding carton business were anything but glamorous. With its limited budget, Federal could only afford to buy marginal facilities. Jack Murphy recalls reporting to the George S. Goerke Company plant shortly after he joined Federal in 1948 as a carton salesman. Goerke had been acquired by Federal a year earlier. Its plant was located in a rundown loft building in lower Manhattan, in a neighborhood now called Tribeca. "I reported down there and when I saw that old building I said, 'Holy Christmas,'" according to Murphy. Once inside, he discovered that the elevator was a human-powered antique; the operator pulled it from floor to floor by means of a rope. Disembarking warily at the Goerke facility, located on the fourth through sixth floors, Murphy was appalled to find "a rat's nest of a carton plant." Murphy adds, "When the manager of the plant saw the look on my face he said, 'Please don't get too discombobulated. We're building a new carton plant in Bogota.'" Ironically, Tribeca is now a fashionable residential neighborhood, and the Goerke building was recently converted to luxury condominiums.

Other small operations were acquired in Manchester, Connecticut, in Steubenville, Ohio, and even in the Greenpoint section of Brooklyn where Kennedy grew up. Throughout the late 1940s, Federal seemed ready to gobble up virtually any carton plant that was for sale — providing the price was right and the plant was located within supply distance of one of Federal's board mills.

Most of these facilities were not much more modern than the Goerke operation. For instance, the Steubenville carton plant was purchased from a preacher and was located in the heart of that city's red light district. "I couldn't believe it, it was something I wasn't quite used to," says Dave Trout, who joined the Steubenville facility in 1951 as a newlywed one year out of college.

The Steubenville plant had a cast of colorful characters not unlike the highly individualistic employees at Federal's first paperboard mills. The plant manager, Jim Farley, wore his hat at all times as a kind of symbol of authority. He was a chain smoker, and the tile floor around his desk was pockmarked with cigarette burns. "It was really a seat-of-the-pants type operation, and we were really divorced from the home office," Trout says. "Somebody from the home office might call once a week or so and ask how everything was going. At that time, there were very few written reports. The managers just kind of did their thing. In some respects it was kind of nice — not a lot of pressure from the administrators. As long as you did reasonably well, nobody was on your back."

From these humble beginnings, Federal's folding carton business became a big succcess. As corporate earnings surged, the company replaced its rundown plants with new facilities. It built a carton factory in Bogota to replace the Manhattan and Brooklyn plants and one in Versailles to replace the Manchester, Connecti-

When visiting Federal's factories, J.R. Kennedy often chatted with employees and sought to learn more about their jobs. Following the chain of command was not as important as getting to the bottom of matters that concerned him.

cut, operation. In 1958, Federal built one of the industry's largest carton plants in Washington, Pennsylvania, consolidating operations from Steubenville and two other locations.

However, Federal's biggest growth in folding cartons was achieved through a series of major acquisitions beginning in 1953. The first and most important of these was the purchase of National Folding Box Company, which described itself as the Tiffany of the folding carton industry. "When we bought them, it sent shock waves through the industry," says Murphy. "Our competitors just couldn't believe that this upstart company, Federal Paper Board, could acquire a company like National." With the acquisition, Federal became a leading player in the carton business for the first time. The National purchase, and the acquisitions that followed, are discussed in the next chapter.

In buying its initial small plants and making its later acquisitions, Federal acquired not only these companies' facilities and equipment but also their customers — and what an exceptional group of customers it turned out to be. By the late 1950s, Federal was manufacturing folding cartons for Colgate toothpaste, General Electric light bulbs, Bayer aspirin, Camel cigarettes, Fab laundry detergent, Eveready batteries, Budweiser beer, and Coca-Cola, Pepsi-Cola and 7-UP, among hundreds of other consumer brands. Federal was now the second-largest producer in the folding carton industry.

Meanwhile, Federal struggled to modernize its paperboard mills, reduce production costs and keep pace with major changes taking place in the board industry. During the 15 years, Federal doubled its paperboard production from 143,000 tons in 1945 to 308,000 tons in 1960, primarily through a series of mill acquisitions beginning in 1953.

Federal did not build any new board mills during this period. It did, however, implement a wide range of quality improvements in response to growing customer demand for higher grades of board. These improvements included investments in equipment for applying clay coatings to improve the whiteness and printability of the company's paperboard, and in equipment to laminate foil, plastic and other materials to board.

J. R. Kennedy reported to Federal's shareholders, "Vast changes are taking place in the packaging field.... Although paperboard and folding cartons comprise major items of the packaging industry, new products and new combinations of products are being introduced almost daily. The development of new chemicals, the rapid growth in the use and application of plastics, the use of various 'polys' instead of wax, the plastic coating of paperboard by the extrusion process, the lamination of light metals and paperboard — all represent the challenges and opportunities of the future."

CONSERVATIVE FINANCIAL STRUCTURE

One of the interesting aspects of Federal during J. R. Kennedy's tenure was his unyielding commitment to prudent financial practices.

When a company expands rapidly, as Federal did in the postwar years, it typically finances this growth through the heavy use of debt. Federal, however, pulled off the rare feat of achieving rapid growth while maintaining an extraordinarily conservative balance sheet. At year-end 1960, Federal's long-term debt was a mere $137,000, or less than one-half of one percent of total capitalization. Its ratio of current assets to current liabilities was an exceptionally solid 4.9 to 1, and its net working capital was $21.5 million, equivalent to about one-quarter of annual sales.

During the entire 15 years, Federal issued debt only twice: in 1946 when it borrowed $900,000 from Guaranty Trust Company to finance its early purchases of folding carton plants, and in 1953 when it borrowed $4 million from Guaranty Trust and New England Mutual Life to help finance the acquisition of National Folding Box Company. Once debt was taken on, repaying it became a top priority of management. The 1953 loan of $4 million was repaid in eight years.

In common with many business executives who had lived through the Depression, J. R. Kennedy espoused a philosophy of financing expansion from cash flow to the degree possible. In cases where the need for external capital was unavoidable, he tended toward the conservative approach of relying on preferred stock rather than debt. By the end of 1960, Federal had issued 560,000 preferred shares with a total par value of $14.1 million, representing 27 percent of the company's capitalization; most of these shares were issued for acquisitions. Common shareholders' equity constituted 72.5 percent of capitalization.

This aversion to debt reminds us just how extraordinary it was, and how nerve-racking it must have been, for Kennedy and his partners to have purchased Federal 17 years earlier in a completely leveraged transaction.

Edward Schrader, right, of Goldman Sachs, was elected to Federal's board in 1953 after the company went public in its initial offering of stock. He is pictured here with J.R. Kennedy.

EMPHASIS ON FINANCIAL DISCLOSURE

Federal "went public" in 1953, when its sales were about $25 million annually. Kennedy originally approached Merrill, Lynch, Pierce, Fenner & Smith to underwrite an offering of stock to be sold by himself, Brown and Freas, but was turned down. He then went to Goldman, Sachs & Co., which agreed to handle the deal. In March 1953, the three partners sold 200,000 shares of common stock in a $3.4 million offering through a 40-firm syndicate headed by Goldman Sachs. Through this offering, each partner sold approximately one-third of his investment in Federal and retained the other two-thirds.

The offering established a market value of $11.9 million for the company, compared with the $1.5 million acquisition price paid by the partners ten years earlier. Today, Federal's market value is nearly $1.2 billion.

Many managements find the transition to public ownership difficult and frustrating, as they enter the unfamiliar world of financial disclosure and shareholder relations. Kennedy, on the other hand, approached these new responsibilities with gusto. An accountant by training, he understood the nuances of financial reporting and seemed to enjoy the intellectual give and take of dealing with security analysts, who can be pesky and cynical if not treated with respect and given access to the information they need.

In 1955, shortly after Federal's common stock was listed on the New York Stock Exchange, he invited nearly 50 analysts to the company's Bogota headquarters for an all-day briefing by senior management and a tour of the mill and carton plant. Two years later, he made his first presentation to the New York Society of Security Analysts, Wall Street's most influential group of investment analysts. Thereafter, he spoke frequently before analyst gatherings.

Federal's shares were listed on the New York Stock Exchange in 1955. From left: William L. Vesce, stock exchange specialist, Kennedy and G. Keith Funston, president of the exchange. J.R. felt at ease in the world of finance and enjoyed the give and take of meeting with investment analysts.

J.R. took great pride in his company's annual report, and the 1959 report was designated one of the six best in American industry. Kennedy is shown receiving an "Oscar-of-Industry" from Richard J. Anderson, editor of Financial World *magazine.*

But J. R. Kennedy's real pride and joy when it came to dealing with investors was the annual shareholder report. Unlike many chief executives, he wrote it personally and got involved in the tiniest details of its design. Federal's first report as a public company, issued at the end of 1953, justified his effort; remarkably, *Financial World* magazine rated it the best in the paperboard industry and one of the 12 best among all 5,000 public companies included in the magazine's survey. Six years later, in 1959, *Financial World* rated the Federal annual report as one of the top six among 5,000 companies.

"He was awfully proud of the annual report," says retired vice president Frank O'Connor. "He spent days on it. The Boss was a very meticulous guy."

THE REWARDS OF SUCCESS

The landscape of the '40s and '50s is littered with companies that were unable to adapt to change and didn't survive as independent companies. Two of Federal's direct competitors, Continental Paper Company and Robert Gair Company, no longer exist as independent businesses today.

Federal survived, and then some. In fact, if ever there was a true-life example to rival the legend of Horatio Alger, a story of hard work leading to financial success, it is the saga of Messrs. Kennedy, Brown and Freas.

The three partners were men of modest means who bought Federal without a penny down — "about half scared to death after they signed the papers," in the words of Guy Freas's son, Arthur. They ranged in age from 42 to 49 at the time and had spent their entire adult lives as salaried employees at relatively modest wages.

Following the acquisition, they took chances, made smart decisions and adapted to change. They also had Lady Luck on their side, as they benefited from a robust postwar economy.

It was not long before Federal made each of them wealthy. The first payoff came in 1948, five years after the acquisition, when Federal declared a cash dividend of $350,000, or nearly $120,000 per man. But that was just the beginning. Over the next four years, the company distributed cash dividends totaling nearly $600,000 per partner. Then in 1953, the partners collected close to $1 million apiece in the initial offering of Federal stock. After the sale, they continued to hold stock worth approximately $2 million per man — stock which appreciated further in the following years and paid each man well over $150,000 annually in dividends.

Not a bad investment!

CHAPTER 7

On the Acquisition Trail

To ACQUIRE or be acquired? That was the question faced by Federal throughout the 1950s and into the early 1960s. The trend within the paperboard industry was toward consolidation, with smaller manufacturers being bought up by larger firms. In this environment, Kennedy and his associates recognized that Federal lacked the size to continue to compete successfully on its own.

Federal was not without suitors. There were plenty of opportunities to be acquired, if management had so chosen. One such opportunity occurred in 1960, when Howard Brown elicited a $50 million bid from Celanese Corporation. Brown was then 68 years old. Although he had retired three years earlier as manager of the Versailles mill, he was still a major stockholder of Federal and a member of its board of directors. He felt the time had come to cash in his Federal shares and, in his view, selling the company to Celanese offered an attractive price to all Federal shareholders.

The idea may have been sound. Unfortunately for Brown, he didn't take into account the opposition of J. R. Kennedy, who was still Federal's chief executive and had no intention of selling the company to anybody.

Exactly what transpired between Brown and Kennedy we do not know. Facts about their dispute are few, although the general thrust is clear. Brown lined up the Celanese bid and obtained the support of Guy Freas. When Kennedy got wind of the plan, he immediately went to Freas and convinced him to change his mind.

The Celanese offer was then rejected by Federal's board of directors, whereupon Brown resigned from the board and sold his Federal stock on the open market.

Thus, the partnership of three, a partnership which had guided Federal for 18 years, came to an abrupt end.

The behind-the-scenes battle had lasted just a few days, and only Federal's directors and its most senior executives were even aware it had occurred. Kennedy issued a brief announcement to employees, stating without elaboration that Brown had sold his stock and left the board. Tough-minded as ever, "the Boss" had dealt with the situation quickly, quietly and decisively.

Was Brown bitter? "I don't think so," says Gardner Macintosh. "He was philosophical about it. He met somebody from Celanese and they were interested in buying Federal Paper Board, and Howard thought, 'Here's a good chance for us. It's a big company.' I can't blame him for that, but it didn't go over because Mr. Kennedy was Mr. Kennedy."

To acquire or be acquired? There was no question which road Federal would take so long as J. R. Kennedy was in charge.

EIGHT ACQUISITIONS IN TEN YEARS

In 1953, with the completion of its initial offering of common shares, Federal possessed the currency — a publicly traded stock — for making acquisitions. And acquire it did. From 1953 through 1961, Federal bought eight companies in the recycled paperboard and folding carton industries, including three of the most important independent corporations in the business — National Folding Box, Morris Paper Mills, and Manchester Board and Paper. A ninth acquisition was Federal Glass Company of Columbus, Ohio — Federal Paper Board's first and only major acquisition in its history outside the field of paperboard and related products. The purchase of Federal Glass and the fate that befell this wonderful company are the subject of Chapter Nine.

Through these acquisitions, Federal quadrupled its sales and became a major national participant in recycled paperboard and folding cartons, not just a leader in the Northeast.

The nine acquired companies were:

1953 - National Folding Box Company, New Haven, Connecticut, a leading paperboard and folding carton manufacturer known as the Tiffany of the industry, purchased for a cash price of $6.9 million;

1954 - Grant Paper Box Company, a Pittsburgh-based manufacturer of folding cartons and a customer of Federal's Steubenville mill, purchased for a cash price of $1.5 million;

1956 - Morris Paper Mills, Morris, Illinois, one of the largest
        integrated producers of paperboard and folding cartons in
        the Midwest, acquired for common and preferred stock
        valued at some $10.5 million;

1957 - Frankenberg Bros., Inc., a small manufacturer of folding
        cartons based in Columbus, Ohio, purchased for
        $650,000 cash;

1958 - Federal Glass Company, Columbus, Ohio, purchased for
        common and preferred stock valued at some $11 million.

1959 - Sweeney Lithograph Company, a small printing operation
        in Belleville, New Jersey, acquired for cash (the exact price
        is unclear, although it was certainly well under $1 million);

1960 - Manchester Board and Paper Company, Inc., Richmond,
        Virginia, an important southern manufacturer of paper-
        board, purchased for common and preferred stock valued
        at approximately $10 million;

        Keystone Paper Box Company of York, Pennsylvania, a
        customer of Federal's Whitehall, Maryland, and Reading,
        Pennsylvania, mills, acquired for common stock valued at
        about $500,000; and

1961 - Worcester Paper Box Company, Medford, Massachusetts,
        a customer of the Versailles mill, acquired for $3 million in
        stock and notes (see pages 32 through 37).

Reflecting Kennedy's belief in conservative financial practices,
only one of these acquisitions, the 1953 purchase of National
Folding Box, was financed with the use of debt. The Morris,
Manchester and Federal Glass acquisitions, on the other hand,
were all financed in large measure through the issuance of common and preferred stock. "Preferred stock with a sinking fund,
that was my father's favorite method for acquiring companies,"
says Jack Kennedy. "The preferred stock was like debt, and the
sinking fund required you to pay it down. You were in effect
making the acquisition for cash over time. In those days, yields on
preferred stock were pretty low so you could do that." In the case
of Morris, for instance, Federal paid 285,529 shares of 4.6 percent
preferred stock and 114,212 shares of common stock. By means
of a sinking fund, Federal was required to repurchase a minimum
of 5,711 preferred shares annually until all the shares were bought
back; the practical effect was to spread this portion of the acquisition price over 50 years at 4.6 percent interest. (In fact, Federal
accelerated its repurchases and bought back the shares in 22 years.)

Through the acquisitions made in the 1950s and early 1960s, Federal Paper Board not only increased its sales, but also broadened its geographic distribution and customer base while adding a large pool of talented employees. Many of these employees went on to play major roles at Federal. By 1970, seven of Federal's 16 senior officers were individuals who had come to the company through its acquisitions and had worked their way up the Federal corporate ladder. "The people side of the acquisitions was the icing on the cake," Jack Kennedy says. "We got some awfully good employees who contributed a great deal to our company." He cites such examples as James C. La Grua, who came from National Folding Box and later served as Federal's vice president in charge of midwest paperboard operations; Burton Wall, also from National Folding Box, who became Federal's vice president for marketing; Ray Hall, who joined Federal from Grant Paper Box and subsequently became senior vice president in charge of the folding carton division; and Kenneth Petersen, who came from Morris Paper Mills and succeeded Hall as senior vice president of Federal in 1968. Moreover, nearly a dozen executives from the acquired companies, including La Grua, Hall and Petersen, were ultimately elected to Federal's board of directors.

All the acquired companies were privately owned and were purchased by Federal in friendly transactions. Most had gotten their start around the turn of the century and were sold to Federal by their founders or by second-generation owner-managers. In some cases, the owners wanted to retire. In others, the companies lacked the capital or technical resources to continue on their own in an increasingly competitive marketplace. In still others, Federal's price was simply too good to turn down.

Although the companies acquired by Federal no longer exist today, what wonderful memories persist — memories of entrepreneurs who were determined to go into business for themselves... of innovation and growth... of people working together to meet customer needs. Like ghosts from the past, these companies remind us of the tens of thousands of privately held businesses, many of which have long since merged into large public companies, that have contributed so richly to the development of American industry.

These are the stories of three of the companies acquired by Federal, each a blue-chip organization with a long tradition in the paperboard and folding carton business:

NATIONAL FOLDING BOX

National Folding Box of New Haven, Connecticut, was one of the pioneering firms in the folding carton industry. In the early 1890s, when folding cartons were still in their infancy and were

being manufactured primarily by small companies for local customers, David S. Walton had a better idea.

Walton, the owner of a paper company in New York, was
convinced the folding carton had a bright future. By 1890, more
than one-third of America's population lived in cities and towns,
up from one-tenth 50 years earlier. Walton recognized the simple
fact that as people moved from farms to cities, they became
dependent on others for such necessities as food and clothing. He
reasoned that, as urbanization continued and living standards
improved, paperboard packaging would be required to distribute
goods efficiently from producers to consumers.

In 1891, Walton invited the principals of six box plants and
one paperboard mill to a meeting in New York and proposed a
deal: why not pool their operations and become a major force in
the emerging folding carton industry? After six months of negotiations, the "National Company" started operations as a combined unit on August 1, 1891. Facilities were located in New
Haven and Derby, Connecticut; Springfield, Massachusetts; and
New York City and Ballston Spa, New York.

Initially, National got along by manufacturing virtually any
type of box it could sell. Its earliest catalog lists such products as
tack, nail and general hardware boxes, egg containers, oyster and
ice cream pails "with and without tape handles," candy boxes,
patent medicine boxes and even charlotte russe cups. The company also entered a business it would eventually dominate: cigarette cartons. Its first products for the tobacco industry were so-
called "shells and slides," which held ten cigarettes and were
printed in rich colors and fanciful designs. It also manufactured

*David S. Walton, the founder
of National Folding Box,
recognized that demand for
paperboard packaging would
grow as people moved from
farms to cities.*

*National's plant was located in
New Haven, Connecticut,
within shipping distance of
major markets throughout the
Northeast.*

the then-famous "One Hundred Rulers" box for Duke's Mixture Smoking Tobacco. This ornate package featured pictures of heads of state from around the world and was printed sumptuously in eight colors.

In 1905, as sales grew, National purchased an entire city block in New Haven and built a state-of-the-art carton plant on a portion of the site, consolidating carton operations from other facilities. Nine years later National erected a paperboard mill on another portion to supply board for the carton plant. A second paperboard machine was installed at the mill in 1920 as demand continued to rise.

By the time Walton retired as president in 1927, National was the largest manufacturer of folding cartons in the world. However, the majority of its sales were standardized "stock" boxes, which were only marginally profitable. Walton's successor, Hutchinson Hinkle, pushed the company more heavily into custom-made cartons for consumer products. Hinkle was succeeded in 1937 by George Mabee, a grandson of one of National's founders.

By the early '40s, National was manufacturing customized folding cartons for a premier list of consumer products, such as Bayer aspirin, Hershey's milk chocolate, Colgate toothpaste, Budweiser beer and General Electric light bulbs. It also produced the cartons for virtually every major brand of cigarette, including Lucky Strike, Camel, Kool, Pall Mall, Viceroy and Old Gold. In addition, National provided start-up capital for a new company called Peter Paul and, consequently, made all the cartons for that company's Almond Joy and Mounds candy bars.

Proud of its blue-chip clientele, National erected a huge illuminated billboard atop its warehouse and each month pictured a different customer's folding carton next to the words "Yes 'National' makes this box!" The sign was situated along the main line of the New Haven Railroad and became a local landmark, viewed each day by tens of thousands of travelers. Customers were delighted to have the free publicity.

National was famous for its giant sign, viewed each day by thousands of passing commuters. There was great competition among customers to be featured. After the acquisition, the sign was changed to read, "Yes 'Federal' makes this box."

During the 1940s, the management reins passed to two brothers, Walton Lynch and Morris Lynch, Jr. Their father, Morris Lynch, Sr., had been one of the founders of the company and its first director of sales, and they themselves had spent their entire adult lives working for National.

Under the Lynches, National continued to pursue a simple strategy: manufacture superior products that commanded premium prices. The company also became known for the lavish way in which it entertained customers. Typical was its annual Kentucky Derby outing, for which it whisked major customers off to Louisville for several days of partying leading up to choice seats at the race itself. National even placed a bet on every horse in the derby for each of its guests, so they'd be sure to have the winner.

Another key element of National's management philosophy was its employee orientation. Growing up near the plant, Francis J. Healy heard from neighbors that National was a good place to work. He landed a job there in 1938, one year after graduating from high school, and was not disappointed. "They paid well and had tremendous respect for their employees," he says.

Healy's first assignment was as a stock booster. "There was a big, rugged lady up on a platform who fed sheets of printed paperboard into the cutting and creasing press," he says. "My job was to keep her supplied with board. I carried stacks of board up four steps to her on my head." After a series of promotions in the carton plant, Healy eventually moved into the white-collar ranks and became National's personnel manager.

Walter Thomann joined National a year after Healy, also as a stock booster, and rose to foreman. Emblematic of the company's concern for employees, he says, was the way it kept in touch with those who served in the armed forces during World War II. National sent these employees a full-color newsletter every other month to update them on the company. After the war, each returning veteran was presented with a hardcover volume containing all the newsletters as a token of gratitude. In addition, every year at Christmas during the war, National sent each of its em-

ployee soldiers a package full of consumer goods in National folding cartons: toothpaste, razor blades, shaving cream, candy, cigarettes, chewing gum and so on.

"National was an extremely successful, extremely profitable company," adds Clark Fisher, who joined National as a summer employee in the early 1940s while attending Yale. "There was no question but that their quality was ever so much better than almost anybody else's." In the 1930s, he notes, National was one of the first companies to begin coating its paperboard with clay, which gives the board a smoother surface for quality printing. National was also one of the first companies in the industry to acquire offset printing presses, which are more efficient than the old gravure presses. "So they had the equipment and the technical knowledge," he states.

Fisher's father, Fred Fisher, had been employed by National since the turn of the century. "He was born in New Haven and was the oldest of five and, as such, in that day and age the oldest had to go to work," Clark Fisher says. "He left high school after his junior year, and his father took him over to National Folding Box Company and asked the president if he felt there was a future with the company. They decided there was, and my father went to work for them."

Fred Fisher became a salesman for National in the Boston area in 1908 and, as of the 1940s, was one of the top producers. Clark followed in his footsteps. "At the end of World War II, I was accepted to Harvard Business School," he says, "but Walton Lynch [National's president] invited me to New York. My father said I should hear him out, and at our meeting Walton Lynch convinced me I would make more money if I worked as a salesman for National Folding Box than if I went to business school. I left there on cloud nine. He was a tremendous salesperson. I went to work immediately in the Boston area." Later, after National was acquired by Federal Paper Board, Clark Fisher went on to become a vice president in Federal's folding carton division.

Walton Lynch knew firsthand just how rewarding a career at National could be. He was a very astute businessman who had negotiated an employment contract under which his compensation was based on a percentage of sales. Thus, as National's sales burgeoned following the war, he became one of the two or three highest-paid executives in America.

Although National was extremely successful, and Walton Lynch was earning a handsome income, there came a time when he decided to sell the business. Two developments prompted this decision. First, as the decade of the '50s began, the Lynch brothers were getting along in years and wanted to retire. Second, they recognized that the folding carton industry was changing and that National, with its aging production facilities, was not well prepared for the new competitive environment. National remained a

John Budinger, a senior vice president of Bankers Trust Company, joined the Federal Board in 1958 as the company was growing rapidly in size. He served until his death in 1966.

top-quality producer, but its costs were high, particularly in comparison to the large, efficient new board mills being built in the South by such companies as Westvaco and International Paper.

Reflecting its high costs as well as new competition from mills in the South, National's once-hefty profits were eroding. Versus earnings well in excess of $1 million annually in the years immediately following World War II, National saw its profits drop to an average of $700,000 in the period from 1950 through 1952 and then to $573,000 in 1953, the year the company was acquired by Federal Paper Board.

Why would Federal acquire an aging beauty? J. R. Kennedy understood perfectly well that he was buying a business whose best years were in the past. However, National gave Federal something the latter desperately needed: credibility in the folding carton business. The transaction brought Federal into the big leagues of the carton industry.

Jack Kennedy recalls, "I remember my father saying, 'This is going to be the greatest thing or the worst thing, I'm not sure which.' But he went ahead and bought National, and it worked out well."

Fisher states, "Mr. Kennedy saw the advantage to Federal of upgrading its image by purchasing National. On the other hand, many people could not understand why National sold out. But that is one of the things Walton Lynch saw coming. Walton saw the handwriting on the wall that a new type of board was coming in — the solid bleached sulphate in the southern mills — and that it would take over the industry. And, of course, it did."

With the acquisition, Federal Paper Board took its own sales of $22 million annually and added National's sales of $14 million annually, creating a combined company that was 64 percent larger than Federal alone. It turned out to be the biggest single acquisition, in terms of percentage addition to revenues, ever made by Federal.

Although there were clear benefits to Federal, integrating the two companies did not go smoothly at first. Almost immediately, there was a clash of cultures between the free-spending management style of National and the cost-conscious approach of Federal. National Folding Box was operated as a separate subsidiary of Federal Paper Board for two years. Subsequently, its operations were consolidated into Federal and the Federal style predominated.

Federal continued to manufacture paperboard and cartons at the National plant in New Haven for 21 years following the acquisition. As the facility became outdated and unprofitable, however, it was closed in 1974. The closing marked the end of an era for one of the most successful companies the folding carton industry has ever known.

With the shutdown, some employees were transferred to other Federal locations, others were laid off. "It was devastating

Joseph H. Taggart, dean of New York University's Graduate School of Business Administration, was well known to J.R. Kennedy, who was active in NYU's alumni organization. Taggart was invited to join Federal's board of directors in 1969 and served with distinction for 12 years.

for some people, because they never got another job that paid the same wages or benefits," says Thomann. "But I can say this much for Federal, when they discharged me they paid me a week's salary for every year I had worked there. They didn't have to do that. They could have just dumped me on the street." Thomann subsequently found a job at a folding carton plant in Ohio. "It was nothing like I was used to," he says. "I finally understood how good National was and how well it paid."

MORRIS PAPER MILLS

Three years after acquiring National, Federal Paper Board purchased Morris Paper Mills of Morris, Illinois. Morris was, in effect, the midwestern counterpart of National. The two companies were similar in size. Moreover, like National, Morris was a quality, integrated producer of recycled paperboard and folding cartons. Morris was owned by three families, the Lebolds, Ballengers and Beckwiths, who had been associated with the company for many years.

Morris was founded in 1916 by William Beckwith and two partners. However, the three men soon discovered they couldn't get along, so they reached an unusual agreement: whoever could raise the money first would buy out the interests of the others.

Meanwhile, Nathan Lebold, a successful Chicago entrepreneur, was seeking to acquire a business for his son and nephew, Foreman Lebold and A. G. Ballenger. "As the story goes, Uncle Nate was having lunch at a restaurant in Chicago when one of his friends from the Standard Club came over and sat down at the table," states A. G. Ballenger's son, William. "He told Uncle Nate what was happening at Morris Paper Mills, and Uncle Nate said, 'I'll buy it.'"

The main plant of Morris Paper Mills was located about 60 miles southwest of Chicago. Federal acquired Morris and other carton companies for a simple reason: the carton business was a tremendous growth industry following World War II. Industry sales soared from $270 million in 1945 to nearly $900 million in 1959, before leveling off in the early 1960s.

There's an interesting story behind the Lebold family and why Nathan Lebold wanted to buy a company. Nathan had made his money in the shipping business; when iron ore was discovered in the Mesabi Range of northern Minnesota in the late nineteenth century, he obtained a concession to ship the ore across the Great Lakes to the steel mills of Gary, Indiana. "Uncle Nate was the one who had the idea to bring the ore down to the steel mills by boat," William Ballenger says. "My dad remembered going up to Milwaukee and buying the first boat with him."

Lebold and his wife had two sons, Foreman and Samuel. Their nephew, A. G. Ballenger, came to live with them when he was 12 years old following the death of his parents, and he became like a third son.

Foreman and A. G. were inseparable. After graduating from high school, the two cousins went off to college together at Michigan Technological University and studied to become mining engineers. On completing college, they joined the army and served in Europe during World War I. Following the war, they worked briefly at Inland Steel and then decided to venture south to Bolivia, where large copper deposits had recently been discovered. However, Foreman's mother was seriously ill and she didn't want them to go, so she asked her husband to buy a business for the boys to keep them close to home. That's how Nathan ended up investing in Morris.

Given a chance to run their own company, the young engineers opened an office in Chicago and took charge of the financial and marketing aspects of the business. Foreman Lebold (known to his friends as Mike) became the president of Morris, his brother Sam was vice president and Ballenger was secretary-treasurer. Beckwith, the founder, was vice president and general manager and had his office at the plant in Morris, Illinois, about 60 miles southwest of Chicago. He was in charge of production.

Morris was a tiny new company with sales about $120,000 when the Lebold brothers and their cousin became involved. In partnership with Beckwith, they expanded it aggressively.

Morris Paper Mills specialized initially in garment boxes for Marshall Field and other retailers in the Midwest. But it soon expanded into other types of folding cartons and developed special skills in lamination — a process for gluing together two or more grades of board, or for combining board and lining paper. A company booklet said of lamination, "This requires an unusual technique that is a specialty of the Company, and is the means of supplying specific characteristics, such as waterproofing, grease-proofing and other special requirements, to its board." The large round containers from which ice cream is scooped at soda fountains are an example of a laminated product; Morris became the dominant supplier of these bulk ice cream containers.

Frank Forester, Jr., an executive vice president of Morgan Guaranty Trust, served on Federal's board from 1976 until 1988. Federal's banking relationship with Morgan extends back more than 60 years.

In the 1930s, Morris Paper Mills developed the first paper-board six-packs for Coca-Cola and subsequently made them for other soft drink brands, including Pepsi-Cola, 7-UP and Canada Dry. In the 1940s, it introduced the first six-packs for beer. In 1943, Morris expanded its operations through the acquisition of the Lindley Box and Paper Company of Marion, Indiana. By the late 1940s, Morris had the strongest customer base of any folding carton company in the Midwest. Its many prestigious accounts included Sears Roebuck, General Motors, Swift & Company, Joseph Schlitz Brewing and Pabst Brewing. "Morris was a wonderful family-run business that did some great things in the packaging industry," says Ballenger.

"One thing about Morris Paper Mills is they were so diverse that they prospered even during the Depression," says Peter Trucano, who joined the company as technical director in 1947 and later became its general sales manager. "There was no letdown. People in this town worked right through the Depression years."

Morris Paper Mills had a strong employee and community orientation. The city of Morris, with a population of just over 8,000, is located in the middle of Illinois farm country. Morris Paper Mills was the largest local employer and became a beacon for many of the good things to happen in the community. Many of its employees served on local school boards and other community groups. The company and its employees provided financial support for the local hospital and community parks. And the

In 1943, Morris expanded its operations by acquiring the Lindley Box plant in Marion, Indiana. This facility primarily made specialty cartons, such as florist, gift and retail store boxes.

Morris Paper Mills had a strong community orientation. Its athletic field was used not only by the company's baseball team, but also by the high school baseball and football teams.

company built an athletic field for use not only by its own industrial league baseball team, but also by the high school baseball and football teams.

By the mid-1950s, Morris Paper Mills had grown into a $16-million-a-year business. However, trouble loomed on the horizon — increased competition and weaker prices, due in large part to the emergence of new paperboard mills in the South. This was, of course, the same challenge faced by the owners of National Folding Box. In addition, Foreman Lebold, long the driving force in Morris's growth, had died in the early '50s. And so it was that the owners accepted Federal's $10.5 million offer to acquire the business in 1956.

In explaining the importance of the acquisition from Federal's perspective, J. R. Kennedy said "it has opened up the Midwest market and broadened the base of our business." Prior to the acquisition, Federal's westernmost facilities were in Steubenville on the eastern edge of Ohio. With the Morris acquisition, Federal became an important factor in the Midwest folding carton market — a position it maintained until the late 1980s.

The Morris Paper Mills facilities were operated by Federal for 26 years until 1980, when they were closed in line with Federal's programs to upgrade to larger, more modern facilities. However, customers of Morris continued to be supplied from other folding carton plants of Federal, and in that sense Morris is still an important part of Federal today even though its name and plants are gone.

Morris produced folding cartons for Sears Roebuck, General Motors, Swift and other leading companies in the Midwest. "Sales which started with a humble beginning in 1916 have multiplied over one hundred-fold," a company booklet stated in 1961.

MANCHESTER BOARD AND PAPER COMPANY

Manchester Board and Paper Company of Richmond, Virginia, was a somewhat different type of operation than National or Morris. Both National and Morris were, first and foremost, manufacturers of folding cartons. While they made recycled paperboard, they did so primarily to supply stock to their carton plants. By contrast, Manchester's primary end product was the board itself. It was only a minor factor in the folding carton business, and primarily sold its board to other companies that converted it to cartons.

Manchester was acquired by Federal in 1960 for $10 million. Through the acquisition, Federal extended its markets into the southern U.S. and acquired Manchester's production facilities — in particular, its large Seaboard mill, then one of the most modern and efficient installations in the recycled paperboard industry.

The early years of National and Morris were filled with opportunity and success. The early history of Manchester, on the other hand, was marked by disasters and setbacks. Founded in 1889 as Manchester Paper Company, the business was reorganized as Manchester Paper and Twine Company shortly thereafter when one of the founders withdrew. In 1899 its plant, situated on the James River in Richmond, was partially wrecked by an ice jam and in 1909 was completely destroyed by fire. Promptly rebuilt, the mill was converted to the production of paperboard and reorganized as Manchester Board and Paper Company, only to be destroyed again by fire in 1912. The mill was rebuilt once more — and this time, finally, survived.

A key event in Manchester's history occurred in 1907, when a young man named Frank E. Brown joined the mill. Slim, handsome and well-mannered, Brown would later become majority owner of Manchester and the driving force in its growth.

Brown was born in North Carolina in 1889, the year of Manchester's founding. He journeyed to Richmond at age 18 to attend business school and happened to take a "temporary" job at Manchester Board and Paper during Christmas vacation. He wound up staying more than 50 years and never did go back to school. He worked his way up through the business and eventually acquired majority ownership in the 1930s.

Brown was a memorable character — a true Southern gentleman who, with his outgoing personality and unpretentious charm, was able to get along with just about anybody. "He loved the whole world and he was quite sure the whole world loved him," says his daughter, Elva Brown Mehaffey . "As a result, they did." He sprinkled his conversation with homespun aphorisms, such as "There's no future in old age," or "There's no use worrying, yesterday is gone and tomorrow hasn't come yet."

But Brown was no pushover. When it came to business, he could be very tough. "He was pretty darn definite about things, I would say," comments Arthur Freas, who worked at Manchester after it was acquired by Federal. "In a very polite way, he could just slice people to death."

Frank Brown, right, was a southern gentleman who built Manchester Board and Paper into one of the region's largest paperboard companies. As a director of Federal, he constantly stressed the importance of productivity improvements and cost control. With him in this photograph are, from left, Bill Reid, Ted Donnan and Vernon Hogan.

His daughter, Elva, adds, "His work was his life. He was determined that his business be successful. He really worked at it and he expected other people to work at it too." At the same time, he was a caring boss who provided a number of amenities that were unusual in their time, such as an in-plant cafeteria that served free hot lunch and an in-plant barbershop. He was an active member of the Methodist Church and became a major contributor to Randolph-Macon College in Ashland, Virginia.

Brown took over Manchester when it was still a small company and built it into a highly profitable, $8-million-a-year enterprise. Under his leadership, the company earned an after-tax return on sales that generally exceeded 10 percent — a very good return in the recycled paperboard industry.

When he took charge, Manchester had three production facilities: its Southern paperboard mill (the one rebuilt in 1912), located on a Southern Railroad siding in Richmond; a second mill in Roanoke Rapids, North Carolina; and the Wing Paper Box Company folding carton plant in Hendersonville, North Carolina. The latter was an architectural gem, designed in 1895 by Stanford White.

In 1954, Brown expanded Manchester's operations by constructing a third paperboard mill. Called the Seaboard mill, it was located along the tracks of the Seaboard Railroad in Richmond. Its capacity was twice that of the nearby Southern facility.

Brown was 71 when he sold the company to Federal in 1960. He received common and preferred stock and became one of Federal's major shareholders. Although he retired from day-to-day management at Manchester, he was elected a director of Federal and remained active in that role, supporting the Kennedys in their expansion plans and counseling at all times on the importance of productivity improvements and cost control. He was

Completed in 1954, the Seaboard mill was one of the most modern and efficient in the recycled paperboard industry.

succeeded as head of the Manchester operations by his son-in-law, Robert A. Mehaffey. Brown retired from Federal's board in April 1976 at age 87, bringing to an end a memorable career spanning nearly 70 years in the paperboard business. He died three months later.

In acquiring Manchester, Federal used the operation as a base to expand into the South. Two years after the acquisition, Federal built a larger carton plant at Hendersonville, North Carolina, and a new plant at Thomaston, Georgia. It sold the old Southern mill in 1978 but continued to operate Manchester's larger and more modern Seaboard facility until 1988, when it was sold.

WHY FEDERAL HAD TO CHANGE

By means of the acquisitions made from 1953 through 1961, Federal became a larger, stronger company. Nonetheless, it still faced the same problem it had faced when it began its acquisition program: it continued to operate a group of primarily older mills making recycled paperboard.

The '50s marked the peak of the recycled board business. The new southern mills were just starting to come into operation, and they manufactured paperboard from wood fiber rather than from wastepaper. They produced high-quality board at a relatively low cost. As the '50s neared an end, the paperboard business was beginning to migrate South. Today, big southern mills dominate the business.

Glover Johnson of White & Case was a director of Federal from 1958 through 1973 and a trusted legal adviser to the company.

J. R. Kennedy saw these changes coming and recognized that if Federal were to survive, the basic character of the company had to change. Many of Federal's mills were more than half a century old and no longer adequate for the increasingly challenging demands of the marketplace. "Federal was a tough little company competing in a marketplace of giants," in the words of Sidney J. Pope, who retired as a vice president in 1990.

Federal had to be more than tough. It had to find ways to compete with the big, low-cost southern mills.

The closing of the Bogota mill in 1960 was a watershed for Federal. It signaled the beginning of the end for the "old" Federal — the type of recycled board company founded by Shortess — and a dramatic transition to larger, more modern facilities. Kennedy said of the Bogota closing, "Sentiment might have dictated otherwise, since it was the first mill the company owned, but it had become an uneconomic operation in a high-cost area. Its continuance could not be justified. Therefore, the tonnage previously produced at this mill was transferred to other more efficient facilities."

Following the shutdown of Bogota, Federal still operated ten recycled board mills in seven states: Connecticut, Illinois, Maryland, North Carolina, Ohio, Pennsylvania and Virginia. These ten mills produced 308,000 tons of board in 1960.

Two decades later, in 1980, Federal would operate just four larger mills producing 825,000 tons of board.

Today, it operates three huge mills — in Georgia, North Carolina and Connecticut — producing 1.2 million tons of board a year. Moreover, Federal's predominant product is now solid bleached sulphate paperboard made from wood pulp. Of the 10 mills owned by Federal in 1960, not a single one is still part of the company today.

In the next chapter, we shall see how Kennedy and his associates began to address the critical challenge of changing the nature of Federal Paper Board Company and assuring its survival and growth in a rapidly evolving marketplace.

CHAPTER 8

The Story of the Sprague Mill

IN EARLY 1961, J. R. Kennedy announced plans to build the largest and most efficient recycled paperboard mill in the world. Thus, Federal Paper Board took its first major step to battle back against growing competition from the southern mills. Kennedy explained, "The increased capacity in our industry coupled with increased competition from 'solid' boards (paperboard made entirely from wood pulp) makes it necessary to adopt new methods or new processes to establish and maintain better earnings."

The new mill, located deep in the Connecticut woods near the town of Sprague, was Kennedy's pride and joy. He personally supervised many of its details and wrote glowingly of the innovative papermaking machine that was being installed there: "Automated for high speed and efficiency, the machine will produce, from reclaimed or virgin fibres, paperboard of the highest quality, possessing weight, strength and printing characteristics not previously obtainable in America. It will enable Federal to make an entirely new product for the boxboard and carton markets. We believe the new machine will revolutionize Federal's segment of the industry, and have named it 'The Yankee Clipper,' deeming it worthy of the name given to those notable ships whose achievements revolutionized world trade."

Today, the Sprague mill is not only a major contributor to Federal's profits, but stands also at the center of one of the important trends of our time: recycling. Everything's coming up roses at Sprague.

The Sprague mill, completed in 1962, is the last recycled paperboard mill to be built in the United States. It is benefiting today from a resurgence of demand for recycled paper.

The papermaking machine at Sprague was christened The Yankee Clipper, "deeming it worthy of the name given to those notable ships whose achievements revolutionized world trade."

On the raw material supply side, conditions have never been better. Just a few years ago, the Sprague mill was paying over $100 a ton for wastepaper. Now the world is awash in wastepaper and Sprague is paying considerably less than $100 a ton. Some Connecticut communities are so swamped with wastepaper because of recycling programs and the closing of landfills that they're happy to give it away. In 1990, the Sprague mill took in over 7,500 tons of loose newspaper from small towns in eastern Connecticut. To them, finding an outlet like Sprague — and avoiding the high "tipping" fees charged by landfills — is like a blessing from heaven.

These conditions will change over time. Jack Kennedy, Federal's president, points out that 32 percent of the paper produced in the United States is reclaimed as wastepaper and recycled into new paper. The paper industry has committed to increase that figure to 40 percent by 1995. When it does so, virtually all available wastepaper will be recycled and Sprague's raw material will no longer be in oversupply. Nonetheless, Sprague will continue to be a viable and productive facility even when the current wastepaper glut ends and wastepaper costs return to more normal levels.

At the same time, Sprague is benefiting from strong demand for its product. Many consumer products companies are rediscovering the virtues of recycled paperboard as they seek to keep in step with the public's environmental concerns. "For instance, McDonald's has an item called Meal Mate — a little box with a handle on it," says Press M. Millen, Jr., sales manager for Federal's recycled paperboard division. "Not long ago, McDonald's mandated that the box has to be made from recycled board. This is starting to happen around the country."

Increasingly, packaging made from recycled materials is viewed as a marketing tool. Many paperboard packages today carry the symbol for recycling (three arrows forming a continuous loop in a circle) and the words, "This package is made from recycled paperboard."

Surprisingly, the Sprague mill is the most recent recycled paperboard mill to be built in the United States. No such mill has been erected by any company since the early 1960s. Most recycled board mills in the U.S. today are old and relatively small. Sprague, by contrast, is large, highly productive and fast. Though the mill was constructed 30 years ago, its capacity has been more than doubled since 1962 and its technology has been updated periodically. It is considered state of the art.

Each day, the mill takes in more than one million pounds of wastepaper — corrugated cartons, newspapers, envelope clippings, data punch cards, cancelled government checks, etc. — and turns it into high-quality recycled paperboard. Pointing to a vast yard filled with bales of wastepaper stacked as high as ten feet, a smile comes upon Millen's face as he sings out cheerfully, "Our forestland."

The Sprague mill processes more than one million pounds of wastepaper a year into high-quality recycled paperboard. It consumes all types of wastepaper — from corrugated cartons to cancelled government checks.

Recycled board will never take the place of the solid bleached sulphate board made from wood pulp at the big southern mills. (It's easy to tell recycled paperboard from solid bleached sulphate board. Typically, recycled board is gray or light brown in color and has a white surface coated with clay. Solid bleached sulphate is white throughout.)

Solid bleached sulphate is stronger and more versatile than recycled and has superior printing characteristics. Recycled board, on the other hand, is less expensive than solid bleached sulphate. It is also gaining favor with some companies because they prefer to use a recycled product where possible for marketing and environmental reasons.

Measured in terms of annual tonnage sales, solid bleached sulphate currently holds more than three-quarters of the U.S. market for clay-coated paperboard while recycled board holds just under one-quarter. The outlook is that the two types of board will continue to coexist, each serving specific market needs.

When it comes to the manufacture of recycled board, the Sprague mill has no equal. "If you interviewed 100 people who buy recycled paperboard and asked them who makes the best recycled, clay-coated board in the United States, I believe this mill would win hands down," Millen asserts. "And the reason it would win is not because the quality of the folding cartons made from our board is superior. And it's not because the printability of our board is better. It's going to be for a simple reason. The reason is that we produce a flat, stable, consistent sheet. High-speed printing presses require board that is consistent in weight and caliper [thickness]. So our quality isn't necessarily that much better. But our runability is sensationally better, and that means money to our customers because they can run their printing presses faster with our product."

THREE PAPERMAKING TECHNOLOGIES

The Sprague mill holds a unique place in the American paper industry. Of the three basic types of papermaking machines in use around the world today, it's the only mill in the United States to use the Inverform process, the so-called "third" machine. There's a good reason why no one else has installed an Inverform machine in the U.S.: nobody has built a recycled paperboard mill since the completion of Sprague, and the Inverform process is used primarily to make recycled board.

To understand Sprague's unusual technology, let's step back for a moment and look at the history of paper and how it's made.

Before paper was invented, people wrote on anything they could lay their hands on: clay tablets in Babylon, wax tablets in Greece, silk and bamboo in China, palm leaves in India. The ancient Egyptians wrote on papyrus, a grasslike plant which they dried into strips and then glued together in two layers to form a sheet.

Paper was invented in China by Ts'ai Lun in 105 AD. While the science of papermaking has advanced enormously since its invention, the basic steps remain the same:

- Plant fiber is reduced to a fine pulp in water.
- The pulp is spread on a fine-mesh screen.
- The screen is agitated to turn the fibers in different directions so they knit into a homogeneous sheet.
- The fibers are pressed and dried, resulting in a sheet of paper.

In 751, the Arabs captured some Chinese papermakers at Samarkand, an Islamic cultural center located in what is now the southern U.S.S.R. Thus, the invention set out on a 400-year journey to the West, finally reaching Europe in 1150 when the Moors introduced it to Spain.

Paper can be made from the cellulose fiber of virtually any type of plant: flax, cotton, sugarcane, esparto grass, etc. Ts'ai Lun made his paper from a mixture of bark and hemp. However, since the invention of the wood pulping process in 1844, most paper has been made from the fiber of trees.

Prior to 105 AD, writing in China was done on expensive silk or bulky bamboo. Ts'ai Lun made the first paper from beaten fibers of tree bark. He also made paper from linen rags, hemp and even fish net.

Papermaking was mechanized in 1798 with Nicholas-Louis Robert's invention of the first "endless wire" machine, a primitive Fourdrinier.

A Guided Tour of a Modern Fourdrinier

A turning point in the history of paper occurred in 1799, when a Frenchman named Nicholas-Louis Robert invented the first papermaking machine, mechanizing a process that until then had been done solely by hand. His invention was perfected four years later by the brothers Henry and Sealy Fourdrinier of London and is named for them.

Today, a highly refined version of the Fourdrinier is the dominant papermaking technology in use throughout the world. Modern Fourdrinier machines are roaring, steaming behemoths up to three stories high and 700 feet long.

The Fourdrinier incorporates the four basic steps of paper-making, with a few extra twists thrown in for good measure. Let's take a guided tour of a Fourdrinier — the No. 1 Machine at Federal's Augusta, Georgia, paperboard mill — with Vann Parker, the mill's technical director. Parker is a slender, articulate, good-natured man in his early forties.

The No. 1 Machine was completed in 1960 by Continental Can Company when it owned the Augusta mill. The machine produces up to 450 tons of paperboard a day.

Our tour begins at the "wet end" of the machine. As we approach this end, the temperature and humidity in the mill building rise steadily until we feel as if we've entered a steam bath.

"Really, the papermaking process is simply one of water removal," Parker explains, shouting to make himself heard. He walks up a few metal steps into the heart of the wet end of the machine and points to the "headbox," which flows a never-ending stream of pulp onto a moving, continuous-loop screen. The thickness, or caliper, of the paperboard is determined by the rate at which the pulp is fed onto the screen. No. 1 Machine can produce board with a thickness of anywhere from 12 to 24 points, or from .012 to .024 inch.

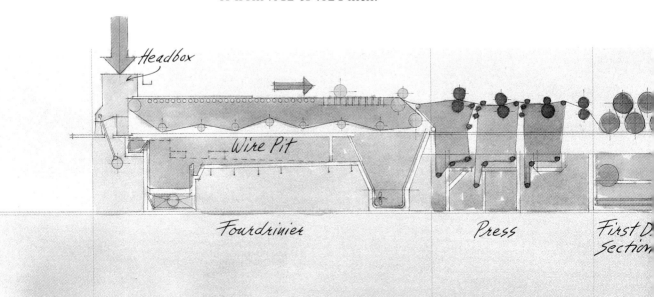

Headbox

Wire Pit

Fourdrinier   Press   First D.
Section

The plastic mesh screen is like a conveyor belt: it moves along at about 12 miles an hour and carries the pulp through the first fifth of No. 1 Machine's length. As it does so, water drains through the screen — aided by pressure and suction — and the pulp turns into a continuous "web" of moist paper with sufficient strength to support itself. When pulp is flowed from the headbox onto the screen, it's comprised of .5 percent fiber and 99.5 percent water. "The reason for having a very dilute solution," Parker says, "is to get a randomly dispersed mixture of fibers." When it leaves the screen, the mixture is 20 percent fiber and 80 percent water.

Next, the moist board is lifted from the screen and fed over, under and around a seemingly endless series of rollers and cylinders. This is the guts of the machine, constituting more than two-thirds of its length. First come dozens of "press rollers" to squeeze out water, reducing the moisture content to about 60 percent. Then the board goes through the "dryer" section: more than 100 hollow, steam-filled cylinders which reduce the water content of the board to 5 percent. After that the board goes through the "calender stack," a series of cast-iron rollers that smooth the paperboard's surface — a process that Parker compares to ironing a shirt.

Finally, the board enters the coating section. By now, the temperature and humidity in the mill are lower, but the noise level remains as high-decibel as ever. "This is probably the most difficult aspect of papermaking," Parker shouts. "We're putting on a coating and scraping off any excess with a blade, and a great many things can go wrong." First, the "size press" coats the paperboard with a solution of starch. "The starch helps hold the coating on the surface of the board so it won't soak in," Parker explains. Then the board is coated with special white clay mixed with adhesive. "The mixture is very similar to latex paint," he notes. "We put on two coats, one on top of the other, much like

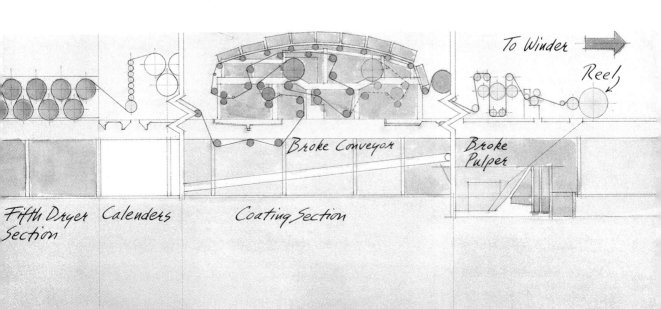

Fifth Dryer Section Calenders Coating Section Broke Conveyor Broke Pulper To Winder Reel

painting your house with a primer and a finishing coat." The clay fills in the tiny voids between the fibers, giving the board an extremely smooth surface for high-quality printing.

Virtually all the clay used by the paper industry in the United States comes from mines in Georgia. This special "kaolin" clay has a very fine texture like talcum powder. (The Augusta mill itself sits on top of a deposit of kaolin, but the deposit has never been mined.) "The adhesive we use is the same as Elmer's Glue," Parker adds with a bit of a chuckle.

Finally, the never-ending sheet of paperboard emerges from the "dry end" of No. 1 Machine and is wound into massive rolls weighing more than 20 tons each. Later, the rolls are slit and rewound for shipment to customers around the United States and the world.

One of the most interesting aspects of a modern, computer-controlled Fourdrinier is the increasing use of high technology to assure product quality. Parker says that, in the past, it was impossible to check the consistency of the product as it was being made on the machine, since there is no way to reach in and grab a piece. As a result, mills would sample some of the paper as it came out the dry end, but would have no idea whether all the paper was up to standards.

The past 20 years have seen major technological advances in the area of in-process quality control. On No. 1 Machine, for instance, the density of the board, as it speeds through the machine, is constantly monitored with the use of beta particles. "We have a source of beta particles on one side of the board," Parker says, "and what is in essence a geiger counter on the other side. By monitoring how many get through, we can measure the board's density."

Cylinder machines were the mainstay of Federal's papermaking operations until the 1970s. Today, the company no longer operates cylinder machines.

Moisture content is continuously measured by shooting infrared light through the board.

Caliper is measured with an eddy current device. A source of eddy current is pressed against one side of the board as it moves through the machine. An eddy current detector is pressed against the opposite side. "The strength of the current received by the detector is dependent on how close it is to the source, so in this way we can gauge the board's thickness," Parker says.

Parker explains the importance of consistent quality as follows: "What's happened in the paperboard industry is that our customers have begun to run their printing equipment faster to improve productivity. They require much closer tolerances to do this. Any disruption in their manufacturing process is very costly, so they want us to deliver a consistent product and absolutely minimize our contribution to their variability. It's certainly a different world now with regard to our customers' expectations, even as opposed to five years ago."

MAKING MULTI-PLY BOARD WITH A CYLINDER MACHINE

Soon after the Fourdrinier came along, the cylinder machine made its debut in 1807. The cylinder machine is the second major technology in use today and is similar to the Fourdrinier in every respect except one: the way in which the pulp is deposited on the moving screen at the wet end.

Remember, in a Fourdrinier a single layer of pulp is flowed onto the top of the continuous-loop screen. To understand how a cylinder machine differs, let's consider an analogy: take a large bowl and fill it part way with diluted cake batter. Then hold a rolling pin horizontally and lower it into the bowl until the bottom half of the pin is dipped into the batter. Turn the pin slowly in one direction and it will become coated with batter.

In a similar manner, a cylinder machine employs large wire cylinders in vats of pulp. A continuous-loop screen runs across the tops of the cylinders. As the cylinders turn, they transfer pulp from the vats to the underside of the moving screen. Most machines have a series of four to eight cylinders, each adding more pulp to the moving screen as it passes over them in succession. By a process of adhesion and pressure, the successive layers of wet fibers form a multi-ply web of paper on the bottom of the screen (similar to the multiple layers of wood in plywood). This web is then peeled from the screen and fed into a series of drying and pressing rollers; this part of the process is virtually identical to a Fourdrinier.

Cylinder machines are slower than Fourdriniers and do not normally match the latter's consistent product quality. Why, then, would anyone use a cylinder machine? The answer lies in its multi-ply capability. One advantage of multiple plies is the ability to reduce costs by making the middle plies from less expensive grades of pulp. Also, the middle plies can be made from materials that give the board special characteristics, such as added stiffness.

Cylinder machines are used primarily to make recycled paperboard. Until 1961, every board mill ever owned by Federal had cylinder machines, but today the company no longer has any cylinder machines, having sold or closed all its older mills.

ENTER THE INVERFORM

For a century and a half, the Fourdrinier, invented in 1799, and the cylinder machine, in 1807, remained the only practical technologies for mass producing paper. Then along came St. Anne's Board Mill of Bristol, England. In 1951, it announced it had invented a new machine, the Inverform.

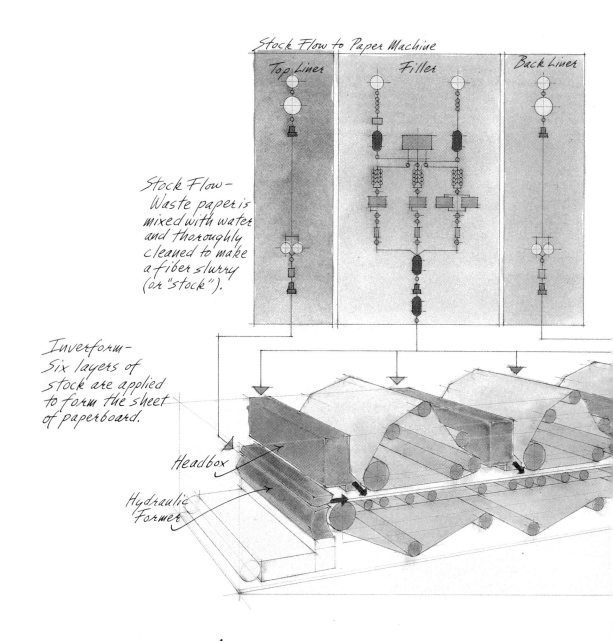

Stock Flow to Paper Machine

Top Liner   Filler   Back Liner

Stock Flow —
Waste paper is
mixed with water
and thoroughly
cleaned to make
a fiber slurry
(or "stock").

Inverform —
Six layers of
stock are applied
to form the sheet
of paperboard.

Headbox

Hydraulic
Former

The Inverform is a modified Fourdrinier — but with quite a difference. The challenge taken up by the engineers at St. Anne's was to design a Fourdrinier that could produce multi-ply paper. That may sound simple enough, but the technical problems were formidable.

Consider the problems this way. A Fourdrinier places a single layer of pulp on top of a moving screen. If a second layer were placed on top of the first, where would the water go? The bottom layer would act as a barrier, preventing the water in the upper layer from draining downward. (In a cylinder machine, this problem is solved by applying pulp to the underside of the screen, so that each successive layer is on the bottom and can drain.)

The engineers at St. Anne's ended up adapting the Fourdrinier as follows: Instead of having just one headbox to deposit pulp onto the moving screen, the Inverform has a series of them in sequence. After the first layer of pulp flows onto the screen from headbox one, a "top screen" comes down over the pulp. Squeezed sandwich-like between the top and bottom screens, the first layer of pulp gives up its water in the normal manner — forced downward under pressure, assisted by suction.

Now comes the modification. As the first ply continues its travel and approaches headbox two, the top screen lifts temporarily to allow a second layer of pulp to be laid down over the first. Returning, the top screen squeezes water from the second, or upper, ply. This water can only go upward, and as it does it is removed by suction boxes above the top screen. The process is repeated as the web of paper continues its trip through the sequence of headboxes. The machine at Sprague has six headboxes and, thus, can make six-ply board. Running at about three times the speed of a conventional cylinder machine, an Inverform can produce high-quality recycled paperboard at low cost.

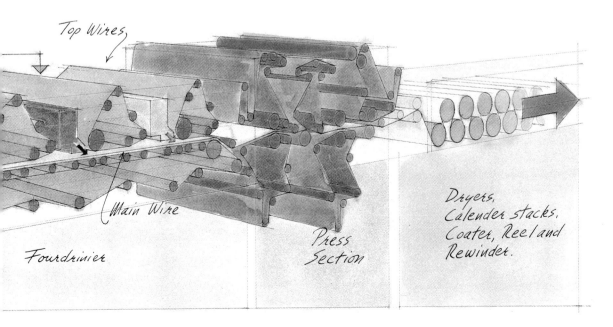

Top Wires

Main Wire

Fourdrinier

Press
Section

Dryers,
Calender stacks,
Coater, Reel and
Rewinder.

J. R. Kennedy was fond of saying, "The Inverform machine combines the speed of the Fourdrinier and the versatility of the cylinder machine without the limitations of either."

Or as *Pulp & Paper* magazine said more lavishly in 1964, following completion of the Sprague mill, "At last, some 165 years later, Nicholas-Louis Robert's Fourdrinier has become a finished masterpiece."

BETTING BIG

With a basic understanding of these technologies, let's go back to 1961 and attempt to put ourselves in the shoes of J. R. Kennedy. The new paperboard mills being built in the South all had high-speed Fourdriniers. By contrast, all of Federal's mills operated with older, slower cylinder machines. Clearly, Federal had to do something to meet the competitive challenge.

Paper mills are built where their raw material is: most recycled board mills are located near the wastepaper-generating urban centers of the North, while solid bleached sulphate board mills are generally situated amidst the vast timberlands of the South and Pacific Northwest. As early as 1955, Federal's directors discussed the possibility of acquiring a southern pulp and board operation, but Federal simply couldn't afford the cost of perhaps $50 million or more.

So Kennedy took a gamble — and a very high stakes one, at that. He decided to compete with the southern mills by making a superior grade of recycled board in the North using the new Inverform technology. "Recycled board was trying to compete with bleached board and having quite a tough time of it," recalls Baxter Chamberlain, who retired as senior vice president of Federal in 1980. "J. R. decided that the Inverform could do what the bleached board did. The potential seemed tremendous. It turned out that way, but he took an awful risk."

The risk was great for two reasons. First, the projected capital cost of Sprague was $15 million. (The actual cost turned out to be approximately $17 million.) The $15 million was small in comparison to the cost of acquiring a southern operation. Nonetheless, it was equivalent to nearly one-third of Federal's total capitalization. With such a heavy investment, Federal's very future depended on the success of the mill. There was little room for error.

Second, the Inverform technology was just a decade old and the first mill using this technology had been completed in England in 1958, only three years before construction began at Sprague. While Inverform offered great promise, it did not have a proven track record.

Not only did J. R. Kennedy select a new technology for Sprague; he also decided that Federal would act as its own general contractor on the project, an unusual step for a company of Federal's size. The task of supervising construction was assigned to Wilfred M. Wyburn, Federal's chief engineer. Bill Wyburn was a quiet, well-liked fellow who was a graduate of the Stevens Institute of Technology in New Jersey. He had served in the Navy during World War II and learned to fly, even though he wasn't a pilot in the service. He joined Federal after the war, as an engineer and part-time pilot of the company plane, and was appointed vice president for engineering in 1959.

While highly respected as an engineer, Wyburn had never before handled a construction project like Sprague. "My father had a very high regard for Bill, which is one reason he was willing to entrust this job to him," Jack Kennedy says. In fact, under Wyburn's guidance, construction at Sprague was completed on schedule in a year and a half. That part of the project went smoothly.

And so it was with high hopes and great anticipation that the first paper rolled off the machine at 10:25 p.m. on Tuesday, October 16, 1962. The Sprague mill was up and running!

What happened next was just about the worst imaginable nightmare: the Inverform technology, being new and complex, didn't work properly. From day one, the Inverform machine was plagued by a seemingly endless series of technical glitches that prevented the mill from operating at its rated capacity or meeting the quality standards expected of it. It is no small task to start a new paper machine. A period of break-in and adjustment is inevitably required. However, the difficulties at Sprague went far beyond any industry norm. Jack Kennedy says, "The problems at Sprague really related to the process itself, which in many respects was a little premature and more complex than anybody had imagined."

Whereas Sprague was designed to produce high-quality, clay-coated paperboard, all it could make at first was "linerboard" — used in the manufacture of corrugated cartons. Recycled linerboard sells for less than clay-coated paperboard. Worse still, the linerboard produced at Sprague wasn't even good enough to meet industry standards. A buyer couldn't be found at any price. "I was dispatched all over New England to find warehouses," says Robert McCabe. "At one point we had 13,000 tons of ware-housed material that was of virtually no value to anybody. When you consider that's equivalent to a year's production at a mill like Reading, and when you consider the financial shape Federal was in, you can begin to understand the problem."

How did J. R. Kennedy respond? He was optimistic about the mill. At the same time, he was impatient for it to operate properly and contribute to Federal's earnings. But most of all, he was exasperated. "It was very frustrating to J. R.," Chamberlain states. "He used to spend a lot of time there. He had his boat on Long Island, and he'd come across Long Island Sound every Monday morning to see how the mill was going."

Kennedy's periodic reports to the board of directors read today like a never-ending saga of high hopes and shattered dreams. In December 1962, two months after the mill began operation, he told a directors' meeting that Sprague was approaching break-even and might contribute $1 a share to Federal's 1963 profits. Just three months later, however, he said the mill still wasn't able to manufacture high-grade board because of "inexperienced crews and continued machine adjustments."

In September 1963, as Federal's earnings sagged because of problems at Sprague, the board of directors reduced the company's dividend from 50 cents per share quarterly to 40 cents — the first cut ever in Federal's dividend as a public company.

In December 1963, Kennedy told a directors' meeting that the mill's difficulties appeared finally to have been resolved. Once again, his optimism proved unfounded, as Sprague continued to have difficulties. Consequently, the dividend was cut again in December 1964 — to 25 cents a share quarterly.

In February 1965, George B. Nicholson, senior vice president, reported to directors that the Sprague mill was finally operating properly and should contribute to earnings in 1965. His optimism was short-lived. Just one month later, J. R. Kennedy said the mill's performance was still disappointing.

In May 1966, Nicholson again reported to the directors that the turning point at Sprague appeared to be at hand, saying the mill was producing "the best profit results since the start of operations." At last, the high hopes proved justified. In mid-1966, after nearly four years of technical problems and repeated operating setbacks, the Sprague mill began to earn a modest profit. From there, operating earnings improved steadily and then surged in mid-1967, after all remaining technical problems had been resolved.

Fred P. Ritchie, who joined Federal in 1965 from Container Corporation of America, played a crucial role in straightening out the mess. "We went through manager after manager, four or five a year," says Millen. "Then Fred Ritchie came in here and solved the problems. He was the first real manager. The ones before him had been technicians more than managers."

Ritchie himself says, "When I looked into the situation, I got the distinct impression that one of the problems was everybody was under such pressure to perform and make the mill operate properly that they all were worried about the big picture and nobody was worrying about the details. What I tried to do in the first two months was tell people, 'Look, you worry about the details. I'll worry about the big picture and we'll see if we can't put this thing together.'"

He says the technical problems involved two primary areas: preparation of the pulp, or stock; and formation of the board at the "wet" end of the machine. "There was a long learning curve for the operators to understand how properly to run the stock preparation equipment," he explains. "And at the wet end, it wasn't fully appreciated initially how sensitive the machine adjustments really were. There are a lot of close tolerance settings that have to be made on that machine, and if they're not made, or if wear and tear change those settings, the machine won't operate properly. It won't produce paper at all. It was a matter of paying attention to the details all the time to keep those things under control."

Baxter Chamberlain, top, and Fred Ritchie and Roger Thorkildsen, left, played major roles in getting the Sprague mill operating properly, ending four years of start-up difficulties.

Ritchie adds, "Over the next couple of years we got it in the black, and today it's a very profitable plant, I'm happy to say." Ritchie retired in 1989 as vice president, manufacturing, recycled paperboard.

DECADE OF SLOW GROWTH

Even though the Sprague mill began to make a major contribution to Federal's profits toward the end of the decade, the '60s were a very difficult period for the company.

Federal experienced slow sales growth and little or no increase in profits or shareholders' equity during the decade, as it struggled to make the transition from an operator of aging cylinder machines to a modern, efficient paperboard company able to compete with the southern mills:

FEDERAL PAPER BOARD COMPANY

	Sales	Net Income	Shareholders' Equity
1960	$ 83.1 million	$ 4.0 million	$ 51.3 million
1965	105.5 million	3.6 million	50.6 million
1970	133.2 million	3.9 million	56.0 million

There has been no decade — from 1943, when Kennedy, Brown and Freas acquired the company, to the present — that turned out so miserably for Federal. The start-up problems at Sprague consumed thousands of hours of executive time and hung over the company like a cloud. Yet, Jack Kennedy says his father never doubted the wisdom of building the facility.

"Federal had a future because of the Sprague mill," Jack Kennedy says. "Without Sprague, Federal had no future. Even in the darkest days, we knew we had something good and knew we could make it work."

SHOW AND TELL

Because the Inverform process was so new in the early 1960s, its installation at Sprague attracted great interest within the paper industry. In response to many requests, Federal finally scheduled an "official opening" for September 1964, two years after the actual opening, and sent out invitations far and wide.

"Everybody involved with the mill was extremely nervous," says Frank O'Connor, who was the mill's sales manager. "So a bunch of us thought we'd get there ahead of J. R. to make sure everything was okay. We arrived at 6:30 in the morning. However, he had arrived at 4:30, two hours ahead of us, to make sure everything was not just okay but perfect. When we arrived, he

J.R. Kennedy enjoyed the give-and-take of dealing with security analysts and often invited groups of analysts to tour the company's facilities.

had already inspected the place. The cleanliness of the floor, the machine, the men's room, the boiler room — just pure as the driven snow — and he was going to make sure himself!"

More than 200 security analysts, paper industry executives and other guests showed up for the ceremony. Federal's corporate minutes report, "Mr. La Grua [James C. La Grua, vice president] stated that the Inverform machine performed perfectly and that the reaction of the visitors was excellent." The opening spawned a host of favorable articles in the business and trade press, including *Pulp & Paper's* comment that the Fourdrinier was now "a finished masterpiece." Imagine, this was said when the machine wasn't even working right!

What Happened to All That Linerboard

There came a time, J. R. Kennedy's relentless optimism notwithstanding, when many others within Federal Paper Board wondered whether the company could survive the start-up problems at Sprague. As Baxter Chamberlain remembers the situation, "Sprague nearly put the company under."

James La Grua joined Federal in the National Folding Box acquisition and went on to become a key executive of the company.

In particular, there was all that substandard linerboard piling up in warehouses and nary a buyer in sight. At the very depths of despair in June 1965, Press Millen recalls negotiating through the night with three potential buyers for the unwanted board, only to fail to come to terms on price. Arriving wearily at his office the next morning, he was greeted by the news that unionized employees at the Southern Kraft Division of International Paper Company had gone on strike. "Suddenly IP was desperate for linerboard," he says. "They paid us $10 more a ton than the price we had asked for, but couldn't get, the night before. They took every pound of it. Saved our lives. We couldn't ship it out fast enough!"

By mid-1967, Sprague was making linerboard about half the time and paperboard the other half. While operations had improved to the point where the mill was capable of producing high-quality paperboard at all times, it didn't have the customers to justify that much production. "Sprague was built primarily to make lightweight recycled paperboard for cigarette cartons," explains David Trout. "By the time the machine was operating

A picnic, opposite, was held on July 26, 1986, for employees, their families and the citizens of Sprague to celebrate the 25th anniversary of the Sprague mill. Also present were, left to right (foreground), Jack Kennedy, Town Selectman Matthew Delaney and Connecticut Governor William O'Neill.

properly, all the cigarette companies had switched to solid bleached sulphate for their cartons. So the market it was built for was no longer there."

J. R. Kennedy, however, was not about to be denied. "On August 1st, 1967, Mr. Kennedy said to me, 'I don't want to make any more linerboard — ever,'" reports Frank O'Connor, the sales manager. "And young Jack said to me, 'If you can find enough customers to keep the mill on paperboard, we're going to pay you a special bonus of $500 a week.' And believe me, we never made another pound of linerboard."

A breakthrough came in 1968, when Nabisco Brands signed a three-year contract to purchase paperboard from Sprague to manufacture folding cartons for its food products. Nabisco continued to increase its board purchases from Sprague after the initial three-year contract expired and, in 1979, agreed to make Sprague the principal source of supply for its paperboard needs. As a result, Nabisco's board purchases from Sprague rose steadily from about 12,000 tons in 1968 to 50,000 tons in 1979. The 1979 agreement was one of the biggest sales contracts in Federal's history.

Subsequently, in 1984, Federal acquired Nabisco's folding carton plants with an agreement to supply Nabisco's carton needs. In 1990, however, Federal announced plans to sell the plants in line with a strategy to reduce its participation in the carton business, which is no longer a growth industry. Jack Kennedy says there should be no problem selling out the Sprague mill's production, even though Federal no longer owns the Nabisco carton plants. The mill is today well established as a leading supplier of quality paperboard and serves dozens of customers manufacturing everything from baseball cards to folding cartons.

DOUBLING THE CAPACITY

When constructed, the Sprague mill had a rated capacity of 230 tons of board a day. Through a series of improvements made over the years, the Inverform machine now has the capacity to produce 600 tons a day. How do you take a machine and more than double its capacity? This has been accomplished primarily through a series of improvements to make the machine run faster.

William Hemans, mill manager at Sprague, says a lot of the credit belongs to the people who designed the facility 30 years ago. "Building this machine took guts," he says. "It was the only machine of its type ever built in this country. But it was a good choice. The machine has been easy to expand and the steam turbine they chose has been easy to update. If they had chosen a different steam turbine, we couldn't have expanded without buying a whole new turbine system. It's cost us very little to increase our capacity. Most of it was good planning on their part and, in a few instances, a little bit of luck on ours."

A sampling of cartons made from Federal board. Included were some of the best-known brands in America. Many of these are made of recycled board from the company's Sprague mill.

CHAPTER 9

The Day Leon Simkins Phoned Jack Kennedy... And the Battle That Followed

B Y LATE 1967, *somebody* noticed that the Sprague mill was performing well. That somebody was 40-year-old Leon J. Simkins, president of Simkins Industries, Inc., a paperboard company located in New Haven, Connecticut. Simkins Industries' annual sales were $28 million at the time, compared with Federal's sales of $108 million a year.

On the morning of Saturday, December 16, 1967, Simkins phoned Jack Kennedy, who had been elected Federal's president two years earlier, and said he had something important to discuss. Simkins suggested they meet on Monday, but Kennedy said he preferred to do so that very day. They got together a few hours later at the Red Coach Inn, a popular restaurant just off the Connecticut Turnpike in Darien, Connecticut. Their meeting was brief and to the point.

"He mentioned the Sprague mill specifically," Kennedy recalls. "He was very interested in that. In the summer of 1967, the mill had really started to take off in terms of demand and profits, and I guess somehow he knew that. It was kind of industry gossip, I suppose. He also made some comments about the quality of the properties we had."

Then Simkins dropped a bombshell. On Monday morning, he informed Kennedy, he would be making a cash tender offer for up to 43 percent of Federal's common stock at a price of $35 a share, or a total of $17.6 million. His price was 30 percent higher than the latest closing market price of $27 a share on the New York Stock Exchange.

"I didn't say much of anything to him," Kennedy recalls. "I think I made some comment that it would be very difficult to acquire our company because the large stockholders weren't interested in selling. That was about it, and I couldn't wait to get out of there to a telephone." As quickly as he could find a phone, Kennedy called his father, J. R. Kennedy (who was still chairman of the board), to give him the news.

Thus began one of the classic takeover battles in American history.

"That Simkins thing should have been a Harvard Business School case study," observes Ken Petersen, now retired as senior vice president in charge of Federal's folding carton division. Press Millen, sales manager at the Sprague mill, has a different description: "It was like the Second World War all over again."

However, before learning about the unusual steps taken by Federal to defeat the Simkins bid, let's meet some of the other unwelcome investors who have come knocking at Federal's door.

UNWELCOME BIDDERS

Federal Paper Board plays tough when it comes to defending its independence. The company has survived several skirmishes with unfriendly investors — most notably, in 1975 with businessman Peter M. Brant and in 1979 with financier Saul Steinberg, as well as in 1967 with Simkins.

In 1975, Brant acquired 8.7 percent of Federal's common shares and was quoted in a magazine interview as saying he should have a seat on its board of directors. Brant is the owner of a newsprint business, Bato Company. He is also a prominent Greenwich, Connecticut, socialite, a champion polo player, a real estate developer, an avid collector of contemporary art and the owner of *Art In America* magazine.

Brant was just 28 years old when he bought his Federal stock in 1975. Management considered his investment unfriendly and sued. Alleging he had manipulated the price of the stock, the company asked a court to require him to sell his holdings. "Then we started taking depositions and found to our amazement that he had borrowed more than 95 percent of the money to purchase the shares," says Edmund J. Kelly, an attorney who represented Federal in the case and now serves on its board of directors. So Federal amended its suit to include an additional allegation — that Brant's financing violated Federal Reserve "margin" rules, which specify how much can be borrowed to purchase securities. It also added First National City Bank (Citibank) and Merrill Lynch as defendants, alleging they were the source of Brant's financing.

Merrill Lynch and Citibank were anxious to resolve the matter amicably, according to Kelly. Federal and Brant, on the other hand, remained at loggerheads. After lengthy negotiations,

Federal agreed in November 1975 to buy Brant's stock at a price of $24.75 a share, or a total of $6.3 million. This was below the market price of $25.375 per share. However, Federal agreed to pay an additional $2.25 per share if the market price rose by a specified amount within six months. The price increased 50 percent in the six months and Brant got his additional $2.25 a share. Of course, Federal shareholders who held onto their stock did even better, receiving the full 50 percent gain. Kelly says the transaction, including the rapid price increase after the buyback, was "a remarkable outcome in this day and age of greenmail."

Four years later, Federal attracted the unwelcome attention of Saul Steinberg, resulting in a classic confrontation between company and raider. Steinberg is a well-known financier who made his first big splash in 1969 when, at age 30, he attempted to take over Chemical Bank, one of the nation's largest commercial banks. Although the bank managed to elude his grasp, the battle between Steinberg and Chemical is widely viewed as the starting point in the era of hostile takeovers. In the years since, Steinberg has purchased sizable stakes in one company after another, often causing concern among executives of his targets. In many instances, he has ended up earning a handsome profit by selling the stock back to the company at a premium over the market price (the so-called "greenmail" referred to by Kelly).

In December 1979, Steinberg revealed in a filing with the Securities and Exchange Commission that he had purchased 11 percent of Federal's stock through Reliance Insurance Company and other members of his Reliance Group. "Before you knew it he owned close to 20 percent of Federal," says Kelly. Steinberg continued buying and eventually increased his position to 24 percent.

Federal fought back. "Our first reaction," says Kelly, "was to tell him he owned restricted stock and we wouldn't allow him to transfer it." This meant Steinberg couldn't freely sell his Federal shares if he wished to do so. More importantly, the restricted stock question went to the heart of a complex legal issue as to whether Leasco Corporation, which owned a controlling interest in Reliance Group, was required to register with the Securities and Exchange Commission (SEC) as an investment company. If forced to register, Leasco and Reliance would be subject to stringent investment company rules limiting their flexibility to buy and sell securities.

The battle between Federal and Reliance raged on for a year and a half, with each side suing the other. At one point, Jack Kennedy arranged to have lunch with Steinberg to ask the latter's intentions and perhaps settle the dispute. "In fact, by the time the lawyers got through with me before this lunch, I didn't know what to talk with him about except the weather," Kennedy says.

By 1980, Saul Steinberg owned 24 percent of Federal through his Reliance Group. Later, in a phone call with Jack Kennedy, he negotiated to sell the shares back to Federal for $74 million.

"It was one of those things. Everybody was so nervous about this meeting. In any event, the conversation went nowhere."

Then in March 1981, Leasco filed a routine application with the SEC seeking a continued exemption from registration as an investment company. Federal saw an opening and petitioned the SEC to hold a public hearing on Leasco's application. This was like grabbing for the jugular, since it raised the possibility that Leasco might not get its exemption without a fight from Federal.

Shortly thereafter, in June 1981, the dispute was quickly settled during a period of 24 hours through some behind-the-scenes maneuvering. The settlement process began one morning when Ed Kelly, the lawyer for Federal, suggested that Jack Kennedy contact John O'Herron of Lazard, Freres & Co., a Wall Street investment banking firm, in the belief that O'Herron might serve as an intermediary with Steinberg. O'Herron, in turn, suggested that he and Kennedy meet with Joseph Flom, an influential takeover attorney who is senior partner in the firm of Skadden, Arps, Slate, Meagher & Flom in New York. Kennedy and O'Herron visited that very day with Flom, who agreed to phone Steinberg on Federal's behalf.

After meeting with Flom, Kennedy flew off on business to Phoenix, where he received a call at his hotel from Flom. "It must have been midnight, and Flom said I ought to talk with Steinberg, that he was ready to make a deal," Kennedy recalls. "I said I'd call Steinberg when I got back to the office in three days, but Flom said, 'No, call him first thing in the morning.' So I phoned Steinberg when I got to Los Angeles the next day, and our deal for the buyback of the stock was done over the phone." Kennedy says he still doesn't know what Flom told Steinberg to make the latter amenable to negotiations.

Under their pact, Federal agreed to repurchase Steinberg's stock for $74.2 million, or $40 a share (half in cash, half in the form of a ten-year note), slightly over the market price. The SEC had not yet held its hearing on Leasco's application, so Federal withdrew its petition. Leasco subsequently got its exemption without a public hearing.

Typically, a buyback of this type triggers a drop in the price of the stock. That's because, with the unfriendly investor out of the way, the company is no longer viewed as an active takeover candidate likely to be acquired at a high price. And indeed, the immediate aftermath of the Steinberg buyback was unfavorable to Federal shareholders. Over the next year, during a period when the stock market generally was down, the price of Federal's shares fell even more precipitously than the market and ended up in August 1982 at less than half the price paid to Steinberg. However, Federal stock then came roaring back and reached a new high of $46 a share ($6 above the buyback price) in late 1983.

Why does Federal defend its independence so ferociously? "I think there's an emotional aspect to it," Quentin Kennedy, Federal's executive vice president, replies. "Jack and I both grew up hearing about nothing but Federal. It's what Dad spoke about most of the time. So there is that factor. The other thing — not just Federal, but generally — is that corporations in America have tried to build enduring institutions for the benefit of their shareholders, their employees, their customers, their suppliers and other constituencies, and the raiders just tear these institutions apart."

"On the other hand," Jack Kennedy acknowledges, "we've been given some opportunities because of raiders." One of the most striking examples involves an Augusta, Georgia, paperboard mill that was owned by Continental Group, Inc. (the former Continental Can Company). In 1982, Federal privately offered to buy the mill and 150,000 acres of associated timberland for $300 million, but was turned down. That seemed to be the end of the matter until Sir James Goldsmith, the well-known British financier and takeover specialist, made a $2.4 billion hostile bid for Continental Group in June 1984. Goldsmith has a reputation for acquiring companies and then dismantling them by selling off individual divisions and plants at a profit. Continental management wanted no part of Goldsmith, so it quickly arranged for the company to be acquired by a more friendly merger partner, Kiewit-Murdock Investment Corp. — a joint venture of Peter Kiewit Sons' Inc., a privately owned construction company in Omaha, Nebraska, and financier David Murdock.

But alas, being acquired by Kiewit-Murdock did not prevent Continental Group, one of the nation's oldest and largest container manufacturers, from being dismantled. To help finance the $2.7 billion purchase, Kiewit-Murdock sold off some of Continental's assets, including the Augusta mill. This was an unexpected stroke of luck for Federal. Federal bid again on the Augusta facility — this time purchasing the facility, together with four sawmills, two folding carton plants and two paper plate plants, from Kiewit-Murdock for $317 million. Federal subsequently acquired 310,000 acres of related timberland from Kiewit for $96 million. Today, Augusta is one of Federal's major properties — made possible by Sir James Goldsmith's attempted takeover of Continental Group.

Despite this indirect benefit from a raid, Jack Kennedy is adamant in his opposition to hostile takeovers. "The raiders have no interest in a company or its stockholders or its employees," he asserts. "They're interested in making a couple of bucks for themselves."

Speaking specifically of Federal, he states, "This is our business. We work at it every day. And we're not about to sit by and let some guy from New York come in and say to himself, 'I think it's worth so much more' and then buy it and do what he damn well pleases with it. I suppose the argument is that they bring value to the stockholders. They do in the short term, but do they really in the long term? My feeling is that, whatever value Federal Paper Board has, we will maximize it as well if not better over the long term than anybody else ever will."

PLANNING ITS COUNTERATTACK

But let's get back to Leon Simkins's attempt to acquire 43 percent of Federal's stock.

When Jack Kennedy phoned his father on that Saturday afternoon in December 1967 after hearing Simkins's intentions, the two Kennedys agreed to call an emergency meeting the next day to plot their defense against the Simkins tender offer. The meeting was held on Sunday afternoon at the Manhattan offices of White & Case, Federal's legal counsel.

Those in attendance included J. R. Kennedy and his two sons, Jack and Quentin; attorneys Larry Morris and Ed Kelly of White & Case, who took charge of the legal side of Federal's defense and helped coordinate overall strategy; and Richard E. Cheney of Hill and Knowlton, Inc., a large public relations firm. Cheney, who is now Hill and Knowlton's chairman, is noted for his innovative strategies both in spearheading and defending raids and had been invited to the meeting at the recommendation of Morris, himself a veteran of several takeover battles.

Cheney had never before met the Kennedys. "They were furious," he recalls. "They had worked hard to build their company. It was like someone coming in and saying, 'I'm going to steal your wife.'" Cheney had just been involved in helping defend another company whose chief executive was confused by a tender offer. That executive had said he wouldn't know what to tell his own mother if she asked whether she should tender her stock to the raider. Not surprisingly, that company lost its independence. Cheney welcomed the fact that the Kennedys were outraged and ready to fight to the bitter end.

As it turned out, however, the bitter end never really came. At the Sunday meeting, a number of ideas were discussed, such as raising Federal's dividend payment and splitting its stock. "And then Dick Cheney said what we should do is buy up as much of the stock as we can and get our friends to buy it to keep it out of Simkins's hands," Jack Kennedy says.

Out of that simple idea came one of the most brilliant and effective corporate defenses ever devised. The Simkins tender offer proved to be a landmark case — the first time an all-cash tender offer was ever defeated. Simkins had lost the war even before the first battle began.

A pool was established at Goldman, Sachs & Co. to buy Federal shares on the New York Stock Exchange. All purchases

Leon Simkins made at least one fatal mistake: He informed Jack Kennedy of his tender offer two days before it was actually made, giving Federal time to plan a counterattack.

were made through G. A. Saxton & Co., a Wall Street trading firm headed by Gerald C. McNamara, a friend and ally of the Kennedys. The pool was created so that individual buyers wouldn't compete against each other and so all would pay the same average price for their stock. The Kennedys and other Federal executives then went to their customers and friends and asked them to contribute to the pool.

The response was amazing. Lever Brothers, a long-time customer of Harry Posner at Worcester Paper Box, put in nearly $2 million. Hess Oil, which supplied fuel oil to Federal, came up with more than $1 million. Other contributors to the fund included Colgate-Palmolive Company, which purchased folding cartons from Federal; Topps Chewing Gum, which bought paperboard to make baseball cards; and American Mutual Liability Insurance Company, which provided workmen's compensation and general liability insurance to the company. R. Earl Roberson, who was American Mutual Liability's chairman, says, "I heard Federal was having the fight of its life. I either called Jack [J. R. Kennedy] or he called me, and he said, 'If you can help us any, we'd appreciate it.' We bought about half a million dollars of stock. I had no compunctions about doing it. Actually, we made money on our investment."

Federal's officers and employees did their part. J. R. Kennedy personally invested close to $1 million to buy 28,500 shares, increasing his holdings to more than 75,000. Guy Freas bought 13,900. Jack and Quentin Kennedy and their sister, Ethel, borrowed money from Bankers Trust to buy stock. Employees bought one or two shares, if that's all they could afford.

It was like the English boats sailing across the Channel to rescue the troops at Dunkirk. On and on the buyers came — an enormous tribute to the esteem in which J. R. Kennedy was held by his friends, employees, customers and those in the industry.

"I called every customer I knew to buy stock, and a lot of them did," says Frank O'Connor, then a sales manager for Federal. "And when the customers would ask how they could help, I'd say you can do two things. You can buy stock through us. And you can buy more board, because we're too busy dealing with Simkins to sell board."

On the other hand, Ken Petersen tells about a Federal salesman in Philadelphia who sold his stock when the price shot up in the wake of the Simkins tender offer. "Jack Kennedy got wind of it and came rushing into my office and said, 'Ken, I want you to fire that SOB,'" Petersen recalls. "But J. R.'s style was different. He always had that wit and biting humor. About 20 minutes later he came in and sat down and chatted. 'How are things going' and so on. And then he said, 'Ken, by the way, we've got a salesman in Philadelphia. I think it would be nice if you found a systematic way to relieve him of his responsibilities.'"

Earl Roberson supported Federal in its dispute with Simkins by purchasing stock. He later served for 14 years as a member of Federal's board.

Today it would be illegal for a company to orchestrate purchases of its stock the way Federal did to fend off an unwanted suitor. But it wasn't illegal then, and Federal used the strategy to perfection, with the purchases driving the price of its stock above Simkins' $35 bid. This was the key; shareholders had no reason to tender to Simkins so long as they could get more by selling their shares on the New York Stock Exchange. "The fact is that the stock opened above his offering price and it stayed there," says Cheney. "It just stayed there. Either he had to raise his bid or forget the whole thing."

Meanwhile, Federal opened new fronts in the war. It sued Simkins on antitrust grounds, charging that the combination of Federal Paper Board and Simkins Industries would create a monopoly in the paperboard business in the Northeast.

One of the keys for any target company in defeating an attempted raid is to keep the company's stock out of the hands of arbitragers, who often accumulate large blocks of stock that they then resell to the raider or other high bidder. (Arbitragers buy and sell securities in hopes of taking advantage of price differentials to make a profit.) Federal got critical help in this regard from Goldman Sachs. Gustave Levy, the legendary securities trader at that firm, phoned one of his industry peers — the equally formidable Salim L. Lewis of Bear, Stearns & Co. — on Federal's behalf. Bear Stearns was acting as adviser to Simkins Industries in the tender offer. Levy warned Lewis that the tender offer posed antitrust problems and that Bear Stearns would therefore be unwise to get involved in arbitraging Federal's stock. (If Simkins Industries ended up being barred from making its purchases because of antitrust violations, the price of Federal stock would almost certainly have declined and arbitragers holding the shares would have lost money.) Although the exact words spoken between Levy and Lewis are today unknown, Bear Stearns apparently heeded Levy's warning and did not buy Federal stock for its arbitrage account.

Gustave Levy was well known as a powerful figure in the Wall Street community. Behind the scenes, he played an important role in discouraging arbitragers from buying Federal stock when Simkins made his tender offer.

That was just the beginning. Turning the screws a little tighter, Federal's board of directors raised the cash dividend rate by 50 percent and split the stock three-for-two to encourage shareholders to hold onto their stock.

J. R. Kennedy wrote to Federal's shareholders, telling them the company's earnings, which were $2.84 per share in 1966, were expected to rise to $3.15 a share in 1967 and were budgeted to increase to $4.00 per share in 1968. (Federal ended up exceeding its 1967 estimate; earnings rose to $3.44 per share on a comparable basis after taking into account the two-for-three stock split. However, it fell short of its 1968 budget; earnings were $3.68 a share.) In the letter giving the earnings forecasts, J. R. Kennedy stated, "Recent market prices for our Common Stock have failed to reflect the Company's substantially higher earnings and its near and long-term prospects for growth." He called the Simkins tender offer "a bizarre attempt to seize upon this situation."

In a hard-hitting advertisement, the company warned ominously about "Five Dangers in Tendering even one Share to Simkins." Danger No. 1, for instance, was: "Simkins has not stated when he will commit himself to purchase if he gets less than 500,000 shares. If he has your shares, he can sit back and watch the market and make up his mind whether he's going to come across with the money, assuming he has it. Even if he decides to buy your shares, he hasn't told you when you'll be paid. The U.S. Congress is now considering legislation that would protect the investor against just these kinds of vague provisions in tender offers."

Danger No. 3: "The total assets of Simkins' company barely exceed the $17.6 million he would be obligated to pay if he got the 500,000 shares he's asking for. This doesn't include the big commission he's paying brokers in an effort to get them to convince you to tender. Simkins won't give you a clear explanation where the money is coming from despite Federal's request that the Federal Reserve Board and the Securities and Exchange Commission investigate the matter."

J. R. Kennedy could think about little except the threat to his company. "We worked nights and Sundays," says one retired executive. "Everybody stopped working on business. We just worked on Simkins."

Federal pulled out all the stops in battling Simkins. This ad posed all kinds of questions about Simkins and his bid.

Federal Paper Board Shareowners
Five Dangers in Tendering even one Share to Simkins

We believe you should be aware of the following dangers in the Simkins tender offer for your Federal stock.

Danger No. 1

Simkins has not stated when he will commit himself to purchase if he gets less than 500,000 shares. If he has your shares, he can sit back and watch the market and make up his mind whether he's going to come across with the money, assuming he has it. Even if he decides to buy your shares, he hasn't told you when you'll be paid. **The U. S. Congress is now considering legislation that would protect the investor against just these kinds of vague provisions in tender offers.**

Danger No. 2

Simkins' company competes with Federal in several different areas of the paperboard industry, and Federal has filed suit under the U. S. antitrust laws to prevent Simkins from holding any Federal stock.

Danger No. 3

The total assets of Simkins' company barely exceed the $17.6-million he would be obligated to pay if he got the 500,000 shares he's asking for. This doesn't include the big commission he's paying brokers in an effort to get them to convince you to tender. Simkins won't give you a clear explanation where the money is coming from despite Federal's request that the Federal Reserve Board and the Securities and Exchange Commission investigate the matter.

Danger No. 4

Simkins hopes that you won't share his high opinion of the future potential of your Federal shares. In 1967 Federal will earn approximately $3.15 a share on record sales of $112,500,000, as compared with earnings of $2.84 a share on sales of $107,691,000

quated. We've already taken business away from him with our new Inverform papermaking machine.

Danger No. 5

If you give up your shares you will miss the full benefits of Federal's stock split and increased dividend.

As previously announced, Federal will distribute to the Company's shareholders of record on December 29, 1967, one additional share of Common Stock for each two shares of Common Stock held of record on such date. This is equivalent to a 3-for-2 stock split.

The Board of Directors also intends to declare quarterly dividends at the rate of 25¢ a share on the shares to be outstanding after the stock split. The new dividend rate will be equivalent to an annual dividend of $1.50 a share on the shares of Common Stock presently outstanding, a 50% increase in cash dividends over the current rate of $1.00 a share.

Simkins is named as a co-conspirator in a lawsuit brought under the anti-fraud provisions of the federal securities laws in U.S. District Court, District of Connecticut. The suit charges that his family's ownership in Simkins Industries, Inc. (formerly New Haven Board & Carton Co., Inc.) was increased from 33 percent to 76 percent by fraudulent means. It is charged that through the use of falsified and misleading reports and proxy statements prepared and distributed under Simkins' direction, the shareholders of New Haven Board and Carton were misled into authorizing New Haven Board and Carton to acquire certain Florida corporations owned by the Simkins, which corporations were worth $2,000,000 less than the New Haven Board and Carton stock issued to the Simkins in the transactions. A motion to dismiss the suit has been denied.

Fellow shareowners, we believe you should turn Simkins back without a single share. Your manage-

JUST "AN INVESTMENT"

Simkins himself initially sought to downplay the dispute, saying Federal was overreacting and that he only wanted to buy the shares as "an investment." It wasn't long, however, before he began turning up the heat. When Federal split its stock and raised its dividend, he commented, "They must be getting a little desperate." A few days later, he said Federal's management "hasn't performed well for stockholders" and suggested he could do a better job. And finally, six days after Federal sued him, he filed a suit of his own, charging Federal with manipulating the price of its stock; he asked that Federal's officers and directors be required to sell all the shares they had bought subsequent to his tender offer.

But in the end, the tender offer was a failure. When the offer finally ran its course in late January 1968, Simkins would not say how much stock he had acquired except that it was less than 3 percent of Federal's total shares. According to Federal's records, 4,622 shares were tendered, about 0.3 percent. Subsequently, Simkins indicated in a newspaper interview that he was considering a proxy fight to gain control of Federal's board of directors, but nothing ever came of this. The suits and countersuits were eventually dropped.

Even so, Federal was not about to let down its defenses. At the annual meeting in April 1968, the company asked for and received shareholder approval to divide its board into four separate classes of directors with staggered terms of office. As a result, only one-quarter of Federal's directors now come up for re-election in any given year, making it tougher for an unfriendly investor to wage a proxy fight for control of the board. Federal is the only company on the New York Stock Exchange with this arrangement; the exchange subsequently barred all other listed companies from adopting four-class boards.

The bylaw relating to the four classes was drafted by Ed Kelly. Following its publication in Federal's proxy statement, an attorney for Simkins Industries kept telling Kelly there was a mistake in the bylaw but wouldn't tell him what it was. This went on for some time until Kelly discovered a minor technical error that required the election of an additional director in one of the four classes. Kelly began pressing Federal to select an additional director, until one day his father — Hugh J. Kelly, executive vice president of McGraw-Hill, Inc. — told Ed, to Ed's great surprise, that he, Hugh, had been asked by Federal to serve on its board. "I was a bit embarrassed that all my pestering led them to choose my own father," he says. When Hugh Kelly retired from the Federal board in 1981, son Ed took his place — indicative of the family feeling that still exists at Federal. Ed Kelly is now vice chairman of Eighteen Seventy Corporation, an investment firm, as well as a member of Federal's board of directors.

Edmund J. Kelly, vice chairman of Eighteen Seventy Corporation, is well known in the investment and legal communities for his staunch opposition to hostile takeovers. He expresses great pride in his long-time association with Federal Paper Board, which he calls a "truly great company."

As a young attorney, Kelly helped defend Federal in 1967 against the attempt by Simkins Industries to purchase Federal stock. Subsequently, he was Federal's principal legal advisor in the 1972 acquisition of the Riegelwood mill.

Since 1981, Kelly has served as a director, succeeding his father, Hugh Kelly, on the Federal board.

Today, Federal's major defense against unfriendly bids is a "fair price" clause devised by Kelly. Approved by shareholders in 1976, this clause requires a controlling stockholder to get a 95 percent favorable vote of all the shares outstanding to authorize a merger. The practical effect would be to make it difficult for a raider, having gained voting control of Federal, to squeeze out the remaining minority holders. The more he tried to acquire these holders' stock, the more expensive doing so would become.

However, whether even the strongest anti-takeover measures would fend off a persistent, well-financed raider is open to question. Unfriendly bids are no longer in their infancy, as they were when Simkins made his offer for Federal shares. Especially important is the dominant role now played by arbitragers; at the first sign a company has been put into play as an active takeover candidate, these speculators tend to buy up its stock. They have no loyalty to the company's management and don't care a whit about its long-term earnings potential. Their only goal is to resell quickly to the highest bidder, whether a raider or a so-called "white knight" acquirer acceptable to management. Common wisdom is that, once the majority of a company's stock is held by arbitragers, the company's days as an independent corporation are almost certainly numbered.

"The reality today," says Jack Kennedy, "is that there is no protection against high cash offers. If someone comes along and is prepared to pay a 40 percent or 50 percent premium, you have to look for another buyer you like better. The ball game has changed."

CHAPTER 10

Shattered Glass

EDERAL Glass was a wonderful little company that came to an odd and tragic end. Its story is a unique chapter in Federal Paper Board's history.

Founded in 1900 in Columbus, Ohio, and family-owned for many years, Federal Glass was known as a quality maker of drinking glasses and inexpensive tableware. The similarity in names between Federal Glass Company and Federal Paper Board Company was purely coincidental; the two had no relationship until Federal Paper Board acquired Federal Glass in 1958. To this day, the acquisition represents the only time Federal Paper Board has ever diversified outside its basic business of paperboard and related products.

The acquisition proved to be a godsend. As Federal Paper Board struggled to earn a profit from the Sprague mill in the 1960s, Federal Glass carried the company financially, accounting for about one-quarter of Federal Paper Board's revenues and up to two-thirds of its operating earnings during the decade.

ORIGINS OF FEDERAL GLASS IN 1900

Federal Glass was established by an inventor and businessman named George Beatty to capitalize on his newly devised glass-blowing machine. Most glassware was still blown by master craftsmen at the turn of the century. Beatty's machine never worked properly, however, so he ended up recruiting glass blowers from Belgium and reverting to traditional manufacturing techniques.

To broaden its markets, in 1969 Federal Glass opened a showroom in New York.

131

Federal Glass started in the business by manufacturing jelly tumblers and other low-cost glassware. This picture of the melting and final selection department was taken in 1913, 13 years after the plant opened.

Beatty died in 1916 and was succeeded as chief executive by his son, James M. Beatty, also an inventor. James ran the company for the next 21 years and introduced many technical innovations. One problem facing glassmakers was the physical transfer of molten glass from the furnace to the forming machines. With two partners, James Beatty invented the Tucker, Reeves and Beatty automatic feeder, installing this technology at Federal Glass in 1916. In 1929, Federal Glass pioneered the manufacture of colored glass made in a continuous tank. During the 1930s, it switched completely to mechanized production, fulfilling the original dream of George Beatty. James Beatty died in 1937 and was succeeded as president by Edmund A. "Ted" Donnan, then 41 years old.

Donnan headed Federal Glass for more than 20 years and was subsequently one of the key personalities in the history of Federal Paper Board Company. He arranged the sale of Federal Glass to Federal Paper Board in 1958. Following the sale, he became a vice president of Federal Paper Board and was an influential member of its board of directors.

A WORLD WAR I AVIATOR

Ted Donnan was born in Washington, Pennsylvania, in 1896. His father was a banker and his paternal grandfather was a Presbyterian minister who had come to the United States from Scotland in the 1860s. His maternal grandfather was a landowner who bought and sold Pennsylvania coal-mining properties. After receiving his bachelor's degree from Washington and Jefferson College, Donnan headed off to graduate school at Harvard, earning an MBA.

On graduation from Harvard, he did something straight out of an Ernest Hemingway novel: barely 21 years old, he sailed to Europe with several classmates to fight with the Allies in World War I. Italy was on the Allied side, and Donnan joined the Italian air force. From a base near Padua, he piloted a biplane bomber and flew across the Dolomite Mountains on missions into southern Austria and Germany. "They only flew at night; he had some close calls," says his son, Edmund "Ted" Donnan, Jr. The elder Donnan retained a lifelong interest in aviation. Although he seldom talked about his experiences in World War I, all his friends and employees knew he had been a pilot and looked upon him with considerable admiration and awe. His venturesomeness during the war was especially striking because he was such a soft-spoken, conservative person by nature.

After the war, he returned to Pennsylvania and worked briefly at his father's bank, while racing cars as a hobby. In 1920, at age 24, he was hired by the Beatty family as general manager of a newly built corrugated box plant at the Federal Glass manufacturing complex in Columbus, Ohio. (Corrugated containers are the familiar shipping boxes made from heavy-duty, light brown board with a ripply center.) Federal Glass had been manufacturing corrugated boxes to ship its glassware since 1911. In 1919, it renamed the operation Hercules Box Company and built a three-story factory to expand production. Part of Donnan's assignment was to increase sales to other companies. He was successful in this effort and was eventually elected a member of the Federal Glass board of directors and then the company's president.

Edmund Donnan was a quiet hero who headed Federal Glass. He flew dangerous missions for the Italian air force in World War I, but seldom talked about them.

Donnan was a small, trim man, standing five feet seven inches and weighing a little over 130 pounds. He was known for his fairness, integrity and natural leadership abilities. "He was just a fine gentleman who was respected by everybody," says Harold Mallett, who joined Federal Glass in 1936 and later became treasurer and controller of Federal Paper Board.

Donnan never swore and seldom raised his voice. "He could get awfully mad and awfully short, but he did it judiciously," according to his son Ted, Jr. Rather than confronting people head-on when he had a complaint, he often made his point in an indirect manner. Russell W. Hughes, who was company controller and was in charge of the heating system in the Federal Glass executive offices, recalls the way in which Donnan would let him know if the temperature was too low. "He would simply walk into my office wearing his topcoat," Hughes says. "He wouldn't mention the cold. He'd talk about something else, and as soon as he left I would make amends and turn the heat up."

Donnan had an analytical mind and was good with numbers. "He could absorb various bits of information and put them together quickly to arrive at a decision," according to Mallett. He was an excellent public speaker, not through humor or theatrics but by means of his ability to lay out facts in a clear, concise manner.

Perhaps reflecting his background as a banker, he was exceedingly conservative financially and insisted that debt be avoided except in the most exceptional circumstances. "He would never endanger a balance sheet," in the words of Mallett. He expanded the operations of Federal Glass slowly, financing capital investments from cash flow and focusing at all times on maintaining adequate profitability. Under his leadership, Federal Glass consistently earned a pretax return on sales of at least 18 percent.

Donnan dressed impeccably in dark, neatly tailored suits. When it came to cars, the only type he ever bought was a dark-colored Cadillac. "When he traded in his car after three years or so, it was hard to tell that he had bought a new one because he always kept the old one so clean," Mallett states.

Unlike many executives, Donnan was not a workaholic. He left home at 7:30 each morning and returned at 5:30 p.m.. Every summer, he took his wife and two sons on a lengthy vacation to Cape Cod, Europe or some other location. He was an expert fly fisherman and, as he grew older, enjoyed spending Saturdays fishing with his grandchildren. Sundays were always set aside for attending church and being with family.

THE $11 MILLION ACQUISITION OF FEDERAL GLASS

Federal Paper Board Company acquired Federal Glass Company out of a mutual need.

In the late 1950s, Federal Paper Board was seeking to diversify into the corrugated box business. Meanwhile, Donnan had decided to put Federal Glass up for sale. The principal owner of Federal Glass was James Beatty's widow, and she was getting along in years. Under the corporate bylaws of Federal Glass, the company's executives would be able to purchase the company at a price based on book value when she died. Donnan believed this price was inadequate. Acting against his own personal interest (after all, he would have been one of the buyers at a bargain price from the Beatty estate) and taking the stance of a fiduciary for the Beatty family, he consulted with Mrs. Beatty and decided to sell the company to a third party to realize its full value for her and her heirs.

However, Donnan was not prepared to sell to just any buyer who happened down the pike. In addition to seeking an adequate price, he wanted a buyer that was financially sound, would support the continued growth of Federal Glass and would treat its employees fairly. He entertained bids for nearly two years before settling on Federal Paper Board.

Donnan and J. R. Kennedy were introduced to each other by officials of Morgan Guaranty Trust Company. However, Donnan was skeptical at first about selling his company to Federal Paper Board, believing Federal Paper Board's balance sheet did not meet his standards. This concern may seem hard to believe, given the fact that Federal Paper Board's debt was less than 3 percent of total capitalization at the time! Donnan finally accepted Federal Paper Board's offer for two reasons: his respect for J. R. Kennedy's integrity and business acumen, and the fact that Federal Paper Board's stock was listed on the New York Stock Exchange. The liquidity of the acquirer's shares was of utmost concern to Donnan, since he wanted the Beattys to receive securities they could resell whenever they wanted.

On June 30, 1958, Federal Paper Board Company acquired Federal Glass Company for common and preferred stock worth

Federal's glass and container facilities in Columbus, Ohio, passed facilities to make glassware, corrugated ship-containers and corrugated paper products. Federal Board acquired the glass company mainly to get into corrugated container business, but this part of the never panned out as expected.

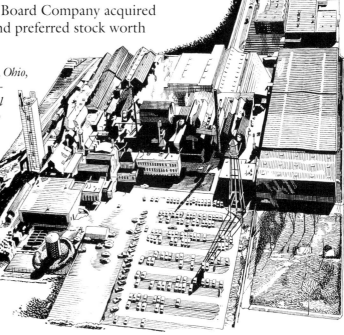

approximately $11 million. Kennedy explained the benefits of the consolidation as follows: "Federal Paper Board is a substantial user of corrugated containers and a supplier of containerboard used in the fabrication of these containers, while the Glass Company is a growing user of folding cartons. The Glass Company and Hercules are now being operated as divisions of Federal Paper Board. Full coordination of operations will result in substantial economies and through intracompany sales, other advantages will accrue."

Donnan continued to head Federal Glass for seven years after the acquisition, retiring in 1965 at age 69. He was also elected to the board of directors of Federal Paper Board following the acquisition and continued in that position until 1976, becoming one of the most respected and influential members of the board. As a director, he supported management's programs to modernize Federal Paper Board's production facilities and was a constant voice for conservative financial practices.

THE FATE OF HERCULES

In 1958, when Federal Glass was acquired by Federal Paper Board, its glassmaking operations had sales of $14 million and the Hercules Box division had sales of $3 million. About two-thirds of corrugated box sales were to outside customers.

Even though Hercules Box was the smaller part of the company, Federal Paper Board made the acquisition primarily to buy Hercules and get a foothold in the corrugated box business. Federal Paper Board's plan was to establish a corrugated shipping box division and expand operations by acquiring more companies.

The new division did well for a time. Federal Paper Board invested in productivity improvements and additional capacity at the Columbus plant of Hercules. In 1966, it purchased majority interest in a corrugated sheet operation in Pittsburgh. And in 1967, it bought a corrugated box plant in Baltimore. As a result, the division's sales rose from $3 million in 1958 to $11 million in 1970.

However, the division never became large enough to justify the management attention it deserved, and its earnings never lived up to Federal Paper Board's expectations. Consequently, the company divested the division in January 1971. In a transaction with Continental Can Company, Federal Paper Board traded the division and $8.4 million for a board mill and folding carton plant in Los Angeles and a carton plant in Piermont, New York; in addition, Federal leased a paperboard mill in Piermont from Continental, with an option to buy. Through this transaction, Federal Paper Board gave up $11 million of yearly sales in the corrugated box business while gaining $30 million of sales in paperboard and folding cartons. Three months later, Federal Paper Board leased a carton plant in Elkhart, Indiana, from Continental for ten years.

The glassware division, on the other hand, turned out to be an excellent investment, far beyond anything Federal Paper Board had anticipated. "Federal Glass was an interesting company," says Oliver F. Runde, who succeeded Donnan as its president. "It was a small company, but it had a great deal of prestige because it was a quality house in the tableware glass industry."

At the heart of Federal Glass was its huge manufacturing facility in Columbus. The size of an airplane hangar, it contained four furnaces and other equipment for the mass production of quality glassware. Glassmaking machines were automatic and, at peak production, operated continuously around the clock seven days a week. Emblazoned by the employees' entrance were the words, "Through these portals pass the best glassmakers in the world."

Federal Paper Board took these operations and expanded them. In 1963, the Glass Company (as Federal Glass was sometimes called) built a highly automated batch plant for preparing raw materials. In 1965, it built a modern furnace room to house a

It was the glassmaking part of the business that turned out to be far more profitable than Federal Paper Board ever anticipated. The Glass Company became an important supplier to the industry and the dominant force in the decoration market. The company's "Sheer Rim" design produced a level of quality usually found only in far more expensive glassware.

redesigned furnace for melting opaque glass. In 1966, it completed a new warehouse. In 1967, it built a fifth furnace. In 1969, it completed another warehouse and opened a showroom in New York City. In 1970, it expanded melting operations and added new finishing machinery. That same year, it secured a long-term lease for 28 acres adjacent to its Columbus operations to provide room for future growth. In 1972, it replaced one of its older furnaces with two new electric-fired furnaces, further increasing melting capacity.

The Glass Company also developed new products and entered new markets. Federal Glass had long been regarded as the industry's quality leader in machine-blown glass. It had developed a unique finishing process called "Sheer Rim." This method gave an even, uniform finish to the lip of each piece of glassware, rather than the heavy beaded finish that was typical of most other machine-made glassware. The company also prided itself on the clarity and uniformity of its products.

Because of its high product quality, Federal Glass was the dominant supplier to the most demanding market segment — independent cutter/decorator companies that embellish glassware with hand-cutting or decoration and resell it to department stores and gift shops. While maintaining this position, Federal Glass began to make inroads into two larger market segments: direct sales to retail outlets such as supermarkets and department stores, and sales to institutional customers such as restaurants and hotels.

At the same time, the so-called "promotion" market — inexpensive glassware given away by gasoline service stations and other retailers to attract customers — began to grow in the 1960s. Federal Glass entered this market aggressively, landing such blue-chip accounts as Shell Oil and Procter & Gamble.

Through these actions, the Glass Company increased its sales from $14 million in 1958 to $39 million in 1972. Meanwhile, earnings rose for 12 consecutive years following the Glass Company's acquisition by Federal Paper Board. Particularly in the mid-1960s, when Federal Paper Board was experiencing start-up problems at its Sprague paperboard mill, earnings from the Glass Company helped carry Federal through this difficult period. Later, in the early 1970s, when Federal Paper Board acquired the Riegelwood, North Carolina, paperboard mill, earnings from the Glass Company provided financial leverage to help make this important acquisition possible. So the Glass Company was more than just a good business in its own right; it gave Federal Paper Board much of the financial wherewithal to upgrade to large, modern paperboard mills. The Glass Company's earnings dipped slightly in 1971, then rebounded to a new high in 1972.

As 1973 began, the outlook seemed rosier than ever for the glassware industry and Federal Glass Company. Federal Paper Board stated in its 1972 annual report to shareholders:

"Notwithstanding competitive materials and imports, the market for table glassware has expanded steadily over the past 20 years. Basic to this growth has been the steady increase in the number of households, in per capita income and in improved living standards. Recognizing these fundamental trends, Federal has accelerated its own growth by continually increasing and improving its production facilities, by developing a flow of imaginative and colorful glassware products, and by expanding and strengthening its marketing activities."

Then, like a bolt out of the blue, the bad times arrived, leading to the eventual collapse of Federal Glass.

LOWER DEMAND AND HIGHER COSTS

The demise of Federal Glass Company had its roots in the 1973 OPEC embargo on oil shipments to the United States. "The embargo did two things to the company, both bad," says Runde. Virtually overnight, it destroyed the petroleum company promotion glassware market, which in 1972 had accounted for more than 15 percent of Federal Glass Company's sales. As gasoline came into short supply and lines formed at service stations, petroleum companies no longer wanted or needed promotional items to attract customers. Second, since glassmaking requires an enormous amount of energy, production costs soared as oil and gas prices climbed.

In 1973, Federal Glass experienced a sharp drop in revenues and earnings for the first time since being acquired by Federal Paper Board; sales sank from $39 million in 1972 to $34 million in 1973 and pretax profits fell from $5.6 million to $1.5 million. Although dollar sales recovered in 1974, unit sales remained depressed and the company lost money in 1974 and 1975.

The entire glassware industry was in turmoil. The abrupt drop in promotion sales had created excess capacity. Additionally, all companies were experiencing sharply higher production costs. To indicate the severity of the cost problem, in 1974 Federal Glass Company's cost of sand increased 9 percent; labor, 12 percent; packaging materials, 22 percent; fuel and electricity, 44 percent; and lime, 72 percent. What's more, a French company named Durand had developed a comparatively inexpensive way to make lead crystal and was rapidly capturing market share in the United States.

"The glassware business was at the front edge of what happened to smokestack industry in America in the '70s," says Jack E. Spengler, Federal Glass Company's final president. "We were decimated by inflation, labor difficulties, overregulation, imports, outdated technology and a long list of other problems."

Federal Glass returned to profitability in 1976, and it looked like the glassware industry might be on the road to recovery. So when John B. Gerlach, president of Lancaster Colony Corporation, another glassmaker, approached Jack Kennedy (who had by

Hugh Kelly was near retirement as an executive of McGraw-Hill when he joined Federal's board in 1969. He served for the next 12 years, bringing his unique perspective as a long-time business executive.

now succeeded his father as Federal's chief executive officer) in the fall of that year and made a bid to acquire Federal Glass, Kennedy wasn't interested. But the recovery proved short-lived. Losses began to mount again in early 1977, and Federal Paper Board was happy to accept Lancaster Colony's $45 million offer.

What followed was one of the most bizarre and controversial antitrust cases in American history. In the words of the *Washington Post*, "Federal Glass was regulated out of business."

ENTER THE FTC

The agreement to sell Federal Glass to Lancaster Colony Corporation was signed in March 1977. Had the sale been completed at that time, it would have just been another mid-sized corporate transaction that would have gone unnoticed outside the glassware industry; chances are Federal Glass would still be alive today as a division of Lancaster. "It was a good deal for everybody involved," says Mallett. For Federal Paper Board, the transaction offered an opportunity to sell Federal Glass at an attractive price. For Federal Glass employees, it meant their company would be acquired by a new owner committed to supporting the growth of the business. And from Lancaster's perspective, buying Federal Glass would give the firm something it wanted — a line of blown glassware such as drinking glasses to complement the line of pressed-glass beer mugs, ashtrays and giftware that Lancaster already made.

Neither Kennedy nor Gerlach anticipated any antitrust problems. Federal Glass was the third largest producer of machine-made glassware in the United States with a market share of approximately 11 percent, while Lancaster was number five with a 7 percent share. Their combined share of 18 percent would still be well behind the two industry leaders, Anchor Hocking Corporation and the Libbey division of Owens-Illinois, Inc., which together held about 60 percent of the U.S. market. Moreover, Federal Glass and Lancaster weren't direct competitors, and there was no overlap among their 25 largest customers. It was even possible to argue that the acquisition of Federal Glass by Lancaster Colony would result in increased competition by creating a strong number three participant in the glassware industry. "The combined companies would have profited from economies of size and a broader line of products," says Spengler. "They would have been able to compete successfully with the two giants."

Nonetheless, in June 1977 the Federal Trade Commission, armed with affidavits from Anchor Hocking and Owens-Illinois, charged that the sale of Federal Glass to Lancaster Colony would be anticompetitive. Noting that there were only seven domestic manufacturers of glass tableware, the FTC argued that any reduction of this number would diminish competition and drive consumer prices higher.

Federal Glass executives were appalled that the FTC was basing its claims largely on the views of the Glass Company's two largest competitors. In a deposition, J. Ray Topper, then head of Anchor Hocking's consumer glassware division, said his company opposed the acquisition because Lancaster Colony was buying production capacity for less than replacement cost — something that Anchor, because of its size, would be barred from doing. "I don't think a competitor should be allowed to do it on a more economic basis than me," he testified.

"The problem was that the FTC never did understand or learn the facts," says Spengler. "They made their decision and then sought to substantiate it." Although the FTC questioned customers of both Federal Glass and Lancaster Colony, not a single one expressed concern that the acquisition would diminish competition. Explaining why the FTC ignored the views of the very parties it was supposedly protecting, Alfred F. Dougherty, Jr., director of the commission's bureau of competition, later told *Fortune* magazine, "Generally what happens is that purchasers are really only concerned about making sure that their supplies are assured.... Competition rarely means the same thing to an antitrust lawyer as it does to someone who is in business."

In July 1977, one month after filing its charges, the FTC obtained an injunction to block the sale pending a trial before an administrative law judge. Faced with the prospect of lengthy and expensive legal proceedings, Federal Paper Board and Lancaster Colony called off the sale.

In opposing the acquisition of Federal Glass by Lancaster Colony, the FTC's Alfred Dougherty, Jr., argued that competition "rarely means the same thing to an antitrust lawyer as it does to someone who is in business."

In the following months, the financial performance of Federal Glass continued to deteriorate, and Federal Paper Board decided to sell the plant or close it. Gerlach, meanwhile, still wanted a blown-glass factory. In an attempt to convince the FTC to change its mind, Gerlach asked Senator Howard Metzenbaum of Ohio for help. The senator arranged for Gerlach and Jack Kennedy to meet with Dougherty of the FTC. At their April 1978 meeting, Kennedy told Dougherty that Federal Glass had lost $567,000 in 1977 and that 1978 losses were likely to be higher. He asked Dougherty to reconsider the FTC's opposition to a purchase by Lancaster, adding that liquidating the company had become a real possibility. Dougherty promised to take another look.

For the next two months, officials of Federal Paper Board attempted to convince FTC attorneys that Federal Glass was no longer viable on its own. They pointed out that the Glass Company's reported financial losses understated the problem because they did not include the cost of financing inventories, receivables and capital investments. Even in 1976, the only year in the previous four that Federal Glass had been profitable, cash flow was negative.

After reconsidering for two months, in June 1978 Dougherty

told Kennedy and Gerlach that he had not changed his mind. Dougherty was unmoved by claims of losses and seemed to disbelieve Kennedy's assertion that the plant faced possible liquidation. Later, Dougherty and his boss, FTC Chairman Michael Pertschuk, accused Federal Paper Board of having purposely exaggerated Federal Glass Company's losses through bookkeeping maneuvers in an attempt to force the sale to Lancaster. "We couldn't convince them that Federal Glass was a drain," says Quentin Kennedy, executive vice president of Federal. "They didn't understand that inventories have to be financed. They thought they were the same thing as cash."

Dealing with the FTC was becoming a nightmare for Federal Paper Board executives. Having supplied cartons full of documentation and having spent many hours answering the FTC's questions, they were no closer to a sale than they had been a year earlier. Speaking of the FTC, Jack Kennedy says, "They had little faith in us, and I can assure you we had no confidence in them."

While declining to reverse himself, Dougherty told Jack Kennedy he would consider the matter again if Federal Paper Board hired an investment banking firm and spent 120 days looking for an alternative buyer. Kennedy is normally calm and charming. But he can also be extremely tough and blunt, and he considered Dougherty's suggestion the final straw, coming as it did after 15 months of effort by Federal Paper Board to sell Federal Glass. "I said that hiring an investment banking firm would be a waste of time and money," Kennedy asserts. Kennedy said there had already been ample opportunity for other buyers to come forward and that Federal Paper Board hadn't been able to identify a single candidate other than Lancaster. Accordingly, he told Dougherty, the plant would be closed as soon as possible.

News of the planned closing hit the city of Columbus like a bombshell. Editorial writers denounced the FTC, bemoaned the fate of the 1,500 workers and expressed hope the plant could be saved. The struggle to keep the plant alive suddenly became one of the hottest news stories in Columbus. President Spengler stopped setting his alarm clock. "I didn't need to," he states. "Literally, for the next several months I was awakened at five or six every morning by a phone call from someone in the media."

It was at this point that Governor James Rhodes of Ohio and Mayor Tom Moody of Columbus got involved. Immediately on hearing of the planned closing, they phoned Kennedy and asked him to meet with them in Columbus. At that meeting, held in June 1988, they prevailed on Kennedy to go partway with Dougherty. "I changed my mind about closing the plant as a result of the intervention of plant management and principally because of Mayor Moody and Governor Rhodes, who indicated they'd do everything they could to help us try to sell the facility," Kennedy says. Consequently, Federal Paper Board retained First

Boston Corporation, the investment banking firm, to spend the next 60 days seeking a new buyer. First Boston contacted 79 candidates, but only one, Durand, was interested enough to inspect the plant, and it didn't make a bid.

With no new buyers in sight, Federal Paper Board was back to square one. So once again it attempted to sell to Lancaster Colony. On August 28, 1978, Federal Paper Board notified the FTC that it planned to make the sale 60 days later. The notification was required under a consent agreement that Federal and Lancaster had signed to settle the original FTC complaint. On October 25, 1978, the FTC issued a second complaint, and Lancaster dropped out again. "To add insult to injury," says Spengler, "the commission barred us from selling equipment to Lancaster Colony in the event of liquidation." Oddly, Federal Glass was free to sell equipment to larger competitors, including Anchor Hocking and Owens-Illinois, or anyone else.

PROPOSED EMPLOYEE BUYOUT

Now, attempts to save the plant took a new turn. In late October, Federal Paper Board agreed to sell the facility to 15 of the Glass Company's senior executives, led by Spengler, at a reduced price. The employees were to put up $500,000 of their own money, with $12 million of the acquisition price to be financed by a loan from Federal Paper Board and $14 million by bank loans. However, the employee group was never able to get the bank financing it needed.

With the aid of Governor Rhodes and Mayor Moody, the group also attempted to obtain financing from the federal Economic Development Administration and the Department of Housing and Urban Development. The EDA regional office in Chicago seemed willing to finance part of the package, but was unable to get the money from Washington. Federal Glass qualified for loans from HUD, but HUD officials said they couldn't reach a final decision until April.

By January 1979, Federal Paper Board was spending $100,000 a week to keep Federal Glass afloat, and it wasn't prepared to wait three months for HUD's decision. On January 31, Kennedy flew to Columbus and closed the plant.

The FTC still seemed to believe Federal Paper Board was bluffing. Maintaining that the shutdown was a ploy to force the sale to Lancaster, a commission spokesman told a press conference that it made economic sense to keep the plant open. Other FTC officials continued to accuse Federal Paper Board of manipulating the books of Federal Glass to make financial results look worse than they really were. However, the FTC's claims were not winning many converts in Columbus. Senator John Glenn of Ohio called the situation "ridiculous" and said antitrust laws should be brought into line with economic realities. A columnist in the Columbus *Citizen-Journal* wrote, "The Federal Glass situation is a classic case of misplaced objectives and government at its worst." And U.S. Representative Chalmers P. Wylie opined, "If I introduced a bill to abolish the Federal Trade Commission, I'd be a hero in Columbus."

Two companies, Eastcliff Corporation and Wheaton Industries, had by now stepped forward and said they might be interested in acquiring the facility. However, they withdrew after looking at the plant and reviewing its financial results, whereupon Dougherty startled Kennedy by offering a modified version of his earlier proposal: if Federal Paper Board would reopen the factory and look for a new buyer for 30 days more, Dougherty would again reconsider his objections to Lancaster. Kennedy declined.

"By late February, even the Federal Trade Commission knew that Lancaster Colony was the only hope for Federal Glass," says Spengler. Bowing to reality, the FTC staff asked administrative law judge Paul R. Teetor to dismiss its complaint and clear the way for the transaction. Dougherty said he still believed the deal violated antitrust law, but that public policy considerations in protecting jobs outweighed those violations. In an ironic twist, Teetor turned down the staff's request, saying the agency's mandate didn't allow for personal philosophy to take precedence over antitrust law. However, the five FTC commissioners sided unanimously with the staff and approved the sale on March 6, 1979, almost two years to the day after the original agreement had been reached by Federal Paper Board and Lancaster Colony.

A FATAL UNION VOTE

Now it was up to Federal Paper Board and Lancaster Colony to work out a new deal. Lancaster's Gerlach was willing to try again, but he estimated that half of Federal Glass Company's 1979 sales had already been lost to Anchor Hocking and Owens-Illinois. Accordingly, he wanted new terms, including a new contract with the six locals of the American Flint Glass Workers Union that represented Federal Glass employees. He insisted on new work rules and temporary pay reductions of up to 9.5 percent.

Union officials refused, and contract negotiations between Lancaster and the union broke down on March 18, 1979. At the urging of federal mediators, the union then submitted the plan to a vote by its membership, but with the recommendation it be rejected.

The vote was held on Sunday, April 1 — April Fool's day — and had its own strange twist: the wording on the ballot was confusingly inverted. A "yes" vote meant the member supported the union and wanted to reject the proposed new contract. A "no" vote was for acceptance of the pact. The measure carried by a vote of 393 to 286, meaning the membership had turned the contract down. One day later, Lancaster withdrew its bid to acquire the plant, and that was the end of Federal Glass.

In August 1979, the plant equipment was sold at auction. Subsequently, the plant site was developed into an industrial park. Federal Paper Board had a total cash gain of $22 million from the liquidation and took a $13 million after-tax charge against earnings to reflect the costs of the shutdown.

Several months later, Federal Paper Board filed an antitrust suit in federal court against Anchor Hocking, Owens-Illinois, the American Flint Glass Workers Union of North America and others, alleging they had conspired to cause the FTC to withhold its approval of the sale to Lancaster. The suit also alleged that the defendants had attempted to monopolize the machine-made soda lime consumer glassware industry. In 1984, Federal settled the suit out of court, receiving $8 million.

"Regulatory Fiasco"

The shutdown became a national cause celebre. In a lengthy postmortem in its July 2, 1979, issue, *Fortune* magazine called it "a regulatory fiasco that would be comic were it not for the economic losses that resulted." *Columbus Monthly* magazine described the closing as "the case of a dying company lying on the ground screaming for help, while the FTC comes along, demands that the company fill out 50 or so forms and then stomps the life out of it."

The FTC, on the other hand, continued to blame Federal Paper Board. At a July 1979 hearing before a Senate Judiciary subcommittee, Daniel Schwartz, deputy director of the FTC Bureau of Competition, said the case was an example of "corporate extortion" by a company wishing to achieve economic objectives contrary to the interests of society. Federal's objective, he said, was to sell the factory at the highest price even though selling to Lancaster would reduce competition in the glassware industry.

But the FTC was in a strange position to make such a charge. For in April 1979, just three months after the closing of Federal Glass, the agency didn't raise the slightest objection when Anchor Hocking acquired the glassmaking operations of Brockway Glass Company in Clarksburg, West Virginia, for $6.25 million. Brockway was the nation's fourth largest producer of glass tableware, with a market share estimated at 9 percent. Like Federal Paper Board, it was losing money in glassware and wanted out of the business. Not only did Anchor Hocking — the same Anchor Hocking that in 1977 joined the FTC in an antitrust suit to block the sale of Federal Glass to Lancaster Colony — acquire the facility at less than replacement cost; it obtained the low-cost federal financing that had eluded the employee group at Federal Glass. To West Virginians, the takeover must have seemed an eminently logical way to save a major business from going under. To those who had watched the agony of Federal Glass in Columbus, it was the ultimate irony.

John Millikin, a senior vice president of Bankers Trust, joined Federal's board of directors in 1967 when annual sales were just $100 million. He actively supported the Riegelwood and Augusta acquisitions and served with distinction for 22 years. The single most difficult decision of that period, he says, was the closing of Federal Glass.

CHAPTER 11

Going South: The 1972 Riegelwood Acquisition

"FOR YEARS, our favorite saying was, 'We've got to get to the tree,'" states Press Millen, sales manager for Federal's recycled paperboard division. "That meant we had to get into solid bleached sulphate (paperboard made from wood fiber). And we finally did get to the tree when we bought Riegelwood."

Riegelwood is Federal's sprawling paperboard mill in south-eastern North Carolina near Wilmington. The company acquired the huge facility and other properties from Riegel Paper Corporation for $115.6 million in 1972.

Federal had been trying to get into the bleached board business for nearly two decades. (Solid bleached sulphate board is 100 percent wood fiber. The pulp used to make the board has been bleached to improve its whiteness and has been made with the sulphate process, which refers to the type of chemicals employed.) All the growth in paperboard demand was occurring in solid bleached sulphate, because of its high quality and competitive costs. Demand for recycled paperboard, on the other hand, was declining.

Time and again, Federal sought to build or acquire a bleached board operation. It explored potential mill sites across the South, at one point reaching a preliminary agreement to purchase acreage in Louisiana. It made bids for existing mills. It even looked into the idea of converting production at Sprague to bleached board and building a pulp mill in Nova Scotia to supply Sprague with wood fiber.

Foresters continuously monitor the growth and health of Federal's trees.

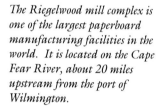

The Riegelwood mill complex is one of the largest paperboard manufacturing facilities in the world. It is located on the Cape Fear River, about 20 miles upstream from the port of Wilmington.

Always, the problem was money. Harold Mallett, who was Federal's treasurer in the late '60s and early '70s, explains, "During that time our price-earnings ratio was only five or six. Because the bleached board companies had P-E's of anywhere from 10 to 18, we couldn't afford to buy them with stock. And we didn't have enough borrowing power to acquire or build a big mill. So we just couldn't swing it."

Thus, when the opportunity to acquire Riegelwood came along, it was a dream come true. "Federal was either going to acquire Riegelwood or become nothing," asserts Richard Lenon, a Federal director.

"The company probably wouldn't exist today without it," Jack Kennedy agrees. "It's a fabulous facility for Federal and was probably the best deal ever made in our industry."

WHY RIEGELWOOD IS IMPORTANT

It is impossible to overstate the importance of Riegelwood to Federal. The acquisition was large in its own right. Federal had annual sales of $160 million, Riegelwood had sales of nearly $80 million. So overnight, the acquisition increased the size of Federal by 50 percent.

Moreover, Riegel Paper shareholders ended up owning nearly a 60 percent equity interest in Federal, assuming conversion of preferred stock into common. The convertible preferred was issued to Riegel shareholders by Federal. Thus, the ownership profile of Federal changed dramatically.

The acquisition had other significant ramifications:

- Most obvious was the move into bleached board and the implications that had for Federal's survival and growth in the 1970s and beyond. Today, with its huge mills in Riegelwood and Augusta, Federal is predominantly a solid bleached sulphate paperboard company.
- The acquisition brought Federal its first timberlands as well as a market pulp operation. Market pulp is processed wood fiber that is sold to other companies for making paper.
- Equally important was Federal's new willingness to take on debt, something it had assiduously avoided in the past. Without the aggressive use of debt, the acquisition of Riegelwood would not have been possible. Today, Federal employs debt as a routine tool to support its growth.
- Riegelwood also brought Federal a cadre of talented people, such as George E. Oakley, Jr., the mill's sales vice president, and C. Cline "Pete" Peters, the highly respected manager of the mill; E. Vernon Hogan, a colorful North Carolina banker who was a major shareholder of Riegel Paper and was elected to Federal's board of directors following the acquisition; and William E. Reid, who joined the Federal board to represent the interests of Riegel shareholders who had received Federal stock in the transaction. Hundreds of skilled men and women, from mill workers to senior executives, came to Federal in what was probably the single greatest influx of talent in its history.

- In addition, the transaction signaled the passing of the management baton from father to son — from the 71-year-old chairman, J. R. Kennedy, to the 41-year-old president, Jack Kennedy. There was no formal announcement that Jack was now in charge. In fact, he did not officially become Federal's chief executive officer until 1976. But Riegelwood was his deal. He championed it from the start and guided it through to completion. Jack Kennedy himself says it's hard to pinpoint an exact time when his father withdrew from day-to-day management of the company and he took over. But to many at Federal, the Riegelwood acquisition was the point of change.

J.R. and Jack Kennedy are pictured in Federal's 1972 annual report, the year the company bought the Riegelwood mill.

Why was Federal able to acquire Riegelwood when it had been unable to acquire other bleached board operations? Several factors came together to present an unusual window of opportunity.

For one, Federal Glass Company was in its peak earning years, providing Federal Paper Board with a source of income to support the assumption of more debt.

Another factor was the depressed market conditions in the paperboard industry. Federal Paper Board acquired the Riegelwood mill at the very bottom of a down market, purchasing the facility for what, in retrospect, was a bargain price.

But most important of all, Riegel Paper Corporation was an eager seller.

THE FOUNDING OF THE TOWN OF RIEGELWOOD

Riegel had a long history in the paper business. It was founded in 1862 by John Leidy Riegel and was known as an innovator in the paper industry. It was known also for its strong family orientation and its concern for employees. During the Depression, Riegel Paper manufactured product at a loss rather than close its facilities and lay off workers.

Like Federal, Riegel Paper had its roots in the Northeast, operating a group of mills in New Jersey. Then in 1937, it acquired a large tract of timberland in North Carolina. The company intended to harvest trees from this land and ship them north for processing at its paper mills. "This was going to be just the growing grounds," says Michael Padrick, public relations manager at Riegelwood. "But they changed their minds and decided to build a small pulp mill and ship pulp to New Jersey."

However, the outbreak of World War II forced Riegel Paper to put its plans for a pulp mill on hold. After the war, Riegel Paper founded the community of Riegelwood on the timberlands and completed its mill in 1952. Banks wouldn't grant mortgage loans in Riegelwood because they thought it was too risky. So Riegel Paper built the houses and sold them to employees through payroll deduction. When employees wanted to build a nine-hole golf course, Riegel Paper gave them a piece of land and let them borrow construction equipment.

John Leidy Riegel was born in 1819 and became a dynamic builder of businesses, Warren Foundry & Machine Co., Bethlehem Iron Works (later to become Bethlehem Steel) and Riegel Paper among them. In 1862, he built his first paper mill in Finesville, New Jersey, for $27,000. It produced one-half ton of rag newsprint a day.

He was known as being scrupulously honest and decreed that any family member working for the company who was not competent should be dismissed.

Banks wouldn't grant mortgage loans in Riegelwood, so Riegel Paper built the homes and sold them to employees through payroll deduction.

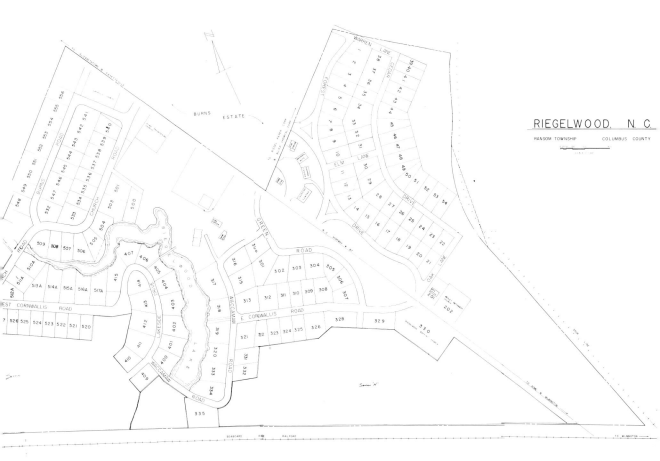

RIEGELWOOD, N.C.

RANSOM TOWNSHIP   COLUMBUS COUNTY

The town of Riegelwood was carved out of the North Carolina forest and was founded, planned and built by Riegel Paper.

Originally, the Riegelwood mill produced up to 250,000 tons of pulp annually. Soon, however, Riegel Paper began to expand the facility and use the pulp to make paperboard at the site. In 1958, it installed a Fourdrinier, christened the Carolina Belle, to make heavier grades of paperboard. In 1967, it installed a second Fourdrinier, the Carolina Queen, to make lighter grades.

Today, those same two Fourdriniers — the Carolina Belle and the Carolina Queen, modernized and greatly expanded — together with a pulp dryer completed in 1979, the Carolina King, are the heart of the Riegelwood mill complex.

In the late 1960s, Riegel's interest in the paper business began to wane. First, the company ran into some cost overruns at a joint venture pulp mill being constructed in Louisiana. And in 1970, it suffered its first net loss in years when the paper market went into recession. The papermaking business is both cyclical and capital-intensive. Riegel decided it no longer had the resources to remain a participant, so it put out quiet feelers to find a buyer for its papermaking operations, including Riegelwood.

Two potential bidders quickly emerged: Hoerner Waldorf Corporation and Southwest Forest Industries. But Hoerner Waldorf never made a formal bid, and on June 10, 1971, Riegel publicly announced some astonishing news. Riegel Paper — one of the oldest and best-known paper companies in America, and an enterprise that had been managed for four generations by members of the Riegel family — said it was getting out of the paper business and had reached an agreement to sell its paper division to Southwest Forest Industries for $112.3 million. That appeared to be the end of the matter — until Federal appeared on the scene.

The Carolina Queen, left, and Carolina Belle, right, are the heart of the Riegelwood mill. Both of these giant papermaking machines are more than 500 feet long.

How Federal Acquired Riegelwood With an 11th-Hour Bid

153

Going South:
The 1972
Riegelwood
Acquisition

The story of how Federal, a johnny-come-lately bidder, took Riegelwood from the grasp of Southwest Forest Industries is really the story of two men: George E. Oakley, Jr., the sales vice president of Riegel's paper division, and Jack Kennedy, the president of Federal.

Oakley was passionate in his belief that the Riegelwood mill should be modernized and expanded, and he feared that Southwest might not invest the necessary capital. So he launched a campaign within Riegel Paper to find a buyer other than Southwest. He was not a member of Riegel's senior management group, and it was unusual for someone at his level to attempt to overturn a major decision by the board of directors. In doing so, he risked getting fired.

Federal became involved when Oakley phoned Jack Kennedy. "He called me and said a lot of the people at Riegelwood didn't like the deal with Southwest," Kennedy recalls. "He asked if we were interested, and I said yes."

Explaining recently why he thought of Federal, Oakley says, "I had known Jack a long time. Also, I could see what Federal's direction was. They were big in paperboard. They wanted to get into bleached paperboard. And Riegelwood needed a home where the people were willing to spend the money and commit to make it the best mill in the world."

At Oakley's suggestion, he and Kennedy met with William M. Riegel, Riegel Paper's executive vice president. Bill Riegel told Kennedy that he, too, was unhappy about the planned sale to Southwest. So Riegel arranged for Kennedy to meet with William J. Scharffenberger, Riegel Paper's president and chief executive officer.

Scharffenberger said the sale to Southwest was not final and that Riegel Paper was willing to entertain a bid from Federal. Federal quickly made a formal offer of $115.6 million.

Federal's bid was only $3.3 million higher than Southwest's, but it was clear that price alone would not win Riegelwood for either bidder. Riegel Paper's management was deeply concerned about placing the paper division with a buyer that would treat the division's employees fairly. Although Riegel Paper was a publicly owned company, listed on the New York Stock Exchange, members of the Riegel family still held 16 percent of its stock and Hogan, the banker, owned another 4 percent. "It was a very family-oriented company and, as such, the Riegels wanted to make sure their employees were well taken care of in any acquisition," says Bill Reid, the Riegel Paper director who joined the Federal board after the transaction.

Riegel Paper's directors had mixed feelings when they received Federal's offer. Some were concerned about Federal's financial condition and whether it was in a position to finance

George Oakley, sales vice president of Riegel's paper division, was instrumental in lining up Federal to buy the Riegelwood mill. He joined Federal in the acquisition and later became a senior vice president and director of the company.

capital projects at Riegelwood. Others wanted to get to know the Kennedys before reaching any judgments. "There wasn't any vehement opposition to Federal, but there were differences of opinion on the board and some directors were a little skeptical about Federal at first," says Reid.

Slowly, the directors came around. "We just kept pushing at it," says Oakley. "Jack was very good. He persisted and hung in there. He did and we did, and it worked out."

J. R. Kennedy already knew Frederick S. Leinbach, a retired president of Riegel Paper who was still on Riegel's board. Jack Kennedy knew Bill Riegel, the executive vice president and a board member, and had met Scharffenberger, the president. Oakley arranged for Jack Kennedy to meet another board member, Thomas D. O'Connor. O'Connor's family had just sold Mohawk Paper Mills to Riegel Paper for Riegel stock and he was very concerned about finding an appropriate buyer for Riegel.

Finally, on August 12, 1971, Riegel Paper's board of directors met at corporate headquarters on Madison Avenue in New York to vote on Federal's offer. J. R. Kennedy and Jack Kennedy ensconsed themselves at the Marco Polo Club at the Waldorf-Astoria Hotel on Park Avenue, awaiting an answer. "My father was in favor of the Riegelwood acquisition, but he also felt the likelihood of being able to do it wasn't great," Jack Kennedy says. "I was waiting for a phone call to say the deal was approved, and I remember him saying, 'I don't think it's going to fly.' I became very annoyed. I said, 'Everything's in place, dammit. We've covered all the bases and this is a formality.' That was my understanding. As it turned out, it wasn't quite a formality. They apparently had some heated discussions."

About an hour later than expected, Jack Kennedy finally received a phone call informing him that Federal's bid had been accepted. The vote by Riegel's directors was unanimous in the end, although at least one director had held out for Southwest until the very last minute.

Reid says there was no single factor that won over Riegel Paper's board of directors. "It was just a general feeling that the Kennedys were very high-quality, impressive people and would do a good job for Riegel employees," he states.

Riegel Paper then announced the news to a business and financial world which, until that moment, still thought Southwest Forest Industries was buying Riegelwood.

WALL STREET SELLOFF

Within Federal, there was great enthusiasm for the transaction — coupled with some nervousness about taking on more than $40 million of debt to finance the purchase. Federal's total debt prior to the acquisition was $30 million, already the highest level in the company's history. "It took a lot of derring-do to make that acquisition," says Earl Roberson, who retired from Federal's board of directors at the end of 1990. "It was very aggressive."

Many Wall Street investors, on the other hand, found it too aggressive. Immediately after the surprise announcement by Riegel Paper, the price of Federal common stock began to tumble. It continued to slide for nearly two weeks, dropping a total of 13 percent over that period. This was at a time when the overall stock market, as measured by the Dow Jones Industrial Average, was rising 7 percent!

American Mutual Liability Insurance Company, of which Roberson was chairman at the time, held 25,000 shares of Federal stock in its pension fund. "When that announcement was made, I remember very well our investment manager coming in and saying, 'Let's get rid of this. They're biting off more than they can chew,'" he reports.

"It was referred to by some as the mouse swallowing the cat," says Mallett, then Federal's treasurer. "In other words, people thought we were taking on more debt than we could handle based on our history."

And, in fact, investors had reason to be concerned. The sticking point, for many, was the prospect — more theoretical than real, as it turned out — that Federal's earnings would be diluted. The startling numbers were stated in a proxy statement for all to see: Federal earned $2.11 a share in 1970. If it had owned Riegelwood, it would have earned only $1.58. Taken at face value, those numbers suggested that Federal was paying too much for Riegelwood.

(Dilution works this way: Let's say your company has 1,000 outstanding shares of common stock and earns $1.00 per share. If you issue a second 1,000 shares to acquire another company, and if the acquired company contributes earnings of only $.50 per share on those 1,000, your per-share earnings have been diluted. You would now be earning an average of $.75 per share on the 2,000 shares, down from your pre-acquisition earnings of $1.00 a share.)

Earnings dilution is common in acquisitions, but in Federal's case the degree of dilution spelled out in the proxy statement was extreme. On the other hand, the Kennedys felt the numbers in the proxy were meaningless, even though government regulations required that they be disclosed. The dilution was related, in large part, to the high corporate overhead costs of Riegel Paper, including yearly costs of $2 million to maintain a New York headquarters for the paper division. Federal was not acquiring this headquarters operation, so right away it would save $2 million annually and lessen the amount of earnings dilution. However, rules of the Securities and Exchange Commission required that the dilution figures in the proxy be presented as if the headquarters operation were being acquired. "In our filings with the SEC we showed our

William Reid joined Federal's board of directors to represent the interests of former Riegel Paper shareholders.

planned cost savings, but the SEC wouldn't let us quantify them in a public document," says Ed Kelly, the White & Case attorney. "J. R. Kennedy was very concerned that the numbers in the proxy were misleading. He was very concerned."

As it turned out, there was no dilution. Federal needed to generate about $14 million of annual operating earnings from Riegelwood to avoid diluting its own per-share results. In 1972, the year of the acquisition, operating profits of Riegelwood were almost exactly $14 million. Consequently, Federal earned $2.47 a share in 1972, equaling its per-share earnings of 1971.

But, of course, investors didn't know at the time of the announcement in August 1971 that no dilution would actually occur.

WHO WILL JOIN THE BOARD?

Under the acquisition agreement, Riegel Paper was to select three of its directors to join Federal's board. Riegel chose Tom O'Connor, Bill Reid and Bill Riegel. (Several months after the acquisition was completed, O'Connor and Riegel resigned to pursue other interests, whereupon Vern Hogan was elected a director of Federal.)

However, between the time when the transaction was announced and it was completed, J. L. Riegel asked to meet with Jack Kennedy. J. L. was a grandson of Riegel Paper's founder and had devoted his life to the company. He had worked at Riegel Paper more than 50 years, having retired as chairman in 1968 and having left the board of directors the following year.

Jack Kennedy describes this meeting as one of the most awkward and difficult of his entire business career. "I was only 40 years old, and J. L. was one of the senior people in the paper industry," Kennedy recalls. "He was probably in his late sixties or early seventies and was heartbroken to see what was happening to his company — the way it was being split up and sold. J. L. said he would like to be on our board and I said, 'I can't do that. The Riegel Paper directors have already selected their three representatives.' That was very sad."

Kennedy continues, "But I would hear from him afterwards. He remained interested in our company and came to our stockholders' meetings. He was a good guy, a wonderful gentleman."

THE FINAL HURDLES

During the fall of 1971, amid continuing skepticism on Wall Street, several hurdles still had to be cleared before the acquisition could be consummated. One of these hurdles was the negotiation of details of the transaction, such as the allocation of specific costs between Riegel and Federal.

"The negotiations on various points were handled by Jack," says Mallett. "Even after we had the agreement, items would come up — involving three quarters of a million dollars, or half a million dollars, or a million. And I'd say to Jack, 'Based on the intent of the agreement, I think Riegel should swallow this.' Several times Jack reversed me. He'd say, 'Well, that's probably right. But go ahead, we'll take that.' Basically, he decided we had to make the acquisition at almost any price." (Kennedy responds, "That's true — I had great interest in seeing the deal go through. But if those final negotiations had gotten out of hand, there would have been a price at which I'd have said no.")

Ultimately, all the details were ironed out to the satisfaction of both sides.

Next, the acquisition required the approval of shareholders of both Riegel and Federal. Both companies scheduled special stockholder meetings for 10 a.m. on Thursday, December 23, 1971, at the Biltmore Hotel in New York — Riegel in the Biltmore Suite, Federal in the Vanderbilt Suite. Shareholders of both companies gave their go-ahead.

Following shareholder approvals, the acquisition was scheduled to take effect on Monday, January 3, 1972. But then a new problem arose as the countdown to closing continued.

Federal was buying Riegel's paper division by issuing common and preferred stock to Riegel shareholders. However, it was also assuming $45 million of Riegel Paper debt, and under the terms of the transaction this debt had to be refinanced by Federal at the time of the closing. Federal planned to do this by taking out a loan from a group of banks headed by Morgan Guaranty Trust Company. It planned later to repay the bank loan by issuing long-term debt and selling off some of Riegel Paper's assets. The acquisition of Riegelwood hinged on Federal's ability to get that bank loan.

Morgan Guaranty Trust originally agreed to provide a 12-month loan. But the acquisition was taking place at a time of tough antitrust enforcement — as Federal would learn so sorrowfully five years later when it began its unsuccessful effort to sell Federal Glass. Morgan became nervous that government regulators would disallow the Riegelwood acquisition after it was completed, in which case Federal might have to dispose of the facility at a fire-sale price and the bank might not get back all its money. Therefore, the bank called a last-minute meeting for the morning of Saturday, January 1, 1972, to discuss the antitrust issue. (Quentin Kennedy still remembers phoning Federal's lawyers and others on New Year's Eve to inform them of the meeting. Not many were excited about the prospect of getting up early the next morning to discuss antitrust enforcement.) At the meeting, seeking assurances that the loan would not entail excessive risk, Morgan asked White & Case — Federal's law firm — to issue an opinion stating that the acquisition would not violate antitrust law. White & Case declined to do so, saying that, given the

antitrust environment, attorneys no longer issued "clean" opinions for large acquisitions. The meeting ended with the matter
unresolved.

Finding itself in a bind, Morgan decided to tighten the terms
of its loan. On Monday morning, just one-half hour before the
scheduled closing of the transaction, a bank official phoned Jack
Kennedy and gave him the bad news: Morgan Guaranty was no
longer prepared to offer a 12-month loan. The maximum term
was now three months.

What did Kennedy do? "I said, 'We agree.'" Kennedy
assumed that anxieties would ease in time and that, if they didn't,
Federal would find one way or another to meet the bank's new
repayment terms. "I think I would have said anything to get the
loan," he recalls. The acquisition was completed on schedule.
Subsequently, the bank extended the term of the loan to six
months. Government trust busters never did challenge the
transaction, and the loan was repaid in just over five months.

ACQUISITION TERMS

Looking back today, Ed Kelly says, "It was far and away the most
complex corporate transaction I've ever worked on." The acquisition was structured to include a spinoff, merger, issuance of
common stock, issuance of convertible preferred stock, debt
refinancing and sale of assets.

First, Riegel Paper split itself into two divisions: the packaging group and the paper group. It then restructured the packaging group as a new company, Rexham Corporation, and spun it
off to Riegel stockholders, who received one Rexham share for
each Riegel share. Bill Scharffenberger, Riegel's president, went
with Rexham as its chief executive officer.

*Riegel Paper's employee
publication announced the
startling news: the Riegelwood
facility was to be acquired by
Federal Paper Board.*

Riegelwood is the world's largest producer of market pulp — processed wood fiber sold to paper manufacturers around the world.

Riegel Paper itself, now consisting solely of the paper group, was merged with Federal. Federal issued three-tenths of a share of common stock and four-tenths of a share of $1.20 convertible preferred stock in exchange for each Riegel share. Following this exchange, Riegel Paper Corporation no longer existed.

Thus, someone who had owned 100 Riegel Paper shares ended up with 100 shares of a new company, Rexham, plus 30 shares of Federal common stock and 40 shares of Federal convertible preferred stock.

Federal assumed all of Riegel Paper's debt and refinanced it with the loan from Morgan Guaranty Trust.

Subsequently, Federal sold all the assets of the Riegel paper group except the Riegelwood mill and the 350,000 acres of related timberland. Divested properties included: four paper mills in New Jersey; Mohawk Paper Mills, Inc., which manufactured book paper at two mills in New York; Techbuilt, which manufactured pre-engineered homes; Community Concepts Corporation, a real estate developer involved in projects in Massachusetts; and a one-sixth interest in 250 acres in Broward County, Florida. The other owners of the acreage were Robert Trent Jones, Sam Snead and Fred Corcoran. Federal sold most of the paper mills to Southwest Forest Industries, which finally got some of the Riegel operations it had wanted.

Proceeds from the property sales were approximately $20 million. Deducting these proceeds from Federal's $115.6 million purchase price for the Riegel paper division, and also deducting the working capital of the division, the net cost of the Riegelwood mill and the timberland came to about $85 million.

In June 1972, Federal raised $40 million through the sale of 25-year debentures. Proceeds from the debentures, together with part of the proceeds from the property sales, were used to repay the bank loan.

Today, about $14 million of the original $40 million of 25-year debentures is still outstanding, the remainder having been repaid by Federal in increments over the past 19 years.

Of the 1,764,814 shares of convertible preferred stock issued by Federal in the acquisition, more than 95 percent have been converted into Federal common stock — and for good reason. An investor who owns 100 shares of the preferred stock receives $120 of cash dividends a year. On the other hand, those same 100 shares can today be converted into 502 shares of Federal common stock that pay total dividends of $502 a year. The huge disparity reflects the simple fact that the dividend on the preferred is fixed, while Federal has increased the dividend on its common stock nearly a dozen times since 1972.

So Much for Earnings Dilution!

For a company that had struggled through a period of slow growth in the 1960s, the Riegelwood acquisition was like a shot of adrenaline. Almost overnight, Riegelwood transformed Federal into a company on a fast growth track.

In the five years prior to the acquisition, Federal had flat earnings, a slight increase in shareholders' equity and moderate growth of sales (per-share earnings in the following two tables are restated for a two-for-one stock split in 1976), as follows:

Federal Paper Board Company, Pre-Riegelwood

	Sales	Net Income	Net Income Per Share	Shareholders' Equity
1967	$ 113,000,000	$ 4,400,000	$ 1.15	$ 53,300,000
1968	125,000,000	4,500,000	1.23	53,000,000
1969	133,000,000	4,200,000	1.13	55,300,000
1970	133,000,000	3,900,000	1.06	56,000,000
1971	157,000,000	4,500,000	1.24	58,000,000

Taking 1971 as a base, Federal's sales and per-share net income more than tripled in the five years following the acquisition, and net income grew fivefold:

Federal Paper Board Company, Post-Riegelwood

	Sales	Net Income	Net Income Per Share	Shareholders' Equity
1972	$ 248,000,000	$ 9,600,000	$ 1.24	$ 127,800,000
1973	276,000,000	12,800,000	1.81	134,700,000
1974	340,000,000	20,900,000	3.22	148,700,000
1975	334,000,000	16,600,000	2.47	152,800,000
1976	394,000,000	22,600,000	3.74	167,300,000

There's a good reason why Federal's financial performance improved so quickly. As luck would have it, Federal bought the Riegelwood mill at the very bottom of a recession in the paper-board industry. "You couldn't have bought a mill at a better time," says Leon "Kirk" Semke, formerly Riegelwood's manager and now a vice president of Federal.

Almost immediately following the acquisition, paperboard demand and prices began to strengthen, with the result that Riegelwood's earnings surged. "When we bought Riegelwood, solid bleached sulphate was selling for $190 a ton," says one retired executive of Federal. "Soon it was up to $250. Today it's nearly $900 a ton. That's the best deal Federal ever made."

But Riegelwood's success reflected much more than lucky timing.

CHANGING OF THE GUARD

The Riegelwood mill is a classic example of Jack Kennedy's management style: he sees an opportunity, goes after it aggressively and then invests heavily to make the acquired property more valuable. Kennedy is an affable, no-nonsense manager who takes large, calculated risks — and knows how to make them pay off. Dick Cheney, the chairman of Hill and Knowlton, Federal's public relations firm, describes Kennedy as "very smooth and charming, but tough, tough, tough."

John R. Kennedy, Jr., was born in 1930 in New York and took his first summer job at Federal when he was 16. In 1952, on graduating from Georgetown University, where he majored in philosophy, he joined the company full time. He has been with Federal ever since.

From day one as a full-time employee, it was clear to everybody in the company that Jack Kennedy was headed for the top. "There's no question my father's design was for me to succeed him," Kennedy states. "He told me that as early as 1955 when I was 25 years old. So that was in his mind."

Initially, Kennedy went through a series of jobs to learn various aspects of the business. But primarily he came up through the marketing department. "In selling paperboard, I worked for a person named John Mousley," Kennedy recalls. "He was a great teacher and had a great understanding of the industry and the company. I spent several years selling paperboard and I enjoyed that. It was fun.

"I also worked in the credit department," he says. "That's a marvelous place to learn the business, because you get to know all the accounts — the good ones, the bad ones, the ones that pay quickly, the ones that never pay on time."

At 29, Kennedy was elected a vice president. At 31, he became senior vice president and a member of the board of

Ethel, Jack and Quentin Kennedy enjoyed a happy childhood, including a birthday pony ride for Quentin. Even when he graduated from high school, Jack Kennedy, bottom, knew he would one day join Federal.

*Jack Kennedy was elected
president of Federal in 1965 at
age 35.*

directors. At 35, he was elected president. He became president
and chief executive officer in 1976, the position he holds today.

Kennedy acknowledges there were disagreements with his
father over policy. This was particularly true after J. R. Kennedy
reached 65 and Jack succeeded him as president. J. R. retained
the title of chairman and was still the company's dominant force.
"We had a lot of conflicts about how the business should be run,"
Jack Kennedy says. The worst moment came when Jack, as
Federal's new president, sent his father a five-year business plan
that called for the closing of unprofitable plants. J. R. stormed
into Jack's office, tore up the memo and raged that no facilities
would ever be closed so long as he was associated with Federal.
J. R. had, after all, built the company, and each plant meant a
great deal to him. Jack says this was the angriest he ever saw his
father. The dispute blew over in a few days, and the unprofitable
facilities were eventually closed.

Disagreements are common in family-oriented businesses where
son succeeds father. However, the Kennedys are a very close-knit
family, and the disagreements that did occur were never allowed to
spill into the open. They were always kept within the family.

In 1972, J. R. Kennedy had the first of several strokes and
was no longer able to play an active, day-to-day role in the business. However, he remained on the board of directors until 1980.
"J. R. kept attending board meetings after his strokes," says Ran
Clerihue, a director of Federal. "He was alert but had difficulty

speaking. Jack was always very deferential to his father. For instance, before starting a board meeting he would always turn to his father and say, 'May we begin?' And his father would nod approval."

Jack's brother, Quentin, three years younger, took a somewhat more circuitous route to Federal. Quentin earned his bachelor's degree from Georgetown University in 1955 and his law degree from Georgetown University Law School in 1957. He then practiced law at White & Case for three years before joining Federal in 1960. Quentin was elected corporate secretary in 1963 at age 30. He was elected vice president and secretary in 1970, was given the additional post of treasurer in 1976 and was elected to the board of directors in 1980, taking the board seat held until that time by his father. Quentin became executive vice president and secretary in 1983.

Jack and Quentin have contrasting personalities. They are similar in some ways: both are tall (Jack is six feet, Quentin is six feet two), and both are extremely bright and down-to-earth. But the similarities end there. Jack is the visionary and planner who sets the corporate direction. Quentin — the financial strategist and trusted adviser — is more cautious and reflective by nature. "Jack is out front leading the troops and he isn't deterred by the investment bankers on the board who worry about taking on too much debt," says Earl Roberson. "He feels Quentin can take care of that. It's an unusual relationship. You have two entirely different people who complement each other and work together as a team."

"Jack tends to say, 'Let's do it,' and worry about the details later," Bill Reid adds. "Quent wants to know before it's done how it's going to be done."

Asked about his reputation for pushing ahead with new ideas and taking risks, Jack Kennedy steals a glance at his brother — who happens to be sitting next to him at a large conference table — and replies, "I'm able to say some outrageous things, knowing others in the company will pull me back."

Quentin Kennedy, seen here in a 1955 picture, took a less direct route to Federal than his brother, spending three years at a law firm before joining the company.

As executive vice president, Quentin Kennedy is Federal's second-in-command.

When Federal acquired Riegelwood, Jack Kennedy swept into the operation like a fresh breeze. He was full of ideas and ready to spend whatever capital was required to make the mill bigger and better.

"It was fantastic," says Pete Peters, then the mill manager. "Jack is a doer. He doesn't have a lot of corporate overhead and he doesn't plan projects to death. He insists that his managers keep him advised, but he stays out of your way. If you mess up, you'll hear about it quickly. You've got to know what you're doing. If you don't, you're out. But as long as you don't spring any surprises on him, he's with you all the way."

Kennedy immediately began pushing to expand the mill. "He came up with that right after purchasing it," says Peters. "He knew that was the way to go, and he was very receptive to any ideas."

When acquired by Federal, Riegelwood had a capacity of approximately 1,050 tons of pulp and 800 tons of paperboard a day. Over the next decade, Federal invested nearly $300 million to modernize production, expand capacity and meet environmental requirements. These investments included:

In 1972, Federal completed a new $13 million recovery boiler and increased pulping capacity by about 100 tons a day. It also began a $12 million project to reduce air pollution.

In 1973, it launched a three-year, $29 million program to increase pulping capacity by another 250 tons a day. It also began construction of a sawmill at Armour, North Carolina, to produce lumber for the building industry and, as a byproduct, supply wood chips to Riegelwood.

In 1974, it installed a new high-speed machine to cut paperboard to customer specifications, installed four new pulp digesters to further increase pulping capacity and made additional investments in pollution control.

In 1975, it invested in better handling equipment for wood chips and began construction of a new turbo generator to supply 90 percent of the facility's power needs.

And in 1977, it launched a five-year, $215 million expansion program to add another 500 tons a day of pulp production. In announcing the expansion, Jack Kennedy wrote, "By 1982, we expect to have mill capacity of at least 2,000 tons of pulp per day, 1,000 tons in the form of market pulp [for sale to other paper companies] and 1,000 tons to be converted into bleached paperboard."

In the 1980s, Federal continued its investments, adding new computerized process controls and further expanding pulping capacity to more than 2,200 tons a day. The company also added a second sawmill — this one at Newberry, South Carolina — to produce lumber and supply wood chips to Riegelwood.

Air emissions at many of Federal's facilities are controlled by sophisticated systems and techniques involving high-tech scrubbing, electrostatic precipitation, incineration and process modification. Here, electrostatic precipitators on the #3 recovery boiler at Riegelwood remove particulate matter from flue gasses.

Today, the Riegelwood mill complex, spread across a 500-acre site, is a major contributor to Federal's earnings and continues to play a central role in the company's growth strategies.

THE VIEW FROM PRUDENTIAL INSURANCE

Prudential Insurance Company of America was one of the major financial supporters of the Riegelwood expansion program and is today Federal Paper Board's largest lender. Prudential first became involved with Federal in 1975, when Federal borrowed $30 million on a 15-year note to refinance bank debt. In 1978, Federal borrowed $105 million from Prudential on an 18-year senior note; this note was Federal's major source of outside financing for the five-year program to expand pulp production at Riegelwood.

Milan Resanovich, who was then a managing director of Prudential, says he felt comfortable granting the $105 million loan, even though it was a relatively large one at that time. "I felt the expansion at Riegelwood made sense and that they could handle it so long as it was done over a time period. The risk you take, of course, is that the cost of completing would exceed budget by a substantial margin. As it was, they did it right and had good people and kept their costs under control."

MERGING TWO CULTURES

One of the interesting aspects of the Riegelwood acquisition was the differing cultures of the two companies, Riegel Paper and Federal Paper Board, and how each company brought something to the other.

Riegel Paper Corporation had built its reputation on quality, while Federal, with its roots in the recycled paperboard business, was known more as a volume operator. "I think Riegelwood opened Jack's eyes to the benefits of quality," George Oakley says. "He saw we could charge a premium of $20 or more a ton because of quality. I think he's changed. I think we helped him change." Indeed, Federal's reputation today is that of a quality producer.

On the other hand, Riegel Paper had a large corporate management group and believed in a structured process of business planning and corporate decision-making. As a result, its corporate overhead was high. Federal Paper Board brought a different style to Riegelwood. It has a lean management organization, and Kennedy personally pushes major decisions to resolution. "Jack Kennedy gets involved and makes decisions fast," says Robert Aranow, who retired in 1986 as personnel director at Riegelwood. "For the people at the mill, it was a fantastic change."

One of the things Kennedy couldn't understand was why all the southern paper mills shut down every year for Christmas. Christmas shutdowns are extremely costly. Restarting operations and getting back into full production often takes a week or more. In addition, when equipment is idled there's a danger it will be damaged in a winter freeze.

"We always had in our union contract that a few people were required to work on Christmas to maintain life and property," Peters says. "There was a contractual rule to pay them triple wages or more."

Kennedy saw that, instead of closing the mill, it would be safer and less expensive to maintain operations over Christmas and pay everybody triple time. He gives credit to the union for help-ing solve the problem.

"Really, there were two issues in getting people to work at Christmas," Kennedy states. "I met with the union and said, 'We have all this capital invested in the facility and we shut it down every Christmas. And last December when we shut down, the storm came through and we had a hell of a time. It took ten days to get this mill up and running again. In addition, we're expand-ing the mill, adding more dollars, and those dollars are shut down for this period of time. They're just idle.'

"So that was one issue," he continues. "The other, I pointed out, is that nobody wants to work on Christmas and I don't blame them. So I asked the union, 'How do we resolve those two issues?' It was left like that." Later, the union came back to Kennedy and said it would allow its members to work over the Christmas holiday on a voluntary basis if Federal didn't raise the issue in contract negotiations.

Barely enough employees showed up the first two years to keep the facility running, but over time the program has been an unqualified success. "The great majority of people now volunteer to work," says Aranow. "The money is too good to turn down."

Kennedy himself showed up that first year and spent the day going from department to department, shaking hands and thank-ing employees for their support. "He also ordered fruit and had it delivered to the mill," says J. T. Bostic, Jr., a senior paper process engineer. "It was a nice touch." Kennedy kept showing up at Riegelwood for the next several Christmases, and subsequently did the same at Sprague and Augusta when employees there agreed to work on a voluntary basis.

"It was amazing to many people here in Augusta that Jack would go through the mill and shake hands with everybody," says Mark Massey, former manager of the Augusta facility who recently became Federal's senior vice president, manufacturing, Forest Products Division. "It gave a flavor that the company was small enough so you could actually meet the guy who was running it. That was very refreshing."

The Riegelwood mill was the first in the paper industry to operate through the Christmas holidays. Since then, Christmas operations have become standard practice throughout the indus-try. However, most other paper companies negotiated the issue with the unions in order to make Christmas operations mandatory.

"A Real Diamond in the Rough"

The Riegelwood acquisition also brought Federal one of the most popular and colorful directors in its history: Vern Hogan, the North Carolina banker. "Old Vern was a real diamond in the rough," says Ran Clerihue, a long-time member of Federal's board. "I don't know how far he went in school, probably grade six or seven. But he was very smart. He had native intelligence. He ended up owning a bank and a big piece of Federal."

Bill Reid adds, "Vern was a country boy from the South, and you'd better watch them when they say, 'I'm just a country boy from the South.'" He was not a fancy dresser nor did he ever brag about his success. Reid says, "If you met Vern Hogan, you wouldn't think he had a dime."

Hogan grew up in poverty and during the Depression traveled by boxcar to North Carolina, settling in Norman. There, he met his wife-to-be while they were picking cotton. Hogan believed in the value of land, particularly timberland, and bought it whenever he could afford to do so. He formed a company, Norman Lumber Company, which eventually owned 25,000 acres of prime North Carolina timberland as well as a lumber mill. "I guess he had the best feel of acreage prices in North Carolina of any man I can think of," Reid says.

In 1957, Hogan sold his company to Riegel Paper Corporation for Riegel common stock valued at nearly $4 million. He became one of Riegel's major stockholders, joined its board of directors and served for a time as vice president in charge of its lumber division. In 1958, however, the Norman Lumber mill burned to the ground and Riegel Paper decided to get out of the lumber business. Consequently, Hogan resigned as a vice president of Riegel but continued as a director and major stockholder.

In the late 1960s, Hogan began to devote full time to the banking business as president and principal owner of the Richmond County Bank in Rockingham, North Carolina. Despite his personal wealth, he never lost his down-home manner. For instance, when the Richmond County Bank needed to transfer cash to another bank, he didn't bother calling an armored truck

Vernon Hogan was a country banker who invested in timberland and became a major shareholder of Riegel Paper. He served on Federal's board for 14 years and was greatly respected.

service; he simply put the money in his car, took along a shotgun and drove it to the other bank himself.

Hogan was very conservative when it came to lending the bank's money. Roberson notes, "He had very little respect for the New York bankers. He said he had charged off only one bad loan in his whole career. We used to kid him that you couldn't borrow money from his bank unless you paid it back before you borrowed it. And he was kind of that way."

On the other hand, Hogan didn't hesitate to dip into his own pocket to help someone in need. "For instance, a widow would come into the bank because she was in trouble financially," says Reid. "The bank lending officer would say, 'I'm just as sorry as can be, but we can't lend you any money.' Vern would overhear the conversation and call the widow into his office and say, 'How much do you really need?' And if she said, 'A thousand dollars' and gave him the reasons, Vern would give her a personal check and say, 'There won't be any interest on it. Just repay me if and when you can.'"

When Federal acquired Riegelwood, Hogan received Federal Paper Board stock for his Riegel Paper shares and became one of Federal's largest individual stockholders, joining the board of directors several months later.

As a director, Hogan was always in favor of buying timberland. "He was very enthusiastic about the Augusta deal," says Roberson. "In fact, the main attraction he saw was not necessarily the papermaking operations but the timberland. He used to quote Will Rogers that 'they ain't making any more of it.' And that was his philosophy."

Vern Hogan died in 1986 after serving on Federal's board for 14 years. Thomas L. Cassidy, a Federal director, went to the funeral with Jack and Quentin Kennedy and others. "It was held in an old country church out in the middle of nowhere," Cassidy recalls. "The whole town turned out for the funeral. We flew into a little airfield about 50 miles away. We didn't know the roads, so we stopped at a gas station 30 miles away and asked the gas attendant how to get to the town. The attendant said, 'Oh, you must be going to Mr. Hogan's funeral.' They knew him all over the countryside."

Riegelwood's Future

"When Federal acquired Riegelwood, they not only got the material assets but they got some awfully good people," says Baxter Chamberlain. "None of those people left Riegelwood following the acquisition. They all stayed. A lot of that is due to the fact that Jack wanted Riegelwood to expand. There's nothing a young engineer likes better than spending money to make paper faster or better."

One of those young engineers was Kirk Semke. He joined Riegelwood in 1963 when it was still owned by Riegel Paper Corporation and moved up steadily in the ranks. He then became the facility's manager and is now a vice president of Federal.

Are there expansion plans in Riegelwood's future? "At this point, from what we know about the limitations of this site, we do not visualize large future expansion here," Semke answers. "You've got to keep everything in perspective. This is already the largest bleached pulp mill in the world."

Nonetheless, Semke says another 10 percent expansion is a possibility. "And when you look at our current production, that's 10 percent of a pretty big number," he says. "So we're talking about a fairly substantial amount, but not real rapid growth."

Semke also sees a continued emphasis on product quality. "It puts more demands on you, but you can get a premium price," he states. He cites two examples of quality improvements.

In 1989, new "blade coaters" were installed on the Carolina Queen, one of the mill's two Fourdriniers. These coaters are used to apply clay coatings to the board. "Now we've got two of the finest blade coaters in the world," Semke says. The benefit is a smoother paper surface that enhances printing quality.

More recently, a new additive room was completed at Riegelwood, replacing one built in 1958. Various types of coatings and additives are prepared in this room. "You can imagine, 30 years ago the state of the art is not what it is now," Semke says. "With our new computer-controlled, highly automated additive room, we're in as good a position as anybody as far as coating."

"About three years ago, we moved up a notch on investments in quality," Semke concludes. "The thrust was to make a better product. I've just mentioned two projects. There are others. We've invested a lot."

CHAPTER 12

The Imperative of Growth: The 1985 Augusta Acquisition

I N A COMPETITIVE economy, there is no resting place for a business that fails to grow. Growth is central to a company's long-term survival and success. It attracts investors, creates opportunities for employees to advance and fosters an atmosphere of innovation and constant renewal.

And so in the early 1980s, as Federal was completing its major expansion program at Riegelwood, Jack Kennedy began to look for a new growth opportunity for the company. Drawing on the success of Riegelwood, he launched a search for a second solid bleached sulphate paperboard mill in the South.

In 1982, without publicity, Federal offered to buy the huge Augusta, Georgia, mill of Continental Group, Inc. and 150,000 acres of surrounding timberland for $300 million. Best known as a manufacturer of metal cans, Continental had diversified into the solid bleached sulphate paperboard business in the late 1950s. By the early 1980s, however, Continental was struggling to earn a satisfactory profit from its paperboard operations, and Kennedy thought Continental might be willing to part with the Augusta facility. But Continental turned Federal's offer down.

Meanwhile, executives of Federal visited mills in Texas and other locations in their search for a new facility, but none was available at a price Federal was willing to pay.

Never one to give up easily, Kennedy kept pushing the search — until Federal finally got its mill in a most unexpected way.

In June 1984, Sir James Goldsmith, the British financier, made a surprise bid to acquire Continental Group for $2.4 billion. Continental's management opposed Goldsmith's offer, fearful that, once he had acquired Continental, he would dismember the 71-year-old company by selling off its divisions and facilities one by one to the highest bidders. The battle for control of Continental Group was brief. To fend off Goldsmith, Continental management arranged for the company to be acquired instead by a "white knight," or friendly merger partner. That partner was Kiewit-Murdock Investment Corp., which paid $2.7 billion for Continental. Kiewit-Murdock completed the transaction in a matter of weeks and then, ironically, began selling off some of Continental's assets to raise cash to finance the purchase. So Continental ended up suffering the very fate, the divestiture of assets, it had sought to avoid.

Among the assets being sold, Kiewit-Murdock asked for bids on a package of nine Continental properties: the Augusta paperboard mill (the same mill Federal had attempted to acquire two years earlier) together with two folding carton plants, four sawmills and two paper plate plants.

Kennedy saw his chance. "When the Augusta mill became available, Jack Kennedy immediately hopped on that," says Pete Peters, who was Federal's vice president in charge of manufacturing. "I went there a number of times with Jack and a number of times alone. We investigated the mill's costs and its expansion possibilities."

Peters says the facility was especially attractive because it provided an expandable mill site well located in terms of raw materials and transportation.

Jack Kennedy single-mindedly pursued the acquisition of the Augusta mill and pushed the deal to a successful conclusion.

How Federal Almost Yielded Its Independence

It did not take Kennedy long to decide he wanted the mill very badly — so badly, in fact, that he considered giving up Federal's independence to get it. This surprising development happened as follows:

Kennedy knew it would take upwards of $300 million to get the facility and believed — mistakenly, as it turned out — that Federal would be unable to raise the money on its own. So he discussed with officials of International Minerals & Chemical Corporation (IMC) the possibility of Federal and IMC jointly buying the Augusta mill. IMC is a major producer of phosphate rock and potash. "Out of that came a discussion that IMC would acquire Federal," Kennedy reveals. "And we brought that along. To get Augusta, I really considered making a deal with IMC that the companies would be merged and IMC would be the surviving company, and we would acquire Augusta at the same time."

But a merger never proved necessary. That's because Kennedy had also approached Morgan Guaranty Trust Company

and asked whether it would lend Federal the funds to acquire
Augusta. To his surprise, the bank said yes. Kennedy notes that,
by happenstance, Morgan was at the time becoming more aggressive in its lending practices and was seeking to increase its business
with mid-sized clients like Federal. He says Morgan's willingness
to provide financing was the key development enabling Federal to
buy the mill by itself.

The mill and other properties were being sold through an
auction process involving sealed bids. Kennedy wanted to bid
aggressively. "We talked with our advisers about the price we
should offer," he recalls, "and I said we wanted the price that
would buy the business. We didn't want to come in second.
Coming in second was a waste of time." Federal bid $317 million
— and when the results of the auction were announced in November 1984, it had won.

Of the $317 million purchase price, an astonishing $315
million was financed through the loan with a syndicate of 11
banks headed by Morgan. Kennedy recalls meeting with David
Murdock, a partner in the Kiewit-Murdock venture that owned
the mill, and being asked by Murdock, "How do I know you can
pay for this?" The meeting took place after Federal had submitted
its bid, but before the bid had been accepted by Kiewit-Murdock.
"There was a guy with me from Morgan who said, 'It shouldn't
be any problem.' That settled the argument pretty quickly,"
Kennedy states.

The large bank loan was a temporary measure. Over the next
two months, Federal refinanced nearly $200 million of the loan
with proceeds from the sale of $75 million of $2.3125 convertible
preferred stock and with most of the proceeds from the sale of
$125 million of subordinated debentures.

In retrospect, Kennedy says, Federal's bid was probably $40
million higher than the nearest competitor. "But I'd rather be
$40 million higher than one dollar lower," he adds.

The purchase was completed in March 1985. (Murdock had
by now sold his interest in Kiewit-Murdock to his partner, Peter

*The massive Augusta complex is
located on the Savannah River.
It manufactures heavier grades
of paperboard for packaging and
supplies pulp in slurry form to a
nearby newsprint facility.*

*On completion of a three-
phase expansion program in the
mid-1990s, Augusta will rank as
the world's largest paperboard
mill.*

Kiewit Sons' Inc., and the venture had been renamed Kiewit Continental, Inc.) Of the nine facilities acquired from Kiewit in the package deal, Federal retained:

- the Augusta mill;
- a folding carton plant in Durham, North Carolina; and
- three sawmills — in Augusta and Washington, Georgia, and Johnston, South Carolina.

Federal Paper Board's five sawmills produce lumber for the building industry and wood chips for the manufacture of paperboard.

Federal's mills consume more than three million cords of wood a year.

The sawmills manufacture lumber for the building market and, as a byproduct, supply wood chips to the Augusta mill.

Federal did not want the four other facilities — an older folding carton plant, a sawmill and two paper plate plants. It sold the paper plate plants for $5 million and closed the carton plant and sawmill.

Twenty-one months later, Federal acquired 310,000 acres of related timberland from Kiewit Continental for $96 million.

Thus, Federal paid a total of $413 million for the Augusta mill, the carton plants, the sawmills, the timberland and the other properties. Of this amount, $330 million was related to the cost of the paperboard mill and timberland, compared with the $300 million offer Federal had made for these same properties in 1982.

A BOLD MANEUVER

The purchase of the Augusta mill was one of the biggest, riskiest decisions ever made by Federal. With the acquisition, Federal nearly doubled its bleached paperboard capacity and catapulted itself from fifth to second place in the U.S. bleached paperboard industry, just behind International Paper Company.

The acquisition was similar in many ways to the earlier purchase of Riegelwood. Kennedy's plan in each case was to acquire a facility that had operational problems, invest heavily in its modernization and expansion, and end up with a highly efficient, world-class mill.

While the idea seemed sound enough, three factors made it risky. First, the Augusta acquisition involved an unprecedented sum of money for Federal — more than triple the price paid for Riegelwood. Second, because the purchase was financed almost entirely with bank debt, it stretched Federal's balance sheet to the limits. Third, the acquisition was made at a time when paperboard demand and prices were softening.

Many investors thought Federal was making a terrible mistake. Reflecting these concerns, the price of the company's stock immediately began to tumble following news of Federal's winning bid.

As you may recall, in 1971 when Federal had announced its plans to acquire the Riegelwood mill, the price of Federal stock dropped 13 percent. That decline was mild, however, in comparison to the aftermath of the Augusta announcement. Over the next month, Federal stock gave up 26 percent of its value — a precipitous drop at a time when the overall stock market, as measured by the Dow Jones Industrial Average, was holding steady.

The Augusta transaction was controversial both inside and outside the company.

One of Federal's directors, Ran Clerihue, says, "In the final analysis, the board voted unanimously to buy Augusta. But there was a lot of debate about whether this was the right thing to do — a lot of concern about taking on too much debt, and weren't we getting too big in the board business?"

Another board member, Tom Cassidy, says, "It was a brave move. I wouldn't say there was any controversy on the board, but there were certainly a lot of skeptics."

"Clearly the Augusta acquisition raised a lot of eyebrows," adds Norman C. Webb, vice president in the corporate finance group of Prudential Insurance Company of America. "I remember at the time I was talking with another company that had been interested in acquiring Augusta, and they just couldn't believe what Federal agreed to pay. They didn't see how it could work out."

The acquisition was especially bold in that it was made at a time when Federal's earnings were sagging. Reflecting weakness in the paperboard market, earnings fell from $37 million in 1984 to $11 million in 1985, the year the acquisition was completed. Soon thereafter, however, the paperboard market strengthened and Federal's earnings took off like a rocket, eventually reaching the stratospheric height of $205 million in 1989. The Augusta mill contributed significantly to this performance.

It took great conviction to see beyond the 1985 cyclical downturn and recognize the long-term benefits of the acquisition. Kennedy had this conviction in spades. At the time, he called the

Federal acquired the Augusta mill and related facilities in a sealed-bid auction for $317 million. This issue of the Augusta News *contains Jack Kennedy's letter to the Augusta employees and a brief history of Federal Paper Board Company.*

acquisition "a very ambitious venture" and one with "great potential" for Federal. "We are convinced," he wrote, "that the acquisition of the Augusta mill will, like the acquisition of Riegelwood 12 years ago, be another stepping stone to Federal's growth."

Milan Resanovich, a senior vice president of Merrill Lynch Interfunding Inc., offers an interesting perspective on the Augusta acquisition. "Most of the history of the paper industry," he states, "is that companies expand during the boom periods and face excess capacity when demand declines." Federal Paper Board, he says, has done the opposite. Both Riegelwood and Augusta were acquired by Federal during periods when paperboard demand and prices were weak. As a result, Federal was able to purchase these facilities at prices that, in retrospect, seem quite cheap.

Speaking of the Augusta acquisition, Resanovich says, "What Jack was looking at was down the road. The immediate economics were not that great."

Ground was broken in 1986 for Phase I of the expansion of the Augusta mill. Beginning second from left are Georgia Governor Joe F. Harris, Jack Kennedy and Paul Kinsey, then Federal's senior vice president, manufacturing, Forest Products Division. The man at far left is unidentified.

ON A FAST TRACK TO MODERNIZATION AND EXPANSION

"I think from day one of the acquisition, Jack Kennedy had a vision of where this mill could go," says W. Mark Massey, Jr., former manager of the Augusta facility who is now Federal's senior vice president, manufacturing, Forest Products Division. "And we've been pretty much on a fast track to carry that vision to completion."

Federal is now in the midst of a decade-long, $1.1 billion expansion and modernization program at Augusta. The mill is a beehive of activity. On any given day, as many as 2,500 engineers, technicians and construction workers are at the site, enlarging existing production facilities and building new ones.

When the expansion program is completed in the mid-1990s,

Federal will have taken the mill from a capacity of 1,400 tons of paperboard a day in 1985 to 2,500 tons a day by 1993 or 1994. For a total price tag of more than $1.4 billion (the acquisition cost plus the expansion costs), Federal will end up with the largest solid bleached sulphate paperboard mill in the world, surpassing Riegelwood.

In explaining the financial benefits of this massive expansion, Kennedy says the cost of building a "greenfield" paperboard mill (a brand-new facility erected from the ground up) would come to about $1 million per daily ton of capacity. Augusta, on the other hand, is being expanded at an average capital cost of about $700,000 per daily ton. "It would be imprudent not to take advantage of that opportunity," he insists.

Expansion at Augusta is the major focus of Federal's growth programs in the early 1990s. It's where the action is at Federal today.

AUGUSTA'S THREE PAPERMAKING MACHINES

The history of the Augusta mill dates back to the mid-1950s, when Robert Gair Company — founded in the late nineteenth century by the inventor of the folding carton — decided to build a solid bleached sulphate paperboard mill in the South. The Gair Company purchased a large tract of undeveloped land on the outskirts of Augusta and began to erect its facility there.

Meanwhile, Continental Group (then called Continental Can Company) had similar notions about owning a southern mill. However, rather than building such a facility from scratch, Continental acquired the Gair firm — including the Augusta mill, which was still under construction — and completed the facility in 1960.

Originally, the mill had one papermaking machine, a Fourdrinier designated No. 1 Machine. Continental doubled the mill's capacity by adding No. 2 Machine, also a Fourdrinier, in the late 1960s. In 1977 it further expanded the mill by adding No. 3 Machine, a unique piece of equipment that, unfortunately, caused all sorts of problems.

The No. 3 Machine was engineered to make a special four-ply paperboard. This board was unusual in the composition of its plies: the two outer plies were solid bleached sulphate to give the board a quality finish, while the two inner plies were made with a cheaper, lower-grade material called "thermomechanical" pulp. By filling the center of No. 3 Machine's paperboard with this pulp, Continental sought to reduce production costs and thereby offer a less expensive product to customers.

However, customers never did take a liking to the new product because it didn't fit well with their production needs. "This product was never well accepted by the marketplace and it really undermined whatever image of quality the Augusta mill might have had," according to Massey.

In addition, the mill was plagued by another problem even more nettlesome than the first. In Kennedy's words, the mill was "severely out of balance" — that is, there was a major disparity between its pulping capacity and its papermaking capacity. Ideally, the mill should have produced enough pulp to feed its papermaking machines so they could operate at full speed around the clock. But for whatever reason, the mill's pulping capacity was only 1,000 tons a day, versus the 1,400 tons needed to run the papermaking machines at capacity. As a result, the papermaking machines either had to be run at less than capacity or pulp had to be purchased from outside sources. The end result, in either case, was to raise costs and reduce operating efficiency.

Both these problems were correctable. But doing so would have required a major investment program, and Continental was targeting the bulk of its capital expenditures to its metal can business rather than to Augusta. Moreover, speaking of the four-ply board, Massey says, "I guess the Continental folks had held onto something they wanted to make work. When you start something yourself and have a lot of emotional investment, sometimes it's hard to give it up."

"When Federal acquired the Augusta mill, it was not a real gem," Webb of the Prudential notes. "There was real potential there, and Jack saw that. But what they bought was not the world's greatest mill."

Having been on Federal's board of directors since 1973, Richard Lenon is today second in service only to Jack Kennedy. He is a former chairman and chief executive of International Minerals & Chemical Corporation.

GOODBYE TO THE THERMOMECHANICAL PULP

Kennedy moved quickly to deal with the mill's problems. Immediately following the acquisition, Federal started shipping pulp from Riegelwood to Augusta — a temporary measure until the pulping capacity at Augusta could be expanded. (Riegelwood is just 300 miles from Augusta and is a major producer of market pulp.) In addition, Kennedy decreed from day one that the thermomechanical pulp had to go. The thermomechanical pulping equipment was dismantled and sold, and the inner plies of the board made on No. 3 Machine were switched to solid bleached sulphate. (More recently, the No. 3 Machine was rebuilt to manufacture a standard single-ply, solid bleached sulphate board.)

With these initial improvements completed, Federal's planners and engineers sat down at their desks and drawing boards and drew up a massive, three-phase investment program to modernize and expand the Augusta mill — the $1.1 billion program that is continuing today.

In Phase I, Federal increased the mill's pulping capacity by 220 tons a day and constructed a new recovery boiler. Phase I was launched in 1986 and completed in 1988 at a total cost of just over $150 million.

In Phase II, currently nearing completion, Federal is increasing the mill's pulping capacity by another 800 tons a day, not only to meet current demands but also to have sufficient pulping capacity for the addition of a fourth papermaking machine at a later date. Moreover, the No. 3 Machine was recently rebuilt and converted to a standard Fourdrinier, eliminating the production of four-ply board. Phase II also involved the upgrading of the mill's woodyard to improve its operating efficiency and assure a high-quality source of wood chips for pulping. Phase II was initiated in 1988 and is scheduled for completion in 1991 at a projected cost of $600 million.

In Phase III, Federal plans to expand the mill by adding the fourth papermaking machine. Two options are under consideration: installation of a machine either to make paperboard or to make uncoated freesheet (primarily copy paper). Robert D. Baldwin, senior vice president, marketing, Forest Products Division, says there are advantages in making copy paper if Federal selects that route: Federal would diversify its product line and achieve certain operating efficiencies at the Augusta mill. One disadvantage, he explains, is that Federal does not currently have a distribution network for copy paper in the United States and would have to develop one. Federal expects to reach a decision by mid-1991 on which type of machine to install. Target date for completing Phase III is 1993-94, subject to market conditions and the availability of financing. Projected capital cost is approximately $400 million.

WHY SO MANY PAPER MILLS ARE IN THE SOUTH

Many of us, when we think of Augusta, have visions of a genteel southern city that is home to the world-renowned Masters Golf Tournament. However, that is just one aspect of Augusta. The city is also an important industrial and trade center located at the head of navigation on the Savannah River. Local industries include textiles, chemicals, fertilizers — and paper. In fact, Augusta is situated in the very heart of the southern papermaking belt, a region that stretches from Virginia south to Florida and west to Texas.

The South is one of the major papermaking regions of the world and a great place for a paper company to be. It not only offers good transportation and a skilled work force. Of critical importance, the South has vast stands of softwood and hardwood trees to furnish raw material for paper.

Because of the warm, moist climate and year-round growing season, pines in the South grow to harvestable size in 20 to 30 years. By contrast, softwoods in Canada and Scandinavia — two other important papermaking regions — must grow for nearly 40 years before being harvested. Also favoring the South is its gentle

terrain. This makes it possible to harvest trees with tractor vehicles that have giant scissor-like pincers to chop down and delimb
the trees. Timber is now grown on many of the same southern
plantations where cotton was once king. It is farmed like any
renewable crop: after trees are harvested, six-month-old seedlings
are planted to take their place and begin the cycle again. Paper
companies also work closely with private landowners to improve,
harvest and regenerate natural stands of timber on their property.

Newly harvested trees are transported by truck or rail to
sawmills and paper mills. At Federal's Augusta paperboard mill,
trucks arrive in a never-ending procession, delivering tree-length
logs for processing into pulp — a mushy, oatmeal-like mixture of
wood fiber and water.

All told, at its various facilities, Federal consumes about
9,000 cords, or 24,000 tons, of wood each day for conversion to
lumber and pulp.

*Pine seedlings are grown in a controlled environment for 12 to 18 months before being
planted in the forest to replace harvested trees.*

AN INSIDE LOOK AT AUGUSTA'S PULPING OPERATIONS

What could be simpler than "cooking" wood to make pulp? You'd be surprised. Let's take a tour of the pulping operations at Augusta with Vann Parker, who in Chapter Eight gave us a guided tour of a Fourdrinier.

"A tree as it stands in the forest is about 50 percent water and 50 percent solid materials," Parker begins. "The material we are after is the cellulose fiber, which is held together with a glue called lignin." In the Kraft (German for "strength") pulping process used at Augusta and most other southern mills, the lignin is dissolved with the aid of a "white" liquor (it's actually clear) containing sodium sulphite and sodium hydroxide. This frees the fibers, which are drawn off and bleached. Finally, the bleached fibers are mixed with water to form the pulp. While the basic steps in the process are straightforward enough, pulping is in practice a complex technology that demands close attention to quality from start to finish.

Parker takes us outdoors to the vast woodyard at the Augusta mill. It is filled with piles of logs and enormous mounds of wood chips awaiting processing. Tree-length logs arrive at the woodyard and are de-barked in a revolving drum. Parker notes there is very little waste in a modern pulping operation; virtually every bit of material is used or recycled. At Augusta, the bark is used to fuel the mill's boilers. In fact,

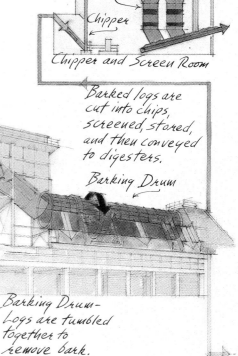

Cyclone

Screens

Chipper

Chipper and Screen Room

Barked logs are cut into chips, screened, stored, and then conveyed to digesters.

Barking Drum

Loqyard Crane

Slasher

Rail Tracks

Longwood Storage

Saw Blades

Log Slasher

Log Loader

Control Room

Conveyors to Barking Drum.

Barking Drum— Logs are tumbled together to remove bark.

Bark Boiler— Burns bark to make steam.

Federal estimates that two-thirds of the energy needs at its mills is met with bark and other waste materials. Through the use of these waste materials, and because of on-site power generation facilities, Federal's mills are close to being energy self-sufficient.

After being de-barked, the logs are fed into a chipper, which cuts the wood into uniform pieces about 1 ½ inches by 1 inch by ¼ inch. Larger chips are screened out and sent through the system a second time.

Parker emphasizes that the quality of the pulp begins with the chips. "In recent years we've learned that chips are not just chips," he observes. "There's a big difference between having a quality chip go into this cooking process and not having a quality

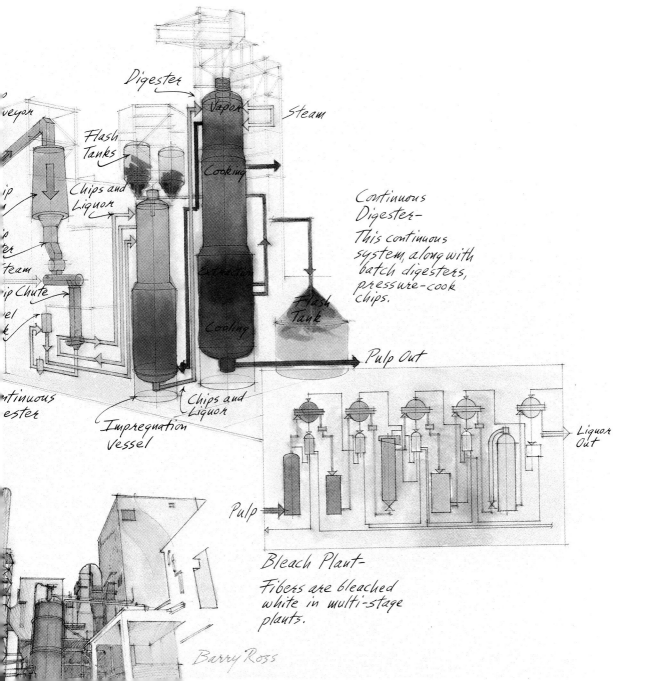

Digester

Vapor

Steam

Flash Tanks

Cooking

Chips and Liquor

Continuous Digester—
This continuous system, along with batch digesters, pressure-cook chips.

Extractor

Flash Tank

Cooling

Pulp Out

Continuous Digester

Impregnation Vessel

Chips and Liquor

Liquor Out

Pulp

Bleach Plant—
Fibers are bleached white in multi-stage plants.

Barry Ross

chip. You might say, what the heck, we're just going to dissolve the lignin. But if I design that cooking process for chips of a certain size and I get a bunch of chips that are a different size, they're going to be underprocessed or overprocessed." The Augusta mill has devoted great attention in the past few years to improving the uniformity of its chips and reducing the amount of handling of the chips so they are less likely to be damaged.

Pulping itself takes place inside a series of tanks and towers that are spread across a major portion of the mill site and are similar in appearance to the towers at an oil refinery or chemical plant. All the tanks and towers are connected by pipe, and the material flows continuously from one step of pulping to the next in a computer-controlled process.

First, the chips are fed into digesters, multi-story-high pressure cookers filled with the white liquor. "Depending on the size of the digester, the chips are cooked for three to six hours," Parker explains. "This part of the process is simply to dissolve the lignin." The fibers emerge from the digester as a dark-colored pulp called brown stock. "Many manufacturers use the stock at this point to make paper for grocery bags and linerboard for corrugated containers," Parker notes. Saleable byproducts include lignin and turpentine. The brown stock is then washed to remove dissolved organic compounds, including tallow, which is sold to make tall oil soaps.

Also in the washing, the cooking liquor — now a molasses-like substance called black liquor — is separated out for recycling as fuel in a recovery boiler. The ash residue from the boiler is in turn processed into green liquor, and the green liquor is processed into white liquor. Completing the cycle, the reconstituted white liquor is sent to a digester to cook a new batch of chips. "One of the problems at this mill, before the acquisition by Federal, was that the recovery area had become run down," Parker recalls. "It was disrupting our operations almost weekly, because we didn't have enough recovery capacity to supply the white liquor to operate the digesters at capacity. Federal came in and immediately refurbished this area."

Parker takes us back to the washers, where the pulp emerges as a slurry that is approximately 3 $\frac{1}{2}$ percent fiber, 96 $\frac{1}{2}$ percent water. "The main reason the pulp is brown," he says, "is that we didn't remove all the lignin." The pulp is therefore sent through a three-stage bleaching operation: in the chlorine tower, the pulp turns yellow as the lignin combines with chlorine; in the caustic tower, the lignin and other colored materials are removed; and in the chlorine dioxide tower, the fibers are bleached. At last, we have white pulp.

The pulp may then be placed in temporary storage. Later, just before being fed into a papermaking machine, it goes through two final processing stages. The first is the refiner. Parker explains that cellulose is a long-chain, carbon-based molecule with hydrogen atoms sticking off it. Hydrogen molecules attract each other. "In the refiner," he says, "the fiber is fibrillated, breaking out little segments of the fiber wall and exposing hydrogen bonding sites." It is this hydrogen bonding that enables the fibers to adhere to each other and form a sheet of paper.

Finally, the pulp is flowed through a cleaner system to remove any foreign material such as sand or debris. From there, it is transmitted to the headbox of one of the mill's three Fourdriniers — beginning the papermaking process, as described in Chapter Eight.

One of the interesting aspects of pulp is the differing qualities imparted by softwood and hardwood. Softwood fiber is long and gives paper strength. Hardwood fiber is short, providing a smooth surface for quality printing. Most paperboard is made with a combination of the two, depending on the customer's needs.

Back in the 1960s, Parker says, the Augusta mill primarily served markets where product strength was a priority. "The mill was making board for frozen shrimp boxes, trays and other products that did not require high-fidelity printing," he says. Therefore, the mill employed a hardwood/softwood mix of approximately 50/50. More recently, as the mill has upgraded its product line to serve more demanding printing applications, such as high-quality packaging for consumer products, it has increased the hardwood content of its board. The typical mix now is 80 percent hardwood, 20 percent softwood — and in some cases, the hardwood content is even higher. This increased hardwood content means that users of the board can print crisp, beautiful graphics on their packaging — graphics that attract consumers, lend an image of quality and help sell products.

The hardwoods used at Augusta are primarily sweetgum and oak, which grow in natural stands throughout the region. The main softwood is pine, cultivated for the most part on plantations.

FEDERAL'S TWO GREAT SOUTHERN OPERATIONS

Augusta and Riegelwood are Federal's two great southern operations. While Riegelwood is currently the world's largest paperboard mill, it will one day be overtaken in that position by Augusta as the latter continues its ambitious expansion program. On visiting the mills, one cannot help but notice that employees at the two facilities work closely together — but also engage in some good-natured rivalry.

Kirk Semke, the former mill manager at Riegelwood, states, "We're very alert to destructive rivalry — people not talking to one another. We don't want that to get started. But I do think there's some spirited rivalry between Riegelwood and Augusta, and that can be healthy if it doesn't get out of control."

He adds, "There's also a lot of helping between the two operations. For instance, if we need to build up an inventory of white liquor for the shutdown of a recovery boiler, they'll ship us tank cars of white liquor. Maybe they'll need green liquor, and we'll ship it down there. The two mills also use a lot of common parts. If we're in a bind and need a certain part, they'll ship it to us. And our maintenance people go back and forth a lot. In addition, our bleached board is marketed by the same overall sales force of Federal."

Each of the mills plays a distinctive role in Federal's operations. Augusta makes heavier grades of paperboard, primarily for packaging, and also supplies cup stock to Federal's paper cup plants. Riegelwood makes lighter grades of paperboard, primarily for brochure covers and other printing applications. Riegelwood is, in addition, a major supplier of market pulp to Federal's Tait mill in Scotland as well as to numerous outside customers.

Together, the two mills generate nearly two-thirds of Federal's annual dollar sales — an indication of just how important the acquisition of Riegelwood in 1972 and the acquisition of Augusta in 1985 have become to the company.

CHAPTER 13

Folding Up the Carton Business

ONCE upon a time, Federal Paper Board was a leading manufacturer of folding cartons. It made cartons for some of the best-known consumer products in America, including Ritz crackers, Pampers diapers, Ivory Snow laundry detergent and Kleenex tissues. By 1985, Federal's carton operations generated sales of $240 million annually. In their best years, these operations provided nearly 25 percent of Federal's operating earnings.

But those times are now in the past. In late 1990, Federal all but withdrew from the carton business, once a mainstay of its operations. The company agreed to sell five of its carton plants to two buyers and declared its intention to sell two other plants. Federal is left with a single folding carton plant in Durham, North Carolina. As of early 1991, Federal's carton sales are less than $25 million annually.

Why did Federal turn away from the carton business? Therein lies a tale of erratic growth, industry overcapacity and a relentless struggle by Federal to achieve adequate profits. Along the way, in the 1970s, came one of the most far-reaching antitrust cases in American history — a case in which Federal and 25 other corporations were accused of fixing carton prices. This landmark case signaled a turning point in antitrust enforcement, with implications for virtually every industry in America.

But let's start at the beginning.

When last we left Federal's folding carton operations, in Chapter Seven, the company had just gone through a period of dramatic expansion by means of acquisition in the 1950s. Diversification into folding cartons was a central element of J. R. Kennedy's master plan for building a larger, stronger Federal, and he succeeded nobly.

Kennedy loved to talk about the growth potential of the folding carton business. In a 1957 speech, he stated:

"The nature of the folding carton, the economy of its use, its suitability for automatic packaging, its display and merchandising values and other advantages have made it practically a 'must' for manufacturers, packagers and retailers alike. It has helped make possible the great growth of supermarkets and the growing trend toward other types of self-service stores. Recently, a survey was made of 307 leading food and grocery companies. These 307 leading companies represented $30 billion in food sales annually. The survey revealed that only 30 percent of these sales are presently packaged in folding cartons. It is understood, of course, that not all products can or should be packaged in folding cartons. Nevertheless, food and grocery products alone, as you may judge, still offer a huge potential market for new or improved cartons."

Federal earned attractive returns in the carton business for nearly two decades. By the mid-1960s, however, competition was increasing as more companies entered the business, adding to capacity and dampening returns. In addition, new materials such

Federal has continuously supplied paperboard for Domino sugar cartons since 1927, first from the Versailles mill and now from Sprague. In this 1950s snapshot, J.R. Kennedy, second from left, and Versailles mill superintendent Arthur Sartori, Sr., far right, meet with officials of American Sugar Company, now called Amstar.

as plastics and foils were making inroads into the packaging market. "The boom years of folding cartons were right after the Second World War through the 1950s," notes Arnold M. Ziroli, Federal's director of marketing and marketing services, Packaging and Printing Division. Since that time, the carton industry has grown at a slower rate and has been plagued by recurrent bouts of overcapacity.

By 1975, Federal's carton sales were well over $100 million annually, accounting for more than one-third of the company's total revenues and consuming 200,000 tons of paperboard a year. These sales were nearly triple those of 15 years earlier. However, Federal's carton operations had become only marginally profitable due to rising costs and excess industry capacity.

Then came what seemed to be the ultimate blow: In February 1976, a federal grand jury in Chicago indicted 23 folding carton companies (later increased to 26) and many of their executives on charges of conspiracy to fix prices. Federal was one of the corporate defendants, along with International Paper Company, Container Corporation of America and all the other leading manufacturers. A vice president and a former vice president of Federal were also indicted, as were executives of other companies.

The government charged, among other allegations, that the defendants had discussed their pricing plans at industry meetings and through phone conversations. Producers of folding cartons had, indeed, been sharing price information for decades; it was a traditional way of business in the industry, as it was in many other industries. Ken Petersen, who headed Federal's carton operations from the late '60s through the early '80s, says, "This was a price list business and, as was true in other industries, everybody had the same published prices. The head of the FTC said, 'It's a strange thing about America. I go into a small town and there are three dry cleaners, but they all have the same prices.'"

Jack Kennedy adds, "My own view is that this so-called market intelligence gathering — through meetings and phone calls — was perhaps illegal but was still viewed as acceptable in business in general. I think the carton industry failed to recognize that what had been acceptable had become both illegal and unacceptable. That's where we missed the boat, because this market intelligence had been going on in the carton industry for as long as anybody could remember."

With the handing up of the indictment, the Justice Department delivered a clear message: it would no longer tolerate the sharing of pricing plans by competitors in any industry. The folding carton case was described by Justice as the largest antitrust criminal action in the department's history.

The criminal indictment was followed by a series of civil suits, by companies that had purchased folding cartons, seeking unspecified treble damages.

Federal was one of the last defendants to settle the cases. Its board of directors wrestled for months with the question of whether the company was culpable, given the fact that the sharing of pricing plans was a long-standing practice in the carton industry. There were many differing opinions among the members of Federal's board. When the company chose to settle, some directors were not completely happy with that decision, believing Federal should have instead fought the criminal charges in court. Even today, some board members insist the company was innocent, while others acknowledge that the company was guilty as charged.

In 1977, Federal pleaded nolo contendere to the criminal charges and was fined $45,000. (Nolo contendere is a pleading that does not admit guilt, but subjects the defendant to punishment as if guilty.) One year later, it agreed to settle the civil suits for $12 million in cash plus $5 million in the form of a five-year note. Additionally, it gave the plaintiffs — buyers of folding cartons — warrants to purchase 181,818 shares of Federal common stock at $27.50 per share, just above the market price at the time. The warrants, if exercised, represented a 2.5 percent equity interest in Federal. The market price rose to $38 a share before the warrants expired in October 1983, and most of them were exercised.

These settlements were similar to those reached by most other corporate defendants in the case. But when it came to the charges filed against its executive and former executive, Federal went its own separate way. Many other carton companies sought to distance themselves from their accused employees. Federal, by contrast, embraced its accused employees as members of the corporate family, providing legal assistance and keeping them on the payroll. And when the two men pleaded nolo contendere, Jack Kennedy flew to Chicago to sit with them at their sentencings. One of the executives received a suspended sentence while the other spent a night in jail and performed community service.

Why did Kennedy take the unusual step of appearing with the executives in court? He replies, "I felt it was a mistake to single these guys out and say, 'They were the bad boys.' They did what many, many other people in our industry and our company did. If they were guilty, then hundreds of other people were equally guilty. It was clearly an industry and a company problem, not an individual problem. It was my feeling they were entitled to my support."

RENEWED GROWTH

Looking back today at the antitrust case, Quentin Kennedy says, "The point is we all got religion. There's no question that in the folding carton industry prices were fixed. It was pretty stupid, because prices were as low as you can imagine yet they were being dictated by a few companies. It cost us a lot of money. I think we would have been far better off if we hadn't been doing it. It was a very costly lesson for us and the industry."

To complicate matters, at the very time when Federal was settling the civil suits, it was also in the midst of its last-ditch effort to sell the Federal Glass Company plant in Columbus, Ohio. The period was a difficult one for the company. Month after month, these two monumental problems — the price-fixing case and the attempted glass plant sale and eventual closing — consumed huge amounts of executive time. In 1978, Federal took an after-tax writeoff of $11.2 million for the lawsuit settlement and one of $14.3 million for the plant closing. As a result, the company suffered a net loss of $3.5 million in 1978, the only yearly loss ever incurred by Federal as a public company.

It was with great relief, then, that members of the Federal management team finally put these two events behind them. Jack Kennedy wrote in March 1979, "The class action suits settlement and the attempted divestiture and subsequent closing of the Glassware Division were time-consuming and expensive. Our major emphasis turns now to our primary product area — the paper and forest products business — and the future looks bright."

Federal produced cartons for many of America's leading marketers, including McDonald's Corporation.

Federal's beleaguered carton operations, it seemed, didn't have much of a role in the company's plans. But then something surprising happened: In the wake of the price-fixing case, Federal's profitability in the carton business began to increase. "That was a turning point for us," Petersen recalls, "because prices were then quoted on the basis of our own efficiencies, not on the basis of protecting other manufacturers' inefficiencies."

In 1975, Federal's carton operations generated a meager 3 percent pretax return on assets. By 1980, that return was up to 10 percent and by 1985 it had increased to 18 percent. This improvement was due partly to better market conditions. But it also reflected a payoff from Federal's programs to improve productivity, reduce costs and increase market share.

In addition, Federal was establishing itself as a technical leader in the carton business. In the 1980s, for instance, Federal developed an innovative approach to the packaging of margarine. Traditionally, most margarine in stick form was marketed in paperboard containers with a foil veneer as a grease barrier. Federal developed a printed ink barrier that replaces the foil and reduces packaging costs. The printed barrier is now widely used in the margarine industry.

However, 1985 proved to be a peak year. Thereafter, the carton industry entered another of its periodic rounds of

Federal's high-speed web presses transform giant rolls of paperboard into packaging for products known across America. Cartons for Kleenex brand facial tissue are on the press, left, while printed rolls of what will become containers for McDonald's and other companies stand in storage, right.

At peak production in the late 1980s, Federal made nearly 100 billion folding cartons annually.

overcapacity. The problem is this: folding cartons are a slow-growth business, yet the ever-faster speed of printing presses keeps adding to capacity whether it's needed or not. An example is provided by Walter L. Vernasco, who headed Federal's carton plant in Palmer, Massachusetts. Twenty years ago, the typical press speed at Palmer was 1,500 to 2,000 sheets an hour. Today's presses at Palmer print about 8,000 sheets an hour, equivalent to a quadrupling of capacity. Industry capacity has not literally grown fourfold during the past 20 years; as new, faster presses have been installed, older ones have been taken out of service. Nonetheless, growth in demand has frequently been exceeded by growth in capacity as press speeds have increased.

As the latest round of overcapacity worsened, Federal's pretax return on assets in the carton business sank to 6 percent in 1987 and then to 4 percent in 1989. Federal fought back by improving productivity, improving product quality, closing un-profitable plants, modernizing equipment, and restructuring its sales and manufacturing organizations. In the end, however, Jack Kennedy decided the time had come to move on to more profit-able business opportunities.

In December 1990, Federal announced plans to sell seven of its eight folding carton plants for a total anticipated price of about $100 million.

Kennedy explains that Federal was a generalist in the carton business, primarily making commodity-type cartons in large volumes, and that it's difficult to achieve adequate profits in this sector. "If we re-enter the market," he says, "it will be in specialty areas where we can add value." Federal's one remaining carton plant — in Durham, North Carolina — makes cigarette cartons from solid bleached sulphate board supplied by the Augusta mill.

Kennedy also notes that Federal's carton plants did not fit well with the company's current direction in solid bleached sulphate paperboard. "For the most part," he says, "these plants made cartons from recycled board, whereas Federal mainly produces bleached board."

Companies change, and certainly Federal is changing as it pulls back from the carton business. The company is today seeking newer, more profitable growth opportunities. Two of those opportunities, as we shall soon discover, are in overseas operations and paper cups.

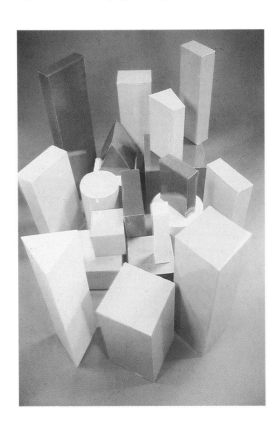

Folding cartons can be much more than simple boxes. Pictured here are samples of the innovative shapes designed by Federal in the late 1960s, when it was one of the nation's premier manufacturers of the versatile paperboard containers.

CHAPTER 14

Thomas Tait
Comes on Board

THE United States, together with Canada and Scandinavia, is one of the heavily forested regions of the world that has "excess fiber" — that is, it produces more pulp and paper than it consumes. Japan and industrialized Europe, on the other hand, are "fiber short" — demand exceeds availability. This fundamental imbalance presents an enormous opportunity to a company like Federal.

One of Federal's key strategies is to capitalize on this opportunity and expand its overseas sales. "Clearly, demand for paper is growing around the world," Jack Kennedy remarks. Successsfully implementing its strategy, Federal has increased its exports by 300 percent in five years — from $53 million in 1985 to $210 million in 1990.

Federal is a major exporter of market pulp (processed wood fiber). More than half the market pulp from Riegelwood is sold to paper companies abroad. In addition, nearly 10 percent of the bleached paperboard manufactured by Federal in the United States is exported to customers in Japan, Europe and other overseas markets, and that percentage continues to climb steadily. Federal's goal is to increase its exports of bleached paperboard from 50,000 tons in 1990 to 75,000 tons in 1992.

To spur its exports, in the late 1980s Federal opened sales offices in Tokyo, London and Zurich.

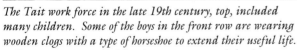

The Tait work force in the late 19th century, top, included many children. Some of the boys in the front row are wearing wooden clogs with a type of horseshoe to extend their useful life.

Esparto grass was Tait's primary raw material prior to World War II. This shed and its contents, right, were destroyed in the war when hit by a tracer bullet during an air battle.

When German U-boats halted the supply of African esparto grass, local straw was harvested for papermaking, above.

Then in April 1989, Federal took an even bigger step: It acquired Thomas Tait & Sons Ltd., which produces uncoated freesheet (primarily paper for copy machines) at a mill in Inverurie, Scotland. The mill is Federal's first production facility outside the United States and opens a new chapter in Federal's global business strategy. Federal paid approximately $60 million in a combination of cash, notes and common stock for the Tait firm.

Tait brings three major benefits to Federal:

- a direct manufacturing and marketing presence in the European Community;
- a new product line to diversify Federal's business; and
- a guaranteed customer for a sizable portion of the market pulp made at Riegelwood.

Tait & Sons earns a 28 percent return on equity. Federal plans to expand the operation aggressively, nearly doubling its capacity over the next three years and raising its sales from $145 million in 1990 to a projected $260 million by 1994. Kennedy points out that Scandinavian paper companies control about 43 percent of the uncoated freesheet market in the U.K. He figures their average production and transportation cost, as of late 1990, was about $530 per ton. By contrast, the Tait mill (with a market share of about 8 percent) had a production and transportation cost of about $385 per ton, representing a $145-per-ton advantage. Kennedy believes the Tait mill's lower cost provides a unique opportunity to expand production and capture market share from the Scandinavians. "One of the reasons we're there is we can beat them from a cost standpoint," he says.

THE HISTORY OF THE TAIT MILL

The Tait firm is one of Scotland's oldest paper manufacturers. The Taits originally settled in the Inverurie area, near the east coast of Scotland, more than 300 years ago as farmers. They became large landowners, developed granite quarries, and went on to build a snuff mill and grain mill. In 1800, seeking an efficient way to ship grain to the booming markets of industrial England, they helped finance the construction of a canal from Inverurie to the port of Aberdeen, some 15 miles away.

Then the railroad came to Inverurie in the mid-nineteenth century. To eliminate competition, it asked the Taits to close their canal and compensated them handsomely for doing so. Looking for a new business opportunity, the Taits used the money from the railroad to found Thomas Tait & Sons and build a paper mill. In the following decades, ownership of the paper company was passed from father to son through five generations — from the original Thomas Tait to William to Thomas to William to the current Thomas Tait, who is the firm's managing director and was recently elected a vice president of Federal.

Thomas Tait, right, took over the family business at age 21 when his father, William Tait, below, was killed in an accident.

The current Thomas, 42, is a charming Scotsman with an impish grin and a deadpan wit. He has headed the company since he was 21 years old. His father, William Tait, had come into the business during the Depression and saved the mill from financial ruin. William increased production slowly until the fall of 1969, when he launched a major program to install a new papermaking machine. However, tragedy struck before he got to see his new machine in operation. Walking over a bridge leading to the mill, William was hit by a truck and killed. He was 63 years old. Young Thomas became the new managing director.

Thomas not only had to deal with the shock of his father's death; he also faced the problem of getting the new machine working properly. "It was a traumatic time," he says. The machine was eventually brought into full production and now makes 30,000 tonnes (metric tons) of paper a year. Thomas expanded the business as it had never been expanded before. When he took charge in 1970, production was 20,000 tonnes a year. In 1986, he installed a world-class papermaking machine with a capacity of 125,000 tonnes; the capacity of this machine is now being doubled by Federal.

The Tait firm was founded in 1852 by Thomas Tait. On his death, he was succeeded by his son, William, who was in turn succeeded by his son, Thomas.

Tait & Sons specializes in business communication paper, such as copy and computer paper. Thomas Tait's face lights up as he speaks about the growth potential of this market. "Laser printers are making a major impact," he says. "Desktop publishing is really in its infancy. We see big, big growth in our marketplace."

Why, then, did he sell the business? One reason is that he and his wife, Sheila, are not planning any family and there is no obvious successor in the Tait family. More importantly, Tait sees benefits in being associated with Federal. In 1986, when Tait & Sons installed its new papermaking machine, it raised the financing by selling an interest in the company to a group of British institutional investors. This reduced the Tait family's ownership from 55 percent to 35 percent. Later, the institutions wanted to sell their stock through an offering to the public, but Thomas Tait was concerned. "We couldn't see ourselves remaining independent if we were publicly owned," he says. "With all the interest by companies in entering the Common Market, we felt we might be taken over."

Tait & Sons also wanted access to the resources of a large, trusted partner to expand its operations and upgrade its product quality.

HEDGING AGAINST THE VOLATILITY OF MARKET PULP

The Tait mill fits well with Federal's plans. Located in "fiber-short" Scotland, the mill produces no pulp of its own. In 1986, it began buying pulp from Riegelwood and soon became one of that facility's largest market pulp customers. Out of that business relationship grew a friendship between Thomas Tait and Jack Kennedy and, eventually, the agreement for Federal to acquire the Tait firm.

Of great importance, the acquisition reduces Federal's exposure to the price volatility of market pulp. Market pulp is an international commodity that, like crude oil, is priced in U.S. dollars. Demand is cyclical and prices sometimes swing sharply. Sid Pope, who retired as a vice president of Federal in 1990, says, "In 1985 we lost $8 million on market pulp and in 1988 we earned $120 million. Now that's volatility!"

Market pulp accounted for about 19 percent of Federal's dollar sales in 1990. To reduce its heavy exposure to the volatility of this commodity, Federal is acquiring businesses — such as Tait — that are pulp users.

Jack Kennedy explains as follows: Federal produces 540,000 tons of market pulp a year. Tait consumes 100,000 tons. Even though Tait buys only 30,000 of these tons from Riegelwood and the rest from other sources, Federal — as the owner of Tait — is effectively hedged against price movements for the full 100,000

In 1983, Thomas Tait was joined by his mother and wife, Sheila, at Buckingham Palace after being appointed an Officer of the British Empire by Queen Elizabeth II.

tons. That's because when pulp prices decline and Riegelwood makes less money, Tait benefits from lower costs and makes more money regardless of where it buys its pulp.

Expansion of the Tait facility will have two favorable consequences for Federal: increased paper sales in the U.K. and a further reduction in Federal's exposure to the volatility of market pulp.

Federal has already increased the mill's production, without any capital cost, by applying American work practices. Paper mills in England traditionally close for Christmas, Easter and a vacation period in July. The Tait mill was closed for 63 days in 1988. "We've changed that," Kennedy states. Applying a method it pioneered in the United States, Federal has begun to keep the mill running through all holiday periods. Kennedy's goal is to reduce shutdowns to 10 days a year, effectively adding capacity without capital investment.

Production at Tait was 95,000 tonnes in 1989, the year the facility was acquired by Federal. It was increased to 135,000 tonnes in 1990 through a variety of actions, including reduced shutdown time. Now, Federal is launching a two-stage capital investment program to add 100,000 tonnes of capacity — 50,000 tonnes by mid-1992 and an additional 50,000 tonnes by the end of 1993. Estimated capital cost is $140 million.

"As Tait expands," Kennedy says, "our market exposure to pulp declines." By 1994, the mill should be consuming 190,000 tons of market pulp a year, equivalent to more than one-third of Federal's market pulp production.

"By acquiring Tait, we now bring our fiber from North Carolina to Scotland to make paper for the European market," Kennedy observes. "Eventually we'd like to do the same thing in the Far East. We might bring our fiber from the U.S. to Taiwan, for instance, and make paper for the Asian market."

For Federal, global expansion is just beginning.

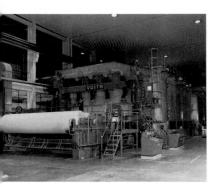

The Tait company's largest papermaking machine, PM4, was completed in 1986 and is being expanded by Federal.

The Tait mill is a major consumer of market pulp shipped from the Riegelwood mill in North Carolina.

CHAPTER 15

Diversification by the Cupful

IN 1989, Federal entered the paper cup business and quickly established an important national presence in this growing industry.

Federal took its first step into the business in October 1989 by acquiring Imperial Cup Corporation, owned by the Allen family of Kenton, Ohio. Eleven months later, it acquired Continental Bondware, Inc., based in Rolling Meadows, Illinois. Combined cost of the two acquisitions was $250 million. Federal merged the two companies to form Imperial Bondware Corp., with plants in Chicago and Shelbyville, Illinois; Kenton, Ohio; LaFayette, Georgia; Salisbury, Maryland; and Visalia, California.

Continental Bondware had an average annual growth rate of 17 percent in the five years prior to its acquisition. Imperial Cup's growth rate was an even more glittering 22 percent a year. Federal intends to build on that momentum.

"Paper cups are going to be a very big part of our company," Jack Kennedy predicts. He notes that the cup market in the U.S. is moving away from styrofoam, back to paper, for environmental reasons. In addition, Fort Howard Corporation, the largest cup producer, went through a leveraged buyout in 1988 and one year later sold its cup operations to Sweetheart Holdings Inc., a new company organized by a private investor group. Kennedy believes these changes have created a temporary leadership vacuum in the cup industry and offer Federal an opportunity to gain market share.

Imperial Bondware's sales were $260 million in 1990, about 14 percent of the U.S. paper cup market. Kennedy's goal is to grow faster than the competition and increase sales to nearly $400 million by 1993.

AN AMERICAN SUCCESS STORY

Federal paid just over $100 million for Imperial. "I think we paid a rather high price, but it was worth it," Kennedy says. He notes that Imperial has quality products, good people, modern facilities and a strong record of profitability.

Imperial Cup is a true-life example of the power of entrepreneurship in America. The company was owned by R. E. Allen, his wife Joanne and their sons, Richard and Rex. The story of the Allens and Imperial begins in the years immediately following World War II. After serving with the Flying Tigers in China, R. E. returned to Ohio, where he enrolled in college and married Joanne. In 1947, with their first child on the way, R. E. and Joanne dropped out of college to go into business. They had $5,000 between them and chose the candy distribution business (selling candy to retail stores) because it didn't require much capital. "We rented an office in Kenton, Ohio, for $10 a month, and my father gave us his 1938 Buick to use as a truck," R. E. recalls.

The candy business did well, and three years later the Allens expanded into the vending business, selling candy, coffee and other products through vending machines at factories. After that, they diversified into the manufacture of packaging for the candy industry, and for a period of time they also made packaging for delicate instruments and delicate wire products.

The Allens got into the paper cup business because they couldn't find a reliable source of cups for their vending machines. They bought their first cup-making machine in 1968, and since it made more cups than they could use, they began selling cups to friends and acquaintances in the vending-machine business. Unsure what to name their new company, R. E. and Joanne happened to drive by an Imperial House Motel and decided Imperial was as good a name as any.

One of the big problems in buying cups, the Allens believed, was that the manufacturers shipped them by common carrier. Shipments were sometimes damaged and often arrived late. So the Allens acquired their own fleet of delivery vehicles. "Our customers were amazed," R. E. recalls. "They'd say, 'We can count on your trucks. We know when they're going to be here. You've got courteous drivers.' So that was an excellent facet of the business."

As their cup business grew, the Allens expanded their plant in Kenton several times and eventually built a new one there. In 1977, they opened a plant in Georgia and the following year sold

R.E. Allen and his family went into business with a $5,000 investment in 1947. Over the next four decades, they built a company worth more than $100 million.

all their other companies to concentrate on the cup business. Subsequently, plants were added in California and Maryland.

By 1989, when Imperial was acquired by Federal, it employed 800 people and had annual sales of $75 million. In just 21 years, the Allens had built one of the larger manufacturers of paper cups in the United States. "We just loved the cup business and had fun doing it," R. E. Allen says today. R. E. is now 70 years old and heads his own investment firm in Florida. Joanne died in July 1990.

Imperial Bondware's plants are large, modern and efficient. The company is taking steps to improve product quality and enhance productivity, aided by an agreement to share technical information with Japan's leading cup manufacturer.

Striking a Bargain With the Allens

R. E. says the Allens never had any intention of selling their company. Federal Paper Board, on the other hand, had identified the paper cup business as a growth opportunity and asked Morgan Guaranty Trust to contact the Allens to see if Imperial might be available. R. E. Allen relates, "I got a call from a banker, and he said, 'I've got some people who are interested in looking at your company.' And I said, 'Our company's not for sale.' The banker said, 'Well, I know the president of the company. His name is

Jack Kennedy and he's a prince of a guy. Why don't you just sit down and talk with him and see what he's got to say?'

"I said, 'Okay,' but I pointed out that I had family in the business. We didn't have any money problems. We didn't have any people problems. The business was going gangbusters. And we didn't have any reason to sell."

The first group of Federal executives to visit Imperial was headed by Bob W. Bowie, senior vice president in charge of the Packaging and Printing Division. Bowie was impressed by what he saw, including the enthusiasm of employees and the cleanliness of the plant and equipment. "Their factories were spotless," he says, "and their truck drivers were just terrific. They were very courteous and their appearance was immaculate."

(Later, after Federal had acquired Imperial, Bowie visited the plants to answer employees' questions. He still remembers a woman in one plant who asked, "Do you have any robots that mop?" When he asked what she meant, the woman suggested he drop by her work area later in the day. He did so and found that she, like everyone else in the plant, always mopped the floor around her work area before going home. She told Bowie, "It sure hurts my back, but I want it to be clean.")

Before leaving Imperial on that first visit, Bowie told Allen, "You should meet Mr. Federal himself — Jack Kennedy." "And I said, 'Bob, I'm not interested because I don't have any problems,'" Allen recalls.

Nonetheless, Jack Kennedy called and arranged to meet Allen a month later. In the interim, R. E. and Joanne had a chance to think about selling. They eventually decided that doing so might not be such a bad idea. "If you keep a family business and don't sell it, and the owners pass away and it has to be sold for tax purposes, it more or less becomes a fire sale," R. E. explains.

When Kennedy visited Imperial, he and Allen got along nicely — after which negotiations started in earnest. "It was a case where Jack kept after me," according to Allen. "He came to California, and he'd call me and say, 'R. E., how about this much, how about that much?' And I kept saying, 'No, here's the price.' And finally Jack called me one day from Jamaica and said, 'R. E., we're going to buy the business.' I guess if you give people a price and finally they say, 'We're going to buy your business,' it's pretty hard to turn around and say, 'I don't want to sell it.'"

Kennedy offers, good-naturedly, a slightly different version of the negotiations. He says the Allens asked a price Federal was unwilling to pay, so Federal called off negotiations. Several months later, Federal looked at other cup properties that were for sale. "But after looking around in the U.S. and overseas, we concluded that Imperial was a better buy," he relates. "That's why we went back to them. I did call from Jamaica, and I told R. E. we had looked at these other properties and our preference was to buy Imperial. And if he would compromise on his price, we would compromise on our last offer. So we did. But I would also add that his idea of compromise and mine were not the same. We did all the compromising."

THE HISTORY OF CONTINENTAL BONDWARE

Continental Bondware was part of Continental Group, Inc., when that company was acquired by Kiewit-Murdock Investment Corp. in 1984. Federal bought the Augusta mill from Kiewit in 1985 and the nearby woodlands in 1986 — and purchased Continental Bondware from the firm for just under $150 million in 1990.

The story of Bondware is one of initial growth, followed by poor financial results and retrenchment in the 1970s, followed by dramatically renewed growth in the 1980s. Bondware was founded by Continental Group (then called Continental Can) in 1946 when Continental acquired two companies: Boothby Container Company of Boston and The Mono Service Company of North Newark, New Jersey. Initially it was called the Paper Container Division.

Continental recognized that the paper cup business was entering a postwar boom. The coffee break was an established fact, created during the war, and the trends toward leisure time and convenience were creating demand for disposable cups.

In 1953, Continental added a line of paper plates to the division by purchasing Bowes Industry Company of Three Rivers, Michigan. (As you may recall, Federal acquired Continental's paper plate factories in 1985 as part of the package of properties purchased with the Augusta mill. However, it sold those factories because it didn't want to be in the plate business.) "Bondware" was a trademark of Bowes. In 1954, Continental acquired another cup manufacturer, The American Paper Goods Company of Kensington, Connecticut.

The division changed its name to Bondware in 1957 in the belief that "Paper Container" was overly broad and had become confusing.

Bondware prospered until the 1970s, when competition intensified and the division's profitability began to sag. Styrofoam was by now capturing a growing share of the cup market, so Bondware fought back by acquiring a styrofoam cup manufacturer. However, this acquisition was not successful and Bondware fell into the red.

"From 1975 through 1979 Bondware lost an average of $7 million a year," according to Denis H. Davidson, the president of Bondware when it was acquired by Federal. Consequently, in 1979 Continental decided to sell the division, but couldn't find a buyer. The final asking price was $6 million, yet still there were no takers. Out of this traumatic period in its history, Bondware rose like a phoenix from the ashes.

Continental Can Company's diversification into the cup business after World War II was spearheaded by General Lucius Clay, the company's chief executive and hero of the Berlin Airlift.

"The management of Bondware sat in a room and said, 'Now what do we do?'" Davidson recalls. "On October 31, 1979, we let go somewhere in the area of 180 salaried people. We closed three plants. We reduced our sales force from 60 people to six. Basically, we retrenched and refocused. Our first year after doing that, we sold $34 million worth of product. When we were acquired by Federal ten years later, our sales were nearly $200 million."

How was this turnaround accomplished? "Basically we got back to what we did best," Davidson replies. Bondware refocused on its most important markets: paper cups and popcorn containers for the fast-food industry and other markets.

The acquisition of Continental by Kiewit-Murdock in 1984 sent a shock wave through Bondware. Kiewit immediately cut employment at Bondware to reduce costs and improve productivity. "We went through three head-count reduction programs in less than three years," Davidson states. But Kiewit also infused nearly $40 million of capital over a five-year period to expand operations — and it was this combination of cost reductions and

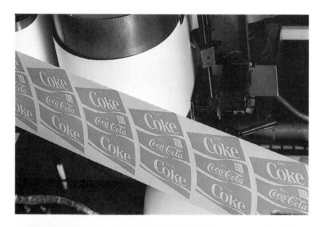

Imperial Bondware's plants have an annual capacity of 12.5 billion paper cups, one billion plastic cups and four billion plastic lids. They employ state-of-the-art manufacturing equipment to produce cups for Coca-Cola and other beverages.

capital investment that, more than any other factor, put Bondware back on a growth path.

"Bondware has had a terrific track record over the past ten years," Davidson states. "But there are a lot of things we still have to accomplish. I think we have a tremendous opportunity for process improvement. I think we have a tremendous opportunity, together with Imperial, to take the leadership position in the paper cup business."

A GOOD FIT

Imperial Cup and Continental Bondware fit well with each other. Imperial is the number one U.S. supplier of paper cups for vending machines. Every time you buy a soft drink or hot chocolate or coffee in a paper cup from a vending machine, there's a better than fifty-fifty chance the cup was manufactured by Imperial. Bondware, on the other hand, manufactures cups and popcorn buckets for the fast food industry, movie theaters and convenience stores. "Even though our products look the same, Imperial and Bondware are really two entirely different businesses," Davidson observes. He says Imperial and Bondware had only three customers in common.

The combined Imperial Bondware, in turn, meshes well with Federal. It not only generates substantial profits, but is a user of paperboard. Federal's mills, principally Augusta, are now supplying about 105,000 tons of cup stock a year to Imperial Bondware's plants, providing a route to market for some 10 percent of Federal's total annual bleached paperboard production. These sales are expected to increase to about 140,000 tons by 1993, which fits in with the expansion of the Augusta mill.

Federal has moved quickly to expand and improve Imperial Bondware's operations. In late 1990 it completed the construction of a poly-extrusion laminating facility in Prosperity, South Carolina, to coat paperboard from Augusta and Riegelwood with a thin, moisture-resistant layer of plastic. As a result, Federal is one of only two paper cup manufacturers in the U.S. that makes and poly-coats its own stock.

Also, Federal is doubling the size of the Visalia, California, cup plant and in late 1990 completed a new 275,000-square-foot plant and warehouse at Kenton, Ohio.

Of equal importance, Federal has signed an agreement to share technical information with Tokan Kogyo Co., Ltd., Japan's leading manufacturer of paper cups. This agreement gives Federal access to Tokan's process engineering and enables Federal to buy manufacturing equipment from Tokan.

"Typical of the Japanese, there is nothing new in what they do," Kennedy says. "But if you take these 20 or so steps to make a cup, they do each one that much better." With the assistance of Japanese technology, Imperial Bondware expects to reduce its

Supporting its growth in the paper cup business, Federal recently built an extrusion coating plant at Prosperity, South Carolina. The $17 million facility applies a plastic, moisture-resistant resin to paperboard. A portion of the coated stock is used by Federal to make cups for hot beverages, while the remainder is sold to outside customers in the packaging industry.

"leakers" (defective cups) by 90 percent, thereby improving productivity and enhancing product quality.

In addition, Federal's Augusta mill has made great strides in improving the quality of its cup stock and thereby qualifying to sell stock to Japanese producers. Initial sales were made in 1990. Kennedy emphasizes that meeting Japanese standards has direct benefit to Imperial Bondware, since the stock that Imperial Bondware buys from Augusta now satisfies the most exacting requirements in the world.

Moreover, in merging the two companies, Kennedy sees a chance to achieve operating efficiencies. He points out, for instance, that both of Bondware's plants are located in Illinois, but its customers are nationwide. Nearly 25 percent of Bondware's sales are to customers in California — "and it's expensive to ship cups," he states. Customers in California are now being served from the Imperial plant at Visalia, which is being expanded.

Kennedy concludes, "The growth in the cup market looks good to us." He says it represents the type of diversification into a related business that Federal might do more of in the future.

CHAPTER 16

Creating Wealth

T HE WORLD into which Federal was born 75 years ago was far different than the world in which we live today.

The Panama Canal had opened two years earlier, in 1914, signaling America's rise as a global power. World War I, "the war to end all wars," was raging in Europe. Russia was still ruled by the tsars. Einstein was about to publish his theory of relativity. King Tut's tomb lay undiscovered in Egypt. Charles Lindbergh was a 14-year-old youth dreaming of aviation. Women still didn't have the right to vote; the Nineteenth Amendment, guaranteeing that right, would not come until four years later.

The era was one of turmoil, change and opportunity. Spurred by technological advances and the growth of consumer and industrial markets, new companies were springing up like wildflowers across America. Some of today's largest corporations, including General Motors, IBM, Shell Oil and ITT, trace their roots to this fertile period of industrial development.

William Shortess stepped boldly onto the stage of American enterprise and sought to play his part, investing every penny he had to launch Federal. He was a true risk-taker and industrial pioneer. His new company survived despite repeated scrapes with potential disaster. Decades later, long after he was gone, it would succeed beyond his wildest dreams through the persistence and talents of numerous individuals.

The history of Federal, then, is a story of America at its best — of what is possible in this land of opportunity. "Federal is an excellent example of how capitalism works," says Tom Cassidy, a member of the company's board of directors. "It shows how a company can take root and grow in a competitive economy. And it's a great example of a company anticipating and adapting to change."

Without doubt, the greatest changes in Federal's history have occurred during the past 20 years, as the company has responded to shifts in the paperboard market to become a leading southern manufacturer of solid bleached sulphate board. The 1972 acquisition of the Riegelwood, North Carolina, mill and the 1985 purchase of the Augusta, Georgia, mill were every bit as daring and visionary as the start-up of the company by Shortess in 1916.

Federal also exemplifies the creation of wealth by the private sector, contributing to an improved standard of living. The free-market system is not an abstract, outdated concept. It is a real-life force in America today. People make it happen. Many of us lose sight of the fact that wealth comes not from government nor from untapped natural resources, but from individuals working together to build successful businesses. The engine of wealth in America is profits, which provide the resources for companies to create jobs, pay dividends, open new factories and develop new products and services.

Federal's total profits during the past decade came to nearly $700 million. Of that amount, the company distributed more than $200 million to its shareholders in the form of dividends and reinvested the remainder in the expansion of its business.

Also during the past decade, Federal paid nearly $500 million in income taxes to federal, state and local governments — taxes based on the company's profits. And it paid $2.5 billion in wages and fringe benefits to employees.

Today, Federal has a market value of nearly $1.2 billion, representing the total value of all the Federal common stock held by investors — still another form of wealth.

The wealth created by Federal has been spread around to the benefit of society. The entrepreneurs associated with the company and its divisions over the past 75 years have not only been highly motivated to succeed, but also to share their success with others. Shortess Chapel in South Carolina, Posner Hall at Tufts University, Freas Hall at Bucknell University, the Breslin-Kennedy wing at Holy Name Hospital in Teaneck, New Jersey, and the Elsie A. Brown Fund in Norwich, Connecticut — these are just a few examples.

None of this wealth would exist if Shortess had not started a company that made a product that met a public need. The free-market system in America is as simple and effective as that, empowering individuals to strike out on their own, take chances, overcome obstacles, seize opportunities, succeed or fail, reap the rewards of their success, and in the process create enduring institutions that add to the economic fabric of the nation.

Today, Federal has sales in excess of $1.3 billion a year and total assets of more than $2.5 billion. It employs almost 8,000 people, compared with fewer than 50 at its founding. Nearly every day, probably without knowing it, you use one or more of the company's products.

Federal is a large private landholder, with nearly 700,000 acres under its control in the southeastern United States — an area a little smaller in size than the state of Rhode Island.

It harvests more than four million cords of timber each year from its own lands and other sources.

It plants over 12 million seedlings each year to replace the trees it harvests.

It turns out nearly 500 million feet of lumber annually, primarily for the building industry.

It produces more than 500,000 tons of market pulp a year.

It produces 170,000 tons of recycled paperboard each year at the world's largest and most efficient recycled paperboard mill in Sprague, Connecticut.

It produces one million tons of bleached paperboard annually at its mills in Riegelwood and Augusta.

It manufactures and prints folding cartons at its plant in Durham, North Carolina.

It manufactures uncoated freesheet, for use in copy machines and laser printers, at a mill in Scotland.

And it holds a rapidly growing position in the manufacture of paper cups.

◆

However, the story of Federal does not end with this book. No company can afford to stand still in a competitive economy. The work of building and creating goes on. Whatever may lie in the future for Federal — whether it be geographic expansion, new mills, new products, new customers (and all of them are likely) — the next 75 years will most certainly be as challenging and eventful as the past 75.

Directors, Officers and Operations

As of April 16, 1991

Federal's current board of directors includes, standing from left: Robert D. Baldwin, Senior Vice President; Richard A. Lenon, former Chairman, International Minerals & Chemical Corporation; W. Mark Massey, Jr., Senior Vice President; Edmund J. Kelly, Vice Chairman, Eighteen Seventy Corporation; John L. Kelsey, Advisory Director, Paine Webber, Incorporated; and Thomas L. Cassidy, Managing Director, Trust Company of the West. Seated, from left, are: James T. Flynn, Chief Financial Officer, J.P. Morgan & Co., Incorporated; B.W. Bowie, Senior Vice President; John R. Kennedy, President; Quentin J. Kennedy, Executive Vice President and Secretary; W. Ran Clerihue, Consultant.

OFFICERS

John R. Kennedy
President,
Chief Executive Officer

Corporate Staff

Quentin J. Kennedy
Executive Vice President
and Secretary

Michael G. Culbreth
Vice President,
Employee Relations

Jack E. Spengler
Vice President,
Purchasing

Thomas L. Cox
Treasurer

Roger L. Sanders II
Controller

John T. Flynn, Jr.
Assistant Secretary

Stephen F. Rizzo
Assistant Controller

Edward M. Werger
Assistant Controller

Converting Operations

B. W. Bowie
Senior Vice President

John E. Abodeely
Vice President,
Manufacturing
Packaging and Printing Division

Carl M. DeFaria
Vice President,
Sales and Marketing
Packaging and Printing Division

Joseph F. Mador
Vice President, General Manager
Imperial Bondware Corp.

Forest Products Division

Robert D. Baldwin
Senior Vice President,
Marketing

W. Mark Massey, Jr.
Senior Vice President,
Manufacturing

Robert F. Dansby
Vice President,
Augusta Operations

Thomas F. Grady, Jr.
Vice President,
Paperboard Sales,
Printing Grades

Louis O. Grissom
Vice President,
Riegelwood Operations

Richard W. Hughes
Vice President,
Woodlands

Stewart Monroe, Jr.
Vice President,
Pulp Sales

Leon K. Semke
Vice President,
Manufacturing Technology

William R. Snellings
Vice President,
Paperboard Sales,
Packaging Grades

Thomas J. Tait
Vice President,
Managing Director,
Thomas Tait & Sons, Ltd.

J. Ronald Tillman
Vice President, Wood Products

FACILITIES

FOREST PRODUCTS DIVISION

Paper, Paperboard and Pulp
Augusta, GA
Riegelwood, NC
Sprague, CT
Inverurie, Scotland
(Thomas Tait & Sons, Ltd.)

Service Distribution Centers
Hazleton, PA
Ontario, CA
Prosperity, SC
Sturgis, MI

Wood Products
Armour, NC
Augusta, GA
Johnston, SC
Newberry, SC
Washington, GA

International Sales Offices
London, England
Tokyo, Japan
Zurich, Switzerland

CONVERTING OPERATIONS

Imperial Bondware Corp.
Chicago, IL
Kenton, OH
LaFayette, GA
Salisbury, MD
Shelbyville, IL
Visalia, CA

Packaging and Printing Division
Durham, NC
Hendersonville, NC
Palmer, MA
Thomaston, GA
Versailles, CT
Wilmington, NC
York, PA

Chronology

1871   William G. Shortess, founder of Federal Paper Board Company, is born in Pennsylvania.

1909   Shortess acquires his first recycled paperboard mill, a small facility in Reading, Pennsylvania, while continuing to work full time for Continental Paper Company as a mill manager.

1916   Shortess quits his job at Continental Paper. On March 3, he founds Federal Paper Board Company, buying a 16-year-old recycled paperboard mill in Bogota, New Jersey, and establishing Federal's headquarters there.

Incorporation papers are drafted by White & Case, beginning a long-standing relationship. White & Case has continuously served for 75 years as Federal's legal counsel.

Late in 1916, Federal buys a second mill — at Versailles, Connecticut.

Howard Brown joins Federal as assistant treasurer, assistant secretary and manager of the Versailles mill.

1917   Federal's sales are $865,000 in its first full year of business.

1920   Federal acquires a mill in Montville, Connecticut.

Sales approach $3 million.

1922   Federal forms a subsidiary, Inland Paper Board Company, to own the Versailles mill.

1923   Shortess organizes Acme Paper Board Company to own his Reading mill.

1924   Shortess organizes Midvale Paper Board Company to acquire a mill in Stockport, New York.

1925   Inland issues $320,000 of first mortgage bonds to finance expansion of the Versailles mill.

1927   Through Acme, Shortess acquires a paperboard mill in White Hall, Maryland.

Shortess organizes Liberty Paper Board Company to acquire a mill in Steubenville, Ohio.

1928   Guy Freas joins Liberty as manager of the Steubenville mill.

Federal obtains a credit line from Guaranty Trust Company of New York (now Morgan Guaranty Trust), establishing an important banking relationship that continues to this day.

Shortess acquires Worcester Paper Box Company, Medford, Massachusetts. Worcester's founder, Harry Posner, continues as president and his wife receives an option to repurchase the company.

1929   Overextended financially, Shortess' various companies and mills come under the control of a creditors' committee on January 30, 1929. Shortess is forced to issue a letter of resignation, which is never exercised by the committee.

1931   At the depth of the Great Depression, Shortess's various companies have a combined loss of $194,000.

1933   Operations return to profitability for the first time in four years and remain profitable for the remainder of the Depression.

Shortess repays all his debts and the creditors' committee is disbanded.

1935   Shortess acquires an 80 percent interest in S-C-S Folding Box Company, Palmer, Massachusetts.

He organizes Windsor Paper Mills, Inc. to acquire a paperboard mill in Newburgh, New York.

J. R. Kennedy joins Federal as assistant to the president.

1941   Through Windsor Paper Mills, Shortess acquires a mill in Walloomsac, New York.

Federal acquires the Packerack mill near Reading, Pennsylvania.

1942   Shortess dies, leaving his various business interests, including Federal, to his widow, Joanna.

A new five-member board of directors takes charge: Joanna Shortess, Archibald Maxwell of Guaranty Trust Company, and three Federal employees — J. R. Kennedy, Howard Brown and Guy Freas.

Harry Posner and his wife, Hannah, reacquire Worcester Paper Box from the Shortess estate.

1943   Joanna Shortess sells her husband's remaining business interests to Kennedy, Brown and Freas for $1.5 million, paid entirely in the form of a note without any down payment.

The new owners consolidate all companies and operations into Federal. Kennedy becomes Federal's president, Brown chairman of the board and Freas executive vice president.

Federal obtains a $1,050,000, 15-year mortgage from Metropolitan Life Insurance Company to repay a portion of the $1.5 million note owed to Mrs. Shortess. She subsequently converts the remainder of her note to $450,000 of preferred stock.

1945   Federal's sales exceed $10 million for the first time.

1946   Federal begins a program of diversification through a series of small acquisitions of folding carton plants. Acquisitions are financed, in part, with a $900,000 loan from Guaranty Trust Company.

1947   The company builds a carton plant adjacent to its Versailles, Connecticut, paperboard mill and acquires a carton plant near its Steubenville, Ohio, mill.

1948   Federal builds a folding carton plant next to its Bogota, New Jersey, paperboard mill.

1952   Jack Kennedy joins Federal.

1953   Federal goes public with a $3.4 million offering of 200,000 shares of common stock through an underwriting group headed by Goldman, Sachs & Co. Edward Schrader of Goldman Sachs joins Federal's board of directors.

The company establishes an annual dividend rate of $1.40 per share on its common stock.

Federal nearly doubles its annual sales through the acquisition of National Folding Box Company for $6.9 million. National operates a board mill and carton plant in New Haven, Connecticut. The acquisition is financed, in part, through a $4 million loan from Guaranty Trust Company and New England Mutual Life.

1954   Federal acquires Grant Paper Box Company, Pittsburgh, for $1.5 million.

Joanna Shortess dies.

Guy Freas retires as executive vice president.

Dividend rate is increased by 28.6 percent.

1955   Federal completes its second offering of common stock.

The company's shares are listed on the New York Stock Exchange.

Archibald Maxwell resigns as a director. John W. Cox, vice president of Diamond Match Company, is elected to the board and later joins Federal as executive vice president.

1956   Federal acquires Morris Paper Mills for common and preferred stock valued at $10.5 million. Morris operates a paperboard mill and folding carton plant in Morris, Illinois, and a carton plant in Marion, Indiana. William Beckwith and A. G. Ballenger of Morris become directors of Federal.

Federal's sales exceed $50 million.

1957   Federal acquires Frankenberg Bros., Inc., a folding carton company in Columbus, Ohio, for $650,000.

Howard Brown retires as chairman of Federal.

Dividend is increased 11 percent.

1958   Federal acquires Federal Glass Company, Columbus, Ohio, for common and preferred stock valued at $11 million. This acquisition gives Federal Paper Board a new product line, glassware. In addition, the Glass Company's Hercules Box division provides entry into the corrugated container field.

Federal Paper Board builds a large plant in Washington, Pennsylvania, to consolidate folding carton operations from Pittsburgh, Steubenville and Columbus.

William Beckwith retires from the board and John Cox resigns. Three new directors are elected: Edward Donnan of Federal Glass; John M. Budinger, senior vice president of Bankers Trust Company; and Glover Johnson, a senior partner in White & Case.

1959 Federal adds to its printing capabilities by purchasing Sweeney Lithograph Company, Belleville, New Jersey.

Samuel N. Lebold of the Morris Paper division is elected to Federal's board, succeeding A. G. Ballenger, who retires.

Earnings reach a new high of $4.7 million.

1960 Federal acquires Manchester Board and Paper Company for common and preferred stock valued at $10 million. Manchester operates two recycled paperboard mills in Richmond, Virginia, and one in Roanoke Rapids, North Carolina, and a folding carton plant — the Wing Paper Box Company — in Hendersonville, North Carolina.

Frank Brown of Manchester joins Federal's board of directors.

Federal acquires Keystone Paper Box Company, York, Pennsylvania, for common stock valued at $500,000.

The Bogota, New Jersey, paperboard mill — Federal's original facility — is closed. J. R. Kennedy explains that the 60-year old mill is outdated and expensive to operate.

Quentin Kennedy joins Federal.

1961 Federal sells $20 million of 20-year debentures in a public offering, primarily to finance construction of a new recycled paperboard mill at Sprague, Connecticut.

The company acquires Worcester Paper Box, Medford, Massachusetts, for the second time, paying $3 million in stock and notes.

Howard Brown resigns from the board. Three new directors are elected: Frederick W. Hesser and Jack Kennedy, senior vice presidents, and Robert A. Wallace, financial vice president.

1962 Federal completes construction of the Sprague mill at a cost of $17 million. Today, the Sprague plant is the largest and most efficient recycled paperboard mill in the world.

Federal expands its folding carton plant in Hendersonville, North Carolina, and builds a new folding carton plant in Thomaston, Georgia.

The folding carton plant in Marion, Indiana, is closed.

1963 Samuel Lebold and Fred Hesser retire as directors. James C. La Grua, vice president, is elected to the board.

Federal reduces the dividend on its common stock by 20 percent, reflecting start-up problems at Sprague.

1964 The Belleville, New Jersey, printing plant is closed.

Federal's sales exceed $100 million.

1965 Jack Kennedy is elected president of Federal. J. R. Kennedy continues as chairman and chief executive officer.

Ray D. Hall and George B. Nicholson, vice presidents, are elected to Federal's board.

Dividend is again reduced, this time by 37.5 percent.

1966 The Sprague mill earns its first profit.

Federal expands its Hercules corrugated container division by purchasing a majority interest in a corrugated sheet operation in Pittsburgh.

John Budinger dies. Robert Wallace resigns from the board.

1967 Federal acquires a corrugated box plant in Baltimore.

Federal Glass expands by completing a fifth glassmaking furnace.

John H. Millikin, senior vice president of Bankers Trust Company, is elected to the board.

Simkins Industries makes an unsuccessful cash tender offer for up to 43 percent of Federal Paper Board's stock.

Federal declares a three-for-two split of its common stock.

1968 With the start-up problems of Sprague behind, and to help defeat the Simkins bid, Federal increases the cash dividend on its common stock by 50 percent.

The company borrows $6 million from banks to increase its working capital.

Corporate headquarters are moved to Montvale, New Jersey.

George Nicholson resigns.

1969   Production capacity is doubled at the Thomaston, Georgia, carton plant.

Production capacity at Sprague is increased by 20 percent, the first of several expansions at the facility.

Hugh J. Kelley, executive vice president of McGraw-Hill, Inc., and Joseph H. Taggart, dean of the Graduate School of Business Administration, New York University, are elected to the board.

1970   The Montville, Connecticut, paperboard mill is closed.

1971   Federal divests its corrugated container division. In a transaction with Continental Can Company, Federal trades the division and $10 million for a folding carton plant in Piermont, New York, and a carton plant and paperboard mill in Los Angeles. Federal also leases a paperboard mill at Piermont from Continental with an option to buy.

Three months later, in a second transaction with Continental Can, Federal leases a carton plant in Elkhart, Indiana, with an option to buy.

1972   In its largest acquisition to date, Federal acquires a solid bleached sulphate paperboard mill in Riegelwood, North Carolina, 350,000 acres of related timberland and other facilities from Riegel Paper Corporation for $115.6 million. Unwanted facilities, including four paper mills in New Jersey, are later sold, reducing the net cost of the mill and timberland to $85 million.

Federal issues 1,323,611 shares of common stock and 1,764,814 shares of convertible preferred stock in the Riegelwood acquisition.

The company also borrows $45 million from Morgan Guaranty Trust to help finance the acquisition. This loan is subsequently refinanced with a $40 million public offering of 25-year debentures.

Three members of Riegel Paper's board of directors — Thomas D. O'Connor, Willliam E. Reid and William M. Riegel — join Federal's board. Subsequently, O'Connor and Riegel resign to pursue other business interests, whereupon E. Vernon Hogan is elected to Federal's board.

The Versailles, Connecticut, paperboard mill is closed and the Piermont, New York, mill is subleased to another company.

Federal Glass Company's sales are $39 million, nearly triple the figure when it was acquired 14 years earlier. Earnings of Federal Glass are at a peak.

Total sales of Federal Paper Board Company approach $250 million.

1973   Ray Hall and James La Grua retire. Glover Johnson dies. Four new directors are elected: Richard A. Lenon, president and chief executive officer of International Minerals and Chemical Corporation, and three senior vice presidents of Federal — L. Baxter Chamberlain, Kenneth A. Petersen and Oliver F. Runde.

Dividend is increased by 20 percent.

1974   Federal opens a folding carton plant in Wilmington, North Carolina, near the Riegelwood mill.

Although Federal Glass Company loses money for the first time, reflecting depressed glass industry conditions, Federal Paper Board's total earnings surge to a new high of $20.9 million, reflecting the growing profitability of Riegelwood.

1975   A sawmill is opened at Armour, North Carolina, two miles from Riegelwood.

Jack Kennedy is elected chief executive officer.

Federal borrows $30 million by issuing a 15-year note to Prudential Insurance Company of America, beginning a relationship with an institution that is today Federal's largest lender.

Peter Brant and Bato Company acquire an 8.7 percent interest in Federal. Federal opposes the purchase and, following a brief legal battle, purchases the Brant and Bato stock.

The New Haven board mill and carton plant are closed.

The dividend is increased by 25 percent.

1976   Frank Brown and Edmund Donnan retire. Three new directors are elected: Frank Forester, Jr., executive vice president of Morgan Guaranty Trust Company; John L. Kelsey, executive vice president of Blyth Eastman Dillon & Co.; and R. Earl Roberson, chairman of American Mutual Liability Insurance Company.

Federal Paper Board and 25 other companies are indicted on charges of conspiring to fix prices of folding cartons.

Stock is split two-for-one. Dividend is increased 6.7 percent and then by 11.1 percent.

1977 Federal launches a five year, $215 million expansion program at Riegelwood.

The company borrows $80 million from eight insurance companies, including Equitable, John Hancock and Travelers, to finance the first phase of the Riegelwood expansion.

Federal Paper Board reaches an agreement to sell Federal Glass to Lancaster Colony Corporation, but the transaction is blocked by the Federal Trade Commission.

Federal Paper Board pleads nolo contendere to folding carton price fixing charges.

The Steubenville, Ohio, paperboard mill and the Medford, Massachusetts, and Washington, Pennsylvania, folding carton plants are closed.

Edward Schrader retires. W. Ran Clerihue, executive vice president of Celanese Corporation, is elected to the board.

1978 Federal borrows an additional $75 million from Prudential Insurance for expansion at Riegelwood.

Federal sells one of its two paperboard mills in Richmond, Virginia.

For the second time, the proposed sale of Federal Glass to Lancaster Colony is blocked by the Federal Trade Commission.

Federal agrees to settle civil suits related to the folding carton antitrust case.

Guy Freas retires as a director. George E. Oakley Jr., vice president of Federal, is elected to the board.

1979 Unable to find a buyer, Federal Paper Board closes Federal Glass.

Saul Steinberg and Reliance Insurance Company acquire a 24 percent interest in Federal.

Howard Brown dies.

1980 J. R. Kennedy retires. Quentin Kennedy is elected to the board of directors.

Federal acquires a sawmill in Newberry, South Carolina, financing the acquisition with $8.5 million of industrial revenue bonds.

Production capacity at the Wilmington, North Carolina, folding carton plant is doubled.

Paperboard mills in Morris, Illinois, Reading, Pennsylvania, Roanoke Rapids, North Carolina, and White Hall, Maryland, are sold or closed.

Federal borrows $40 million from Prudential to finance capital programs.

Sales exceed $500 million. Earnings reach a new high of $29.1 million. Dividend is increased 11.1 percent.

1981 Federal acquires the stock held by Steinberg and Reliance.

The company borrows $50 million from Prudential Insurance, Metropolitan Life and Teachers Insurance and Annuity Association through the issuance of convertible notes. Proceeds are used to repay short-term debt and finance capital projects.

Hugh Kelly and Joseph Taggart retire. Thomas L. Cassidy, a managing director of First Boston Corporation, and Edmund J. Kelly, a partner in White & Case, are elected to the board.

Dividend is increased 10 percent.

1982 The five-year expansion program at Riegelwood is completed on schedule, making the facility the largest solid bleached sulphate paperboard and pulp mill in the world.

Baxter Chamberlain retires as a director. William R. Hartman, chairman of Interpace Corporation, is elected to the board.

Guy Freas dies.

Dividend is increased 9.1 percent.

1983 Federal borrows $10 million from Teachers Insurance and Annuity Association.

Quentin Kennedy is elected executive vice president.

1984 Federal acquires folding carton plants in Beacon, New York, and Marseilles, Illinois, from Nabisco Brands, Inc., with a contract to continue to supply Nabisco's folding carton needs.

The Piermont, New York, folding carton plant is closed.

Willam Hartman resigns from the board.

J. R. Kennedy dies.

Earnings reach $37.1 million. Stock is split two-for-one. Dividend is increased 16.7 percent.

1985   Federal acquires a group of properties —
including a bleached paperboard mill in Augusta,
Georgia — from Continental Group for $317
million. The transaction is financed with a $315
million loan from a group of 11 banks led by
Morgan Guaranty Trust.

Also included in the acquisition are two folding
carton plants, four sawmills and two paper plate
plants. The newly acquired Durham, North
Carolina, plant is expanded. The other carton
plant is closed. Three of the sawmills — in
Augusta and Washington, Georgia, and Johnston,
South Carolina — are retained. The other is
closed. The two paper plate plants are sold.

Subsequently, Federal issues $75 million of
convertible preferred stock and $125 million of
15-year debentures to refinance a portion of the
bank loan.

1986   Federal begins a major, eight-year program to
increase production capacity at the Augusta
paperboard mill by 80 percent. Projected capital
cost is $1.1 billion. On completion of this project
in the mid-1990s, Augusta will be the largest solid
bleached sulphate paperboard mill in the world,
exceeding Riegelwood.

Federal acquires 310,000 acres of timberland near
Augusta for $96 million.

The company sells 2.25 million shares of common
stock in a public offering, using the proceeds to
redeem the $50 million of convertible notes
issued in 1981.

Vernon Hogan dies. George Oakley and Ken
Petersen retire as directors. Robert D. Baldwin,
B. W. Bowie and Paul R. Kinsey, senior vice
presidents, are elected to the board.

1987   To support its growing export business, Federal
opens sales offices in London and Tokyo.

The company redeems its convertible preferred
stock (issued in 1985), forcing its conversion into
3.6 million shares of common stock.
Subsequently, it sells a new series of convertible
preferred stock, using the proceeds to redeem the
$125 million of debentures issued in 1985.

The net effect of the financial transactions in 1986
and 1987 is to reduce Federal's ratio of long-term
debt to total capitalization from 60 percent to 42
percent.

Earnings are $65.8 million. Sales exceed $1
billion. Dividend is increased 14.3 percent, then
by 25 percent.

1988   A sales office is established in Zurich, Switzerland.

Federal acquires United Paper Inc., which has
paper sheeting operations in Sturgis, Michigan,
and Ontario, California.

The Richmond, Virginia, and Los Angeles
paperboard mills are sold. The Elkhart, Indiana,
and Los Angeles folding carton plans are closed.

Federal borrows $200 million from Prudential
and other lenders to finance expansion at
Augusta.

Frank Forester dies.

Stock is split two-for-one. Dividend is increased
28 percent, then by 25 percent.

1989   Federal acquires Thomas Tait & Sons Ltd.,
Inverurie, Scotland, which manufactures copy
paper and other uncoated freesheet. Tait is
Federal's first manufacturing facility outside the
United States and gives Federal a direct presence
in the European Common Market.

Federal acquires Imperial Cup Corp., Kenton,
Ohio. Imperial makes paper cups at plants in
Kenton, Ohio, LaFayette, Georgia, Salisbury,
Maryland, and Visalia, California.

Federal constructs a third sheeting operation — at
Hazleton, Pennsylvania.

The company borrows an additional $200 million
from Prudential and other lenders to reduce bank
debt, finance continued expansion at Augusta and
help finance the acquisition of Imperial Cup.

John Millikin and William Reid retire as directors.

Sales exceed $1.3 billion. Earnings reach a record
$205 million. Dividend is increased
25 percent.

1990   Federal expands its position in the paper cup
business by acquiring Continental Bondware, Inc.

A poly-extrusion laminating facility is completed
in Prosperity, South Carolina, to coat paperboard
being shipped from the Augusta mill to Federal's
paper cup plants.

Federal announces plans to sell seven of its eight
folding carton plants, retaining only the plant in
Durham, North Carolina.

Earl Roberson retires from the board. Paul
Kinsey retires as senior vice president and a
member of the board. W. Mark Massey, Jr., is
elected senior vice president and a director.

Index

*Boldface listings
indicate photographs.*